TRADE-ROUTES
AND COMMERCE OF
THE ROMAN EMPIRE

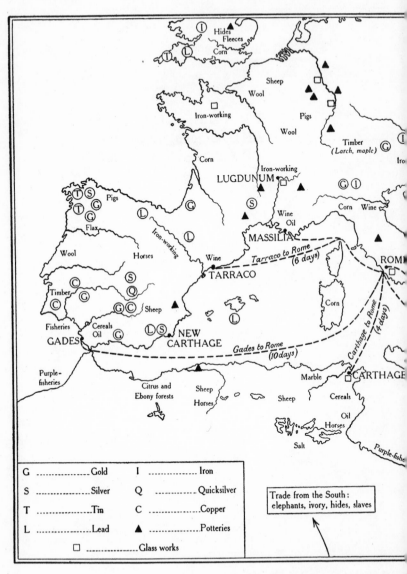

TRADE ROUTES AND COMME

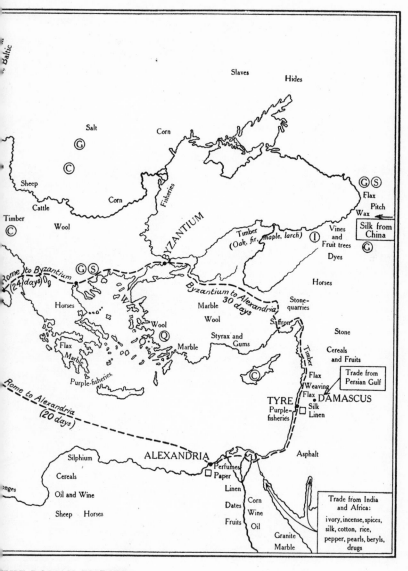

Baltic

Slaves   Hides

Salt   Corn
Ⓖ
Ⓒ   ⒼⓈ

Sheep   Flax   Pitch
Cattle   Corn   Wax
Timber   Wool   Vines   Silk from
Ⓒ   Timber   and   China
                    (Oak, fir, maple, larch) ⒾFruit trees
            BYZANTIUM   Dyes   Ⓖ

Rome to Byzantium   Horses
(24 days)   ⒼⓈ
                    Byzantium to Alexandria   Stone-
Horses   30 days   quarries
                Marble   Stone
            Wool
        Wool   Cereals
    Ⓠ   Saffron   and Fruits
    Marble   Styrax and   Trade from
Flax   Gums   Ⓒ   Flax   Persian Gulf
Marble   Weaving
Purple-fisheries   TYRE   Flax   DAMASCUS
                        Purple-   Silk
Rome to Alexandria   fisheries   Linen
(20 days)
                            Asphalt
            ALEXANDRIA
Silphium   Perfumes
                Paper
Cereals   Linen
Oil and Wine   Dates   Corn   Trade from India
                    Wine   and Africa:
Sheep   Horses   Fruits   Oil   ivory, incense, spices,
                        silk, cotton, rice,
                Granite   pepper, pearls, beryls,
                Marble   drugs

THE ROMAN EMPIRE

TRADE-ROUTES
AND COMMERCE OF
THE ROMAN EMPIRE

By M. P. CHARLESWORTH, M.A.

FELLOW AND TUTOR OF ST JOHN'S COLLEGE
AND FORMERLY FELLOW OF JESUS COLLEGE, CAMBRIDGE;
SOMETIME PROCTER FELLOW OF PRINCETON
UNIVERSITY, U.S.A.

SECOND EDITION, REVISED

COOPER SQUARE PUBLISHERS, INC.
NEW YORK
1970

To

WILLIAM COOPER PROCTER
TRUSTEE OF PRINCETON UNIVERSITY

ⲉⲩⲉⲣⲅⲉⲧⲏ

Originally Published 1926
Published by Cooper Square Publishers, Inc.
59 Fourth Avenue, New York, N. Y. 10003
Standard Book No. 8154-0328-3
Library of Congress Catalog Card No. 79-118637

Printed in U.S.A. by
NOBLE OFFSET PRINTERS, INC.
NEW YORK 3, N. Y.

73-12301

PREFACE

IN this book I have tried briefly to outline a part of the economic life of the Roman Empire during its first two centuries. I cannot claim to have done full justice to the period: the subject is too interesting, the problems too many, to be treated adequately in two hundred and forty pages; but I trust that the book gives a reasonably true picture, and that it will prove useful, even if merely as a collection of facts. I have given, without any idea of fullness, such references as seemed to me necessary; these I have gathered in the course of my own reading save a few which I owe to the works of M. Jullian and M. Pârvan.

I have enjoyed writing this book for two reasons: firstly because I believe in the Roman Empire, and secondly because the work has been done in three pleasant places of this world—in the Graduate College of Princeton University in America, in Jesus College, and finally in St John's College, Cambridge. To the governing bodies of all these great societies I must express my thanks for their kindness, and to many friends for their ready help. More especially would I thank Professor F. F. Abbott, and Professor David Magie, of Princeton, for generous aid and advice, and Mr Wilfrid Schoff, of Philadelphia, for kind permission to draw on his published papers; the examiners for the Hare Prize, Mr T. R. Glover and Mr F. E. Adcock, for criticism and suggestions: Mr R. S. Marsden and Mr P. S. Noble, scholars of Jesus and St John's Colleges respectively, for assistance with references, and last but not least Mr B. L Manning, of Jesus College, who has helped me far more than I can describe or acknowledge.

It is hardly possible that a first book such as this should not contain many faults—inaccuracies, over-statements, reiteration; I have done my best to correct this, but where errors still remain I must ask the reader, as does Odoric of Pordenone, "if he find anything too hard for belief, or wherein he judgeth me to stray from truth, let him remark thereon with a student's charity and not with insolent bitterness and spiteful snarling."

M. P. CHARLESWORTH

June 1924

PREFACE TO SECOND EDITION

A NEW edition has been called for far sooner than I thought likely. I have gladly seized the opportunity to correct some of the grosser blunders, to make some additions, to render some misunderstood passages more intelligible, to improve the Index, and to add a small map. No one knows the faults of this work better than I, but the conditions of reprinting did not allow that thorough revision which I should have liked to give it. But I hope the book may still prove useful, in a modest way.

M. P. C.

March 1926

CONTENTS

INTRODUCTION

τίς ἀμείνων καὶ λυσιτελέστερα γένοιτ'
ἂν ταύτης κατάστασις; νῦν πᾶσα μὲν
ἄδεια πᾶσιν ὅπῃ βούλεταί τις, πάντες
δὲ οἱ πανταχοῦ λίμενες ἐνεργοί, νῦν
τὰ μὲν ὄρη τὴν αὐτὴν ἔχει τοῖς ὁδεύου-
σιν ἥνπερ αἱ πόλεις τοῖς οἰκοῦσιν
αὐτὰς ἀσφάλειαν.   ARISTIDES
            Speech before Marcus Aurelius.

What could be better or more
profitable than the present state
of affairs? Now any man can go
whither he pleases with absolute
confidence, the harbours all over
the empire are full of business,
even the mountains are as safe for
those who journey over them as
the cities are to those who dwell
in them.

INTRODUCTION

THE history of how ancient commerce arose and of how man after many centuries of painful endeavour and of adventurous enterprise in lands and upon seas unknown succeeded finally in establishing those trade-routes, many of which are followed still by the modern world, is a fascinating one to study, and would prove delightful reading were it ever written down in its entirety. But unfortunately there are many obstacles to the completion of such a work, the chief one being that it would require an almost encyclopaedic mind to control and master the mass of multifarious detail that goes to form the whole. Yet it may still be possible to throw some light on the story by a consideration of Trade and of Routes at different periods of history, and it is the purpose of the present essay to discuss, however inadequately, the economic resources of the Roman Empire during the first two centuries of its existence, to indicate the various routes—old and new—by which the products of the different provinces were conveyed and interchanged, and to consider the amount of intercourse between peoples within the Empire itself. Only in this way can we obtain a glimpse of the true greatness of the Roman Empire, as a power, which, by giving freedom from enemies without and from brigandage or piracy within, and by improving all means of communication, fostered trade and commerce, and so promoted the well-being and happiness of its citizens and subjects.

It is only in recent years, however, that this interpretation has won any acceptance. In almost any older history of the period we find ourselves taught to regard it as a "necessary evil," and we are regaled with accounts of tyrannical rule in Rome and with petty court scandals, interspersed with occasional frontier wars. Some historians, indeed, have realised the absurdity of such a picture, but they in their turn are so possessed with the idea of Municipal Self-Government that they appear to regard it as the sole hope for which the ancient world was longing. Indeed, people are usually surprised to hear that any considerable commerce even existed, for their thoughts have never turned in that direction.

Such a notion of the Empire is quite fallacious, and due almost entirely to the brilliant but biassed writing of one ancient Roman historian. Tacitus was a pessimist of genius: his conception of the history of the period has prevailed over all others by virtue of his supreme art, and because of the indolence of modern historians. We do not rely for our knowledge of Queen Mary upon Foxe's *Book of Martyrs*; if we did, we should possess a very one-sided view of her character and of her whole reign. Yet in accepting meekly the Tacitean picture of the Early Empire —and many modern historians of that period are Tacitus and water—we are making quite as great a mistake. If we are to gain for ourselves a just estimate, we must turn to other authors and use epigraphic evidence. This is not easy, but it is worth the effort. If we make it, a new picture of the Empire begins to emerge. Between the strife and desolation of the Civil Wars and the later exhausting struggle against the inroads of the Northern barbarians we can descry two centuries of unexampled peace and prosperity under one far-reaching and efficient government. Indeed we may reasonably doubt whether at any other time in the history of the world so large a portion of the earth has enjoyed so long a visit of peace; it does not seem likely that a Roman, were he permitted to observe—and compare—the condition of present-day Macedonia and Thrace, or of Anatolia and the interior of Asia Minor, would be favourably impressed. To those who lament that it was an age of decadence and despair, we can reply that this may be true of the literary classes or of the vanishing nobility, but it is utterly false of the mercantile population; to them it was an age of hope, the dawn of a new era of stable government, of an amazing development of industrial activity, and of pushing far into unknown lands in the promotion of trade. People who are in despair and unhappiness, carrying out hated tasks in a grudging spirit, do not take the trouble to raise magnificent monuments or make imposing dedications; they have not the heart for it. But a large portion of the Latin Corpus—apart from epitaphs—is filled with the inscriptions of merchants who made votive offerings after successful voyages, gave splendid buildings to their native cities, and set up monuments to the emperor, sometimes as private individuals, sometimes as members of a guild or a corporation. Again, the study of the first two centuries makes it possible to watch the development of roads and industries, which is in itself fascinating: when we reach the age of Constantine everything has hardened down into a monotonous routine and a dull hopelessness, and private enterprise has been almost stifled.

In order to carry out this study properly we must first consider the material upon which we can base our conclusions. Unfortunately, at the outset our task is made difficult by the very smallness of this material; the ordinary Roman writer or historian took little heed of such things as trade or traders, and our authorities are all too few. We must gather our evidence as best we can from various authors; deductions must be drawn from hints carelessly thrown out, meaning wrung from scattered milestones and from fragmentary inscriptions. There is no body of precise statistics, such as those upon which the recorder of modern movements can rely, no collection of papers and manorial accounts, such as the mediaevalist can ransack—save in Egypt, which was an exceptional province—and hence we must suggest and indicate rather than employ dogmatic assertion. The authorities fall into two main classes; literary, and what we may term archaeological.

Among literary sources those of the greatest value to the historian of trade are the geographer Strabo and the

omniscient elder Pliny. The former was an Asiatic Greek
of good education; he travelled extensively and mixed with
friends and officers of the emperor Augustus; where his
personal knowledge was lacking he had numerous monographs and guide-books on which he could fall back, and
doubtless had oral information from Gallus and his noble
friends. Pliny—who comes about fifty years later—had an
encyclopaedic mind; in the vast register of his *Natural
History* where he "has deposited the discoveries, the arts,
and the errors of mankind," he has at the same time presented us with personal contributions from his own times
and circumstances. Both are reliable men, who had travelled
and gained experience of the world; without their volumes
it would be almost impossible to form a clear conception
of the condition of the provinces during the first century
of our era: they are real contemporary authorities. In the
second century there is much to be gleaned from the pages
of the geographer Ptolemy, and—for the affairs of Greece—
from the handbook of Pausanias. It is true that something
can be gathered from such writers as Columella, Varro,
and Dio Chrysostom, and from the poets, Vergil and
Horace, Statius, Martial, and Juvenal, but these tend to
confirm evidence already collected rather than to introduce
new facts of importance. Apart from literary authors, there
come certain geographical monographs and travellers'
handbooks, which are only too rare, but, where they are
available, throw a flood of light upon trade conditions: the
description of the voyage down the Red Sea to India left
us by some unnamed sea-captain, the itinerary through
Parthia, drawn up by Isidore of Charax, or the *Periplus
of the Black Sea*, ascribed to Arrian, teem with valuable
information.

When our literary sources are exhausted we can still
fall back upon the archaeological; these include not only
inscriptions, but also finds of pottery, vases, and other
articles. Since they can be dated, and often assigned to

definite firms or makers, they afford valuable evidence for the extent of transport. Then there is the vast mass of inscriptions, collected by the patient labours of Mommsen and his helpers: if they are milestones they are usually dateable and so shew us what were the means of communication available at various periods; if they are dedications or epitaphs of merchants and traders, they throw valuable light upon the nationality, position, and business of these men, and upon the distances they travelled.

For such works as the *Tabula Peutingerana* or the *Antonine Itineraries*, though rightly used for giving an account of the roads of the Empire as they existed in the fourth and subsequent centuries, are naturally no evidence for their extent in the first or second, and besides afford no indication of how the complex system grew up and developed. To trace that out is an absorbing task; when we observe Tiberius constructing a special road to serve recently-acquired gold-mines near the Sierra Morena in Spain, Claudius opening up the rich iron-smelting districts of Brittany and Normandy and improving communication with the new province of Britain, garrisons placed in the passes of the Caucasus to protect travellers to and from the Caspian, new trade-roads established in Egypt by Hadrian, and expeditions being despatched, either down the Red Sea to protect merchant-ships from pirates, or across Parthia to get into closer touch with the Chinese silk-trade, we can almost see commerce developing before our eyes, and this is a thing that no map can shew us. Even roads that were originally built for frontier defence, for the quick transportation of troops from point to point, soon came to serve as highways for commerce, as the flourishing towns that sprang up along the Rhine or on the outskirts of Syria and Africa in the second century prove.

Again, to archaeological evidence we can give almost more than its full weight. It is unfortunately not likely that our literary sources will ever be greatly increased, even from the discovery of papyri. But no one could claim that archaeological exploration is complete: many sites have been but half explored, many are still unopened, fresh stones and inscriptions are coming to light almost daily. The knowledge we derive from archaeology is even more certain and explicit than a literary statement; the latter may be challenged, but the vases and jars are visible and tangible and cannot be disputed. Chance so often yields unexpected treasures that we may hope for further information as the years go on, long after the last drop of meaning has been squeezed from the words of Varro or Strabo or Pliny.

For the sake of convenience I have adopted one uniform method in dealing with the subject. After a short introduction upon Italy, I review each province or region in turn, discussing successively routes, agricultural resources, mineral wealth, industries, and the intercourse of different peoples within that province. At the end of the narrative portion will be found Notes, dealing with each chapter, which are intended to support and sometimes to amplify the text itself or to deal more fully with disputed points. But neither narrative nor notes make any claim to completeness: this is a handbook, not an encyclopaedia; I have therefore stressed essentials only, deliberately omitting matters of minor importance. Thus the Danubian lands and Britain are only treated summarily: they only developed late, and though not lacking in importance, could never rival France, or Spain, or Syria. In addition, for Britain, there are so many books and articles available in English that only the briefest outline seemed necessary.

SELECT BIBLIOGRAPHY

THIS is, as its title implies, a select list only. Indeed a complete one is almost unthinkable, for it would mean reference to articles in all archaeological periodicals published during the last fifty years. But all the books mentioned will be found useful.

M. BESNIER. Commerce de plomb dans l'Antiquité. *Revue Archéologique*, XII. pp. 211 ff. 1920, XIII. pp. 36 ff., XIV. pp. 98 ff.

—— Lexique de Géographie Ancienne. 1914.

VIDAL DE LA BLACHE. Voies de commerce dans la Géographie de Ptolémée. Ac. des Inscr. et B.-L. 1896.

BLÜMNER. Technologie und Terminologie der Gewerbe und Künste bei Griechen und Römern. 1875–85. (New edition of Vol. 1, 1913.)

E. S. BOUCHIER. Spain under the Roman Empire. 1914.

—— Syria as a Roman Province. 1916.

E. H. BREWSTER. Roman Craftsmen and Tradesmen of the Early Empire. University of Pennsylvania, 1917.

V. CHAPOT. La Province Romaine d'Asie. Paris, 1904.

CLARK. Hellenism in India. *Classical Philology*. 1919, 1920.

COHEN. Description historique des monnaies frappées sous l'Empire Romain. Paris, 1859.

F. CUMONT. Études Syriennes. 1917.

—— Comment la Belgique fut Romanisée. 1919.

J. DÉCHELETTE. Les Vases Céramiques Ornés de la Gaule. 1904.

—— Manuel d'Archéologie préhistorique.... 1910 ff.

DUBOIS. L'Administration et l'Exploitation des carrières dans le monde romain. 1908.

ECKHEL. Doctrina numorum veterum. 1792–8.

T. FRANK. An Economic History of Rome. 1920.

FRIEDLÄNDER. Darstellungen aus der Sittengeschichte Roms. 4th edition. 1910.

GRENFELL-MAHAFFY. Revenue Law of Ptolemy Philadelphus. 1896.

GSELL. Histoire Ancienne de l'Afrique du Nord. Tome IV. 1920.

HATZFELD. Les Trafiquants Italiens de l'Orient Hellénique. 1919.

HAVERFIELD. The Romanisation of Roman Britain. 3rd Ed. 1915.

—— The Roman Occupation of Britain. 1924.

C. HERFURTH. De Aquileiae Commercio. Halis Saxonum, 1889.

HIRSCHFELD. Die Kaiserlichen Verwaltungsbeamte. 2nd Ed. 1905.
—— Kleine Schriften. 1913.
HIRTH. China and the Roman Orient. Shanghai, 1885.
C. JULLIAN. Histoire de la Gaule. Tomes IV–VI. 1920.
ANTON KISA. Das Glas im Alterthum. Leipzig, 1908.
LOUIS. Le Travail dans le monde romain. 1912.
J. G. MILNE. A History of Egypt under Roman Rule. 1898.
MITTEIS-WILCKEN. Grundzüge und Chrestomathie der Papyrus-kunde. 1912.
MOMMSEN. The Provinces of the Roman Empire. Eng. trans. 2nd Ed. 1909.
OSWALD and PRYCE. Terra Sigillata. 1922.
V. PÂRVAN. Die Nationalität der Kaufleute in Römische Kaiserreiche. Breslau, 1909.
SIR W. RAMSAY. The Historical Geography of Asia Minor. 1890.
H. G. RAWLINSON. Intercourse between India and the Western World. 1916.
J. S. REID. The Municipalities of the Roman Empire. 1913.
RIEPL. Das Nachrichtenwesen des Altertums. 1913.
W. SCHOFF. The Periplus of the Erythraean Sea. 1912.
—— Parthian Stations of Isidore of Charax. Philadelphia, 1914.
E. SPECK. Handelsgeschichte des Altertums. Leipzig, 1900 ff.
J. WARD. The Roman Era in Britain. 1911.
L. C. WEST. Roman Egypt. *Journal of Roman Studies*, VII. p. 45.
—— Commercial Syria under the Roman Empire. (*Transactions of the American Philological Association*, vol. LV.) 1924.

Many articles in the two great classical dictionaries of PAULY-WISSOWA (e.g. Frumentum, Industrie) and DAREMBERG-SAGLIO (e.g. Mercator, Via) will be found extremely useful also.

The small sketch-map included here is meant merely as a suggestive outline. Easily the best economic map of the ancient world is that attached to the article by Vidal de la Blache mentioned above. Handy maps will be found in Putzger's "Historischer Schul-Atlas," in Johnston's "Atlas of Ancient History," and in Murray's "Classical Atlas."

In the text itself I have often used modern names, where they are well known, that is, Rhine and Lyons instead of Rhenus and Lugdunum: but it seemed absurd to let Halys or Orontes masquerade as Kizil Irmak or as Nahr-el-Asi. I have not troubled, however, to be scrupulously consistent.

ADDENDA

Conditions of reprinting have made it impossible to alter and amplify the text as I should have liked: I add here, therefore, references to books and articles not previously mentioned.

GENERAL

CURTEL. Kulturpflanzen und Hausthiere (6th Ed.). 1894.
FRANK. Race Mixture in the Roman Empire. (*Amer. Hist. Rev.* 1916.)
HAHN. Rom und Romanismus im griechischen-römischen Osten. 1906.
HEHN. La Vigne et le Vin chez les Romains. 1903.
MILLER. Itineraria Romana. 1916.

CHAPTER TWO

MURRAY. Roman Roads and Stations in the Eastern Desert of Egypt. (*Journ. Egypt. Arch.* XI, 1925.)
RICCI. La coltura della vite e la fabbricazione del vino nell' Egitto Greco-Romano. 1924.
VÖGT. Römische Politik in Aegypten. 1924.

CHAPTER THREE

SOLARI. I Siri nell' Emilia Antica. (*Rivista Indo-grec-ital.* 1921.)

CHAPTERS FOUR AND SIX

HERRMANN. Die Alten Seidenstrassen zwischen China und Syrien. 1910.
SCHMIDT. Drogen und Drogenhandel im Altertum. 1924.
ZOLTÂN. Les anciennes routes de commerce à caravanes en Eurasie. (*Dolgozatok az erd. nem. múz. erém-és regisegtarabol.* 1919.)
As a useful corrective against idea of Greek loan-words in the East consult LAUFER, Sino-Iranica. 1919.

CHAPTER NINE

ALBERTINI. Les étrangers résidants en Espagne à l'époque romaine. (*Mélanges Cagnat*, 1912.)
SOLARI. Articles upon roads in Spain to be found in *Bullet. Comun. Arch.* 1918 and *Rendiconti Inst. Lomb.* 1920.

CHAPTER TEN

There are many gaps here which I hope one day to fill, but on Dacia and the Danubian regions see

MATEESCU. I Traci nelle epigrafi di Roma. (*Ephemeris Dacoromana*, I, 1923.)

NISCHER. Die Römer im Gebiete des ehemaligen Österreichs-Ungarn. 1923.

PÂRVAN. I Primordi della Civiltà Romena alle foci del Danubio. (*Ausonia*, 1921.)

—— Archäologische Funde in Rumänien. (*Arch. Anzeig.* 1913, 1914, 1915.)

—— Ţara Noastra. (In Roumanian.) 1923.

TOCILESCU. Fouilles et Recherches archéologiques en Roumanie. 1900

For the Alpine passes see

CARTELLIERI. Die Römischen Alpenstrassen. 1926.

For Germany and the North see

ALMGREN and NERMAN. Die ältere Eisenzeit Gotlands. I, II. 1914-1923.

DRAGENDORFF. Westdeutschland zur Römerzeit. 1912.

HAGEN. Römerstrasse der Rheinprovinz. 1923.

JUNGKLAUS. Römische Funde in Pommern. 1924.

MONTELIUS. Kulturgeschichte Schwedens. 1906.

WAGNER. Die Römer in Bayern. 1924.

For the early trade- and amber-routes see

de NAVARRO. Prehistoric Routes between Northern Europe and Italy. (*Geographical Journal*, 1925.)

MONTELIUS. Der Handel in der Vorzeit. (*Prähistorische Zeitschrift*, II, 1910.)

CHAPTER ELEVEN

BESNIER. Le point de départ des grandes routes de la Gaule romaine à Lyon. (*Bull. Arch.* 1925.)

de RICCI. Deux Nouveaux Milliaires de Claude. (*Rev. Et. Anc.* 1925.)

CORRECTIONS TO TEXT

p. 17. "No strong forces..." The phrase is misleading: Syria had only four legions in all, and three legions were a considerable force.

p. 32. "Keep away from the Jews." It is only fair to add that this is, so far as I know, a solitary example of such feeling.

p. 89. "the white marble of Synnada." Another slip, due to hasty writing: the marble was a beautiful red-veined variety: cf. Stat. *Silv.* I, 5. 37.

p. 101. "it was here that Tigranes set Tigranocerta": the word 'here' is misleading, but the city lay in the region of these routes, between the Southern and Northern branches. So much is certain, though I forbear to touch on the vexed question of the site of the city itself; see the exhaustive treatment in Rice-Holmes, *The Roman Republic*, I, pp. 409–425.

p. 211. On one stage in the early conquest of Britain see "The Fosse" by R. G. Collingwood in *J.R.S.*, XIV, pp. 252–256.

p. 213. On the Roman roads in Cornwall see Collingwood in *Antiq. Journ.* IV, pp. 101–112.

p. 236. For parallels to the 'amphorae' of Crispinilla, cf. the finds of vases made by Publius Cipius Polybius in Croatia, Hungary, Switzerland, Schleswig, and Denmark, or of the vases of Lucius Ansius Epaphroditus in Croatia, Denmark, and Sweden (Montelius, *Kulturg. Schwedens*, p. 168). Cf. also two silver vases of Augustan age (marked Χειρίσοφος ἐπόει) found on the island of Lolland in Denmark (*Supp. Epig. Graec.* II, p. 152, no. 885).

CHAPTER ONE

ITALY AND THE ESTABLISHMENT OF THE EMPIRE

"τοσαῦται δὲ ἀφικνοῦνται δεῦρο
(Rome)... ὁλκάδες ὡς ἐοικέναι τὴν
πόλιν κοινῷ τινι τῆς γῆς ἐργαστηρίῳ
... κατάπλοοι δὲ καὶ ἀπόπλοοι οὔποτε
λείπουσιν."   ARISTIDES

So many are the merchant vessels
that arrive here that Rome has
practically become a common
workshop for the whole world....
There are always ships putting into
or sailing out of the harbour.

"Ite in orbem universum et de
omni eius continentia referte ad
Senatum, et ad istam confirman-
dam huic scripto sigillum meum
apposui." Words of figure of Augustus in
the Hereford "Mappa Mundi."

ITALY AND THE ESTABLISHMENT OF THE EMPIRE

THE history of Roman trade before the establishment of the Empire can be summed up in a few words. The civilisation of Latium and of Rome during the first five centuries of its existence was predominantly agricultural: industry hardly existed. The Romans who conquered Italy were a race of sturdy peasant farmers and little else. Inhabiting the fertile plain of Latium they had to be continually on the watch to preserve their farms and their crops from the raids of the less fortunate hill tribes, who coveted their good corn-land. Yet it would not be altogether untrue to say that their very conquest of Italy was brought about by their devotion to peaceful commerce: the Roman Empire was not so much the result of a reasoned policy of imperialism carried out by far-seeing statesmen, as the natural outcome of certain qualities implanted deep in the Roman character. Their strong feeling for law and order was coupled with an extraordinary devotion to duty; though slow to rouse they were tenacious of their rights and keen bargainers (a trait which they carried even into their religion). All they desired was to sow and reap on their small farms in peace and undisturbed; it was always to drive back the predatory incursions of some hungry hill tribe that they had recourse to arms, when diplomacy had failed (as the fetial ritual shews). In order to carry on their normal intercourse securely they not only trained themselves as a nation of warriors, but they exercised their legal genius in drawing allies to themselves by covenants, contracts, and treaties. Thus gradually they surrounded themselves with a ring of allies whom it was their duty to protect when attacked by less civilised tribes. Their relations with the Greeks of Campania—which was at that time the commercial centre of Italy—brought them up against the Samnites; the extension of their sphere of influence over the South of Italy and their friendship with Massilia threw them into conflict with the Carthaginians, and made them the champions of the cause of Hellenism. And so the slow process went on; to protect their traders and settlers in Spain they had to wage warfare against savage tribes for many years, to aid Massilia they drove back the Allobroges and paved the way for the creation of a province, to help their Greek allies they put down the pirate kingdoms of the Adriatic, and in answer to appeals from the mercantile states of Pergamum and Rhodes they were led first to conquer Philip of Macedon and divide up his kingdom, and later to curtail the ambitions of the Seleucids. Yet it is worthy of careful notice that there are no signs of a mercantile policy; Rome's aim was to protect her own rights and those of her allies rather than to gain new ones; even after the sack of Carthage and the destruction of Corinth she claimed little for herself; Utica was allowed to usurp the trade of her former mistress, and Delos was proclaimed a free port. Greeks and Asiatics and their brethren in Campania drew most profit from her victories. But a change is observable towards the close of the second century before Christ, a change due to the legislation of Gaius Gracchus. This extraordinary genius, whose career marks an epoch in history as great as that of Augustus or Constantine, was quick to grasp the opportunities provided by the annexation of Asia; all his measures, the tax-bills, the colonies which were to be founded at important commercial and maritime centres, the provision of new roads, even the grain dole, shew that he had a clear vision of the future of commerce and that he intended to raise up a commercial party for his own support. From his time the number of Italians resident in Delos steadily increases, Roman knights and financiers become a power to be reckoned with, and the formation of the province of Narbonese Gaul is an echo of his policy. Agricultural interests had formerly been predominant at Rome, but now the knights began to claim a voice in the governance of affairs; Cicero needed them for his "Concordia Ordinum," their agents were widespread throughout Greece and Asia Minor, and their indignation with Lucullus' measures resulted in the appointment of Pompey and the opening of new fields for their activity in the annexation of Pontus, Bithynia, and Syria. Narbonese Gaul swarmed with Roman merchants and traders, and many more followed Caesar on his brilliant campaigns; Pliny's dictum that the Roman generals in their warfare always thought of commerce now begins to be true, but only now.

It is not necessary to enumerate at length the resources of the Italian peninsula and its trade possibilities: the subject has been discussed so often, and so large a literature exists concerning it, that we shall only treat of it summarily here, presuming a general acquaintance with it on the part of the reader. The praises of Italy have been sung by many, by none more nobly than by Vergil in the Second Georgic, and Strabo and Pliny follow with their humbler prose panegyrics. Its coast had few harbours, but those large ones; its climate was good and varied; it had abundance of minerals and of timber, for fuel or shipping, and was prolific in food for man and beast.

In the North the Padus valley was a region of rivers and intersecting canals; it was fertile in corn, vines, and millet: it had herds of cattle and flocks of sheep in abundance; it produced much wine and the wool of Mutina was famous. It surpassed all the rest of Italy in its thick population, in the number of its cities, and in its wealth; the proportion of knights in a town like Patavium was extraordinarily high. Over the Apennines lay Etruria, with its abundance of ship-timber, and its clays for pottery: up in the Sabine hills vine and olive were cultivated, while of the fertility of the Latian plain there is little need to speak; in the midst stood Rome at the junction of many roads and rivers to receive the crops and the timber of the lands around. But the Southern parts were even more prolific; the plain of Campania, with its warm climate, its crops of wheat and barley, of olive and vine, produced the finest wine and oil in all the world; from here came the Massic and Caecuban brands, the newly-favoured Surrentine, and most famous of all the Falernian; "what wine can compete with the Falernian, what oil with the Venafran?" as Varro proudly asks. On the Adriatic side there was fertile soil around Brundisium and the wool and honey that it exported were alike excellent; the hilly pastures of Calabria supported large flocks of sheep, while the finest wool was obtainable from those of Tarentum. The land of Apulia is described by Strabo as bearing everything in abundance and giving grazing for horses and cattle, while the wool was of a soft and delicate texture.

> Sed gravidae fruges et Bacchi Massicus umor
> implevere; tenent oleae armentaque laeta.
> hinc bellator equus campo sese arduus infert,
> hinc albi, Clitumne. greges et maxima taurus
> victima,...
> hic ver assiduum atque alienis mensibus aestas:
> bis gravidae pecudes, bis pomis utilis arbos.

But in addition the country possessed, or had once possessed, abundance of minerals of every kind; Pliny declares that the mines of Italy were second to none, so long as they were worked, and his tone suggests that by his time the exhausted veins of ore could not compete with the larger resources of Spain and Britain. Even during the Republic the Senate had at times forbidden mining altogether; in the North the output of the gold-mines of Vercellae had been thus limited. But copper was still to be found among the Bergomates, and iron near Comum, where it was extensively worked, while further South the waters of Sulmo were excellent for tempering iron and steel. The most prolific mineral district, however, was the island of Ilva (Elba), whence iron ore was obtained in large quantities; it could not be smelted there, but was conveyed across to the Italian ports; a certain amount of working was done at the near-by harbour of Populonia, but the most important centre, to which the bulk of the ore was shipped, was the port of Puteoli. Here the manufacturers gathered together a vast host of workmen who were busily employed in the production of weapons and all sorts of iron tools, such as spades, forks, mattocks, and sickles, which were widely exported.

The two most important regions for industry were the valley of the Padus and the plain of Campania. In the former, apart from the wool which was exported from the whole district and extensively spun at Patavium, cheeses and pork were despatched to Rome, and a busy trade went on in wine, which was sent out in huge casks; timber, too, was shipped down the Padus and to the South. At Patavium the wool was made into clothes and hangings, into rugs and carpets and blankets, which were in great demand at the capital and made the fortunes of its wealthy knights. Cups were manufactured at Pollentia, and Arretine ware, originally a product of Etruscan labour, had been transplanted to the North. Another flourishing town was Aquileia, which received the steel and iron of Noricum, and the wines of Istria and Rhaetia, together with the hides of the Northern country, and exported Italian pottery and goods to the barbarian. In the midlands was the thriving pottery centre of Arretium, and the famous marble quarries of Luna and Carrara, which began to be used during the last years of the Republic; these together with the stone of Tibur and Gabii were to afford Augustus material for his rebuilding and beautification of old Rome. In the South, besides the ironworks and factories of Puteoli, a considerable industry appears to have existed in and around Capua for the manufacture of articles of bronze and of copper, which were used all over Italy; silver ware too was probably produced on a large scale, and the red-glazed Arretine ware was made at Puteoli, while there were glass-factories newly founded on the Volturnus. Puteoli itself was the largest and busiest port of Italy and contained a cosmopolitan population; Lucilius called it "a smaller Delos," which was the great international mart of those days. Yet even so we must remember that all this activity and industry was of comparatively recent date, that it was only after Gracchan days that Italian merchants begin to play an important part in Aegean and Mediterranean trade, and that the greater part even of these Italians came of Campanian and Southern stock, few being of Latin blood. Again, even in the most flourishing days of the Republic, Puteoli, in spite of its manifold occupations, was never able to send out to the East a cargo equal to that she received; the Alexandrine and Asiatic ships always drew out of her harbour considerably lighter than they had put in.

Such then, summarily, were the resources of Italy and such the state of her industries in the time of Caesar and Pompey. Within the last few decades new prospects seemed to have dawned for Roman industry and finance; Pompey had opened up new provinces such as Bithynia and Syria, Caesar had annexed the vast territory of Gaul; pottery was being manufactured on an extensive scale, and the discovery of glass-blowing had brought an immense increase to the trade besides greatly cheapening the cost of glass ware. Though her agriculture might be declining, and though vast areas of land were left for sheep and cattle to wander over, the cultivation of the olive was being encouraged, and about the year 52 B.C. the first cargo of oil had been exported from Italy. But then there broke out the terrible and desolating storm of civil war, which raged almost without interruption for close on twenty years; the provinces were the scene of bloody fighting, and Italy was drained of her best stock; farms lay neglected in the absence of their masters, there were sudden requisitions, burning of towns and villages, and all those wanton acts which war lets loose; piracy began to lift its head again upon the sea, and brigands overran the land; then came a flood of confiscations and evictions to satisfy the greed of the triumvirs and to provide the wherewithal to reward their soldiery; no man's goods could be thought safe, no man's land was secure, property sank to a ridiculous value, the rate of interest soared high, credit was impaired: the promise of a few years before seemed hideously blighted.

But there was a deliverer at hand. The young Octavian, who had been a member of the Triumvirate formed after the death of Caesar, who had sanctioned the confiscations and proscriptions and murders of the time with a cruelty that appears more appalling than that of Antony or Lepidus, was reserved by destiny for nobler things. He began to realise the work that was appointed him, the task of rescuing Italy and the provinces from the ravages of the war and bringing them back to a normal basis once more. The labour was appalling. We in our generation—though we have tasted all the bitterness of war and of its aftermath—feel that the titles bestowed upon him, and the praises lavished by poets and orators are too extravagant; we are apt to ascribe them to "courtly adulation" or to "poetical exaggeration." But men were in sober solemn earnest, for they knew what had to be done, and what Augustus had done. The wounds of civil war had to be healed, a jealous body of the old *noblesse* had to be conciliated, the Senate had to be assured of power and respect, payment had to

be found for the veterans, the frontiers defended, piracy
overcome and brigandage put down, the hungry populace
of Rome fed, the provincials won over by good and settled
government, trade and commerce and industry restored to
their prosperity, and credit brought back; above all, the
whole population of the Empire had to be given that feeling
of security and freedom from fear without which men will
never embark on any undertaking of commerce. All this
Augustus did and so brought about the renascence of
intercourse and of trade. That is the reason why sailors of
Alexandria once approached him near Puteoli and clad in
festal garments offered incense to him as a god; it was
thanks to him, they said, that they could live and make
their voyages, thanks to him that they could enjoy their
freedom and their fortunes. So, too, Philo, who may be
reasonably supposed to mirror the feeling of Alexandria,
has no words of praise too high for Augustus: he had found
the world in confusion and turmoil, the human race almost
spent by mutual slaughter and by war; it was he who had
loosed the world from its chains and put down every form
of strife; he had emptied the sea of pirates and covered it
with the fleets of merchants; he had brought cities back
into freedom, turned disorder into order, tamed savage
races; he was the guardian of peace and dispenser of all
good things. It is not surprising that in Alexandria there
was raised to him a splendid gleaming temple, facing the
great harbours, that was filled with offerings and dedications and votive gifts in gold and silver; nor that at Philae
the grateful people should set up a temple to him as
"Saviour and Benefactor." The provinces fully appreciated the blessings of his rule, as did Italy. We have multi-
tudinous references to him in contemporary poets, and
upon his return from Gaul in 13 B.C. an altar was dedicated
to "Fortuna Redux." Horace, on the occasion of this same
return, sums up the matter in an ode every phrase of which

should be given its full weight; most significant are the
lines:

> Sic desideriis icta fidelibus
>   Quaerit patria Caesarem.
> Tutus bos etenim rura perambulat,
> Nutrit rura Ceres almaque Faustitas,
> Pacatum volitant per mare navitae,
>   Culpari metuit *Fides*....
> Condit quisque diem collibus in suis,
> Et vitem viduas ducit ad arbores;
> Hinc ad vina redit laetus et alteris
>   Te mensis adhibet deum.

Such measures came naturally to Augustus. He was
sprung from an Italian middle-class family, and had not
the aristocratic contempt for trade which was inborn in
the consulars; he could appreciate the point of view of the
merchant and middle-class business man; one of his main
achievements was to revive the ancient glories of the equites
and fit them for holding governmental appointments, while
wealthy merchants of the freedman class were made to feel
that they too had a stake in the Empire by the creation of
the order of "Seviri Augustales." His family and his
friends, among the enormous property they possessed,
owned various mines—such as those of Livia in Gaul, or
of Sallust among the Centrones—or fertile pieces of territory (such as the rich region of Jamneia, bequeathed to
the imperial family), and so could understand the need for
security throughout the provinces and for quick communication of news. Above all, his control of Egypt, and
the necessity of regular and assured corn-supply therefrom
in order to feed the populace of Rome, made him take such
measures as the cleaning out and repair of the neglected
Nile irrigation channels and the constitution of the Alexandrine corn-fleet.

The essentials of a flourishing trade are, firstly, a peaceable population living unhindered by fear of invasion or

brigandage, secondly, the assurance of easy means of inter-communication, and thirdly, a good coinage. To all these essentials Augustus paid careful attention: the Northern and Eastern frontiers were garrisoned and protected, in the mountainous country of Gaul and Spain the natives were persuaded to leave their hill-fortresses and come down to new towns lying in the valley on natural trade-routes, measures were taken against the brigands who infested Italy and kidnapped travellers into the slave-prisons; client-kings, such as Juba or Herod, policed their own territories, roads which had fallen into disrepair were solidly relaid (Augustus undertaking the restoration of the important Northern highway, the Via Flaminia, and apportioning the others to various nobles), and the pirates were chased off the Mediterranean. All this was done without laying an extra burden of taxation upon either Italy or the provinces; it was carried out thanks to the cool resolution and clear vision of a ruler who saw what remedies were necessary for a suffering world, possessed the patience and energy to apply them, knew how to choose and keep his friends and agents, and above all had confidence in himself.

There was another matter which needed his attention. Outside the territory of the Empire itself lay many rich lands which, if trade was to be properly fostered, should be brought within the Roman sphere of influence. Augustus faced the task with energy: in some cases direct conquest was the result, in others the opening up of commercial relations; the emperor himself declares, "while I was princeps, the good faith of the Roman people was experienced by a large number of other nations, with whom before that time there had been no diplomatic or friendly intercourse." That explains how Roman merchants found their way to Petra or to the courts of the kings of the Cimmerian Bosphorus, or took up their abode permanently in the capital of the Marcomannic king, Maroboduus.

Treaties of commerce and intercourse doubtless existed, and perhaps even closer relations; otherwise it would be hard to account for the presence of what looks suspiciously like a Roman Resident Adviser at Palmyra.

Indeed, we are apt to get a wrong impression of Augustus' foreign policy; historians usually inform us that he exhibited a wise moderation in not extending the bounds of the Empire but consolidating what had been gained, and that he passed this advice on to his successors. Such a view is only partially true; it would be more correct to say that this was the policy of his old age. When he was younger far-reaching schemes of conquest had presented themselves to him, and only great misfortunes had prevented their realisation. Only when he was broken by age and infirmity, when his nerve had been shattered by the Varian disaster, did he definitely renounce his German trans-Rhenane schemes; before that date the expeditions of Drusus, Tiberius, Domitius, and others reveal his intention of extending the frontier to the Elbe. We may compare, too, in the East his treatment of Armenia; when Tiberius was despatched there with full powers in 20 B.C., he placed the Roman nominee on the throne of that distracted country, made a satisfying display of Roman power, and enormously increased the prestige of the Empire. But this was not enough: we can scarcely doubt that something like the annexation of Armenia was planned and reserved for the emperor's grandson, Gaius; poets and writers of the age took up the scheme with extravagant enthusiasm; "nunc, Oriens ultime, noster eris" was the burden of their cry. Not only was Armenia to become a province, but another cherished project was to be realised, the conquest of Arabia and the control of the Red Sea routes. Twenty-five years before, Aelius Gallus had been sent on a similar expedition, which had miscarried disastrously owing to native treachery: there was to be no mistake now; explorers and geographers were called upon to gather information for the forthcoming invasion, and a fleet was sent to operate in the Red Sea (if we read a passage of Pliny correctly). The deaths of Gaius and Lucius wrecked these schemes; a formidable rebellion broke out upon the North-Eastern frontier, the province of Germany was lost by Varus, and the aged emperor had no more courage. Then it was that he advised his successors against any extension of the bounds of the realm, but hardly till then.

For the creation of the Empire and its trade one man alone was responsible; others before him had shewn how to conquer, but the Republic had never learnt how to govern. In his efforts to ensure good governance Augustus visited nearly all the provinces, and it is typical of the man that he could remark, à propos of Alexander's desire for more worlds to conquer, that "he was surprised that Alexander did not regard the right ordering of the empire he had won a heavier task than winning it." And in order to secure the right ordering of his vast realm great pains must have been taken with the information and intelligence service: we know that at his death the emperor left a document called the "Breviarium totius Imperii," in which was contained an exact account of the state of the Empire, the number of soldiers, the money in the treasury, amounts due to it and so on, and we must not forget either the great map which Agrippa had drawn up under his direction. We can scarcely doubt that geographers like Strabo or the erudite Juba, and explorers such as Dionysius or Isidore of Charax were encouraged by the court; Strabo, who had travelled extensively in Armenia, Cappadocia, and Syria, and had voyaged up the Nile, or Isidore, who knew and had described the Eastern trade-route through Parthia, must have supplied invaluable information upon frontier problems or the state of the bordering kingdoms. It has been said that the Republic conquered the world without maps: it is certain that the Empire governed the world by using them.

CHAPTER TWO
EGYPT

"Percrebuerat antiquitus urbem nostram nisi opibus Aegypti ali sustentarique non posse. Superbiebat ventosa et insolens natio quod victorem quidem populum pasceret tamen quodque in suo flumine, in suis navibus, vel abundantia nostra vel fames esset."

PLINY

"Loquax et in contumelias praefectorum ingeniosa provincia."

SENECA

CHAPTER TWO

EGYPT

TO describe the economic relations of Egypt to Rome during our period is by no means an easy task, firstly owing to the vast and almost embarrassing wealth of material at our command and secondly owing to the peculiar nature of the province itself. Over two thousand years ago Herodotus saw and enunciated the truth that "Egypt is the gift of the Nile," and although he referred only to the Delta his words are true of the whole country. Its prosperity depended wholly on the river, and in consequence the management of the irrigation, the control of the crops and of the agricultural produce, and even of industry lay wholly in the care of a centralised administration at the head of which stood the king. The ownership of all land by the ruler, the policy of royal monopolies, the careful exclusion of foreign trade and importation, are all natural results of the position and peculiar nature of the country.

When the Ptolemies came into possession of the land we find that their chief efforts were directed to improving its internal resources and encouraging trade with outside countries, especially those of the South and East. Egypt was absolutely independent of foreign help for grain and could export its surplus; trade with the South provided not only elephants for the royal armies but also ivory and costly Eastern spices and gums which could be sold at a high profit to foreigners. The wealth of the realm rapidly multiplied and this together with the importance of its corn for the supply of Rome excited the cupidity of Italian statesmen. As Egypt was one of the three great granaries of the city it was imperative that its rulers should be friendly and its agriculture in a prosperous condition. So we can well understand how Rome regarded with increasing

disgust the feeble rule of the later Lagids and their neglect
of the country. Caesar early in his career had thoughts of
annexing it. Neither Antony nor Cleopatra knew how to
handle properly the immense power which their control
of Egypt and its resources gave them, otherwise the history
of Rome might have been very different. But their conqueror, Augustus, realised to the full the position and
importance of the country, its wealth, its volume of trade,
its immunity from invasion, its contribution to the corn-
supply. No other Roman of rank except the emperor's
servants was allowed to set foot there without special leave;
Augustus became the ruler of Egypt and controller of all
its revenues; there was—apparently—no break in the suc-
cession, and his own statement that he had added
"Egypt to the empire of the Roman people" was a politic
fiction.

Few defensive forces were needed, for there was no
frontier line open to invasion; on the East approach was
difficult; on the South two years' fighting convinced the
Aethiopians that it was unprofitable to make raids on Roman
possessions. No strong forces were placed in the land;
three legions and nine auxiliary cohorts were left there by
Augustus, and even these were employed mostly upon
works of peace and police, and their number decreased by
successive rulers. The irrigation channels upon which the
fertility of the country depended and which had been
allowed to fall into disrepair during the "drunken debauch" of the later Lagid rule, were cleaned out and put
in order by the soldiery, and the same was done with the
navigable canals. The results were soon apparent; under
one of the early governors a low inundation which would
have spelt famine in former days produced one of the
largest crops known, owing to careful conservation and dis-
tribution of the precious waters. The security of travellers
and merchants was also watched over by cohorts placed at

suitable spots. The Eastern trade will be discussed in another section, but it may be remarked that an enormous increase took place; few ships had dared formerly to shew themselves in the Red Sea, but now, with conditions of greater peace and security, their number increased sixfold and many undertook the hazardous voyage to the Indies. Furthermore this policy was continued by succeeding emperors; both under Nero and under Trajan canals and ditches were carefully cleaned and kept in repair and even fresh ones made where it became necessary. Meanwhile the fiscus received rich revenues and dues from the country and from the trade passing through it; the emperors owned monopolies on the production and sale of innumerable articles and commodities, such as linen, oil, paper, bricks, alum, beer, and so on. Organised commercialism prevailed and it must be confessed that little or nothing was done to ameliorate the life of the natives; municipal institutions were little known until the end of the first century of our era. But for this we must perhaps blame more the nature of the country than any lack of humanity on the part of the emperors. The letters and documents we possess by no means suggest a downtrodden population groaning under an oppressive tyranny, but rather a busy and thriving people far too much occupied to ask itself whether it is happy or not.

For Egypt the great highway of commerce was the Nile. The ease with which goods could be transported upon it made roads superfluous; the usual method of travel was by boat and barge, as we can discern from references in Strabo and the contemporary writers, and vehicular traffic can have been little used. Where the narrow river valley widens out into the Delta a network of artificial channels had been constructed to supplement the river ways and these were employed both for business and pleasure. An important canal led from the easternmost branch of the

Nile to the Red Sea, upon which that Eastern merchandise
was conveyed which made the inner harbour of Alexandria
a more crowded one than the outer. Thus while traffic
between the North and the South was provided for by the
river, artificial waterways catered for the cross traffic. But
there is one natural exception to the rule that water was
used for transport. The mountains lying to the East of the
Nile were rich in porphyry, granite, and building stone,
and also in gems and jewels; furthermore, beyond them
lay the Red Sea and its ports. Certain gaps in this mountain chain afforded easy passes and through these man had
early established routes, which were turned into regular
thoroughfares by the Ptolemies; by this way the ivory of
Africa, the gums and spices of Arabia, the pearls, cottons
and silks of India were conveyed into Egypt. But that is
not to say that roads existed paved in the Roman manner;
they were probably hard-beaten tracks in the sand, though
certain special causes—to which we shall call attention later
—may have demanded a better road-bed, and of course in
Alexandria there were broad roads of great magnificence,
extending far, suitable for horse or vehicular traffic. But
the camel was, then as now, the animal most used for
transport, and paved roads are antagonistic to him. Again,
it must be borne in mind that Egypt, since it did not
require large military forces, never had to face the problem
of moving big bodies of troops; all such movement as was
necessary could be carried out on shipboard, and an elaborate system of frontier and strategic roads would have been
useless.

With this consideration we may proceed to investigate
more in detail the system of roads and waterways. The
chief ports of the land lay all to the West and East of the
Delta itself, for the mouths of the Nile were not large
enough to accommodate big ships and so had no harbours,
and those between the Delta and Gaza in Palestine were

very poor. We know of several havens such as Paraetonium, Drepanon, Dermis, and Leucaspis in the West,
and Pelusium in the East, but all these paled into in-
significance before the famous harbour of Alexandria, the
largest in the world and the busiest mart of the whole
Empire. The several mouths of the Nile were all inter-
connected by cross-channels, so that, as Strabo says, the
whole Delta was navigable, and it was possible to go from
Alexandria to Pelusium by canal. These canals were
crowded always, by day with the ships of the traders and
contractors, and at night-time with swarms of pleasure-
boats bearing revellers from the towns. But the most important of all was that which led from the Easternmost
branch of the Nile through the Bitter Lakes to Arsinoe on
the Red Sea—near the site of the modern Suez—and which
was connected by a branch channel with Pelusium. This
had originally been dug in very early times and restored and
improved by various Pharaohs and Lagids; Augustus put
it in order again and Trajan appears to have constructed
a new channel entering the Red Sea at Clysmon, which
was called after its author "Trajan's River." This canal,
which carried a vast volume of traffic to Alexandria, was
150 feet wide and capable of taking the largest merchant
ships: other channels also connected it with Memphis and
the South. South of this point traffic followed the course
of the river in its narrowing valley; at different points
channels diverged to important towns, as to Arsinoe on
Lake Moeris, or to Abydos—whence a caravan route
struck out into the Western desert towards the Theban
oasis—to Tanis or to Coptos.

Such was the water system of Egypt, and where it was
not sufficient it was supplemented by the roads. The purpose of these was to make trade possible where waterways
were not available and especially to bring the Red Sea
commerce over the mountains down into the valley of the

Nile. Ports on the coast were chosen in preference to
Arsinoe, because the head of the Gulf of Suez did not
afford good navigation; originally Berenice, founded by
Ptolemy Philadelphus, and distant eleven days' journey
from Coptos, had been the principal harbour, but it was
far from being an ideal site both owing to its distance from
the Nile and also to shoals at the entrance and violent
winds. Subsequently Myos Hormos took its place; it lay
only seven days' journey from Coptos, the road was carefully marked out into stages, water collected in large reservoirs, and stations provided for traders. But further along
this route there lay porphyry and granite quarries which
were opened under the emperor Claudius and called from
him Mons Claudianus; as these were only thirty miles
from the sea we must suppose that some form of paved or
prepared road led thence to Myos Hormos, for it would
indeed have been difficult to cart huge blocks across the
intervening desert to the Nile. In the North at the head of
the Gulf of Suez lay Arsinoe, upon which three land routes
converged; one led from the town of Gerrha, upon the
Persian Gulf, across the waterless sands, and was much
frequented; the second came down from Casium and was
the route used by those coming South from Syria and
Palestine; the third struck across from Pelusium, its path-
way through the desert being marked by staves set in the
sands, marks which were often obliterated by storms. For
those who were bound from Northern Asia to Alexandria
the route lay from Gaza or Ascalon in one-day journeys
through Raphia and Rhinocolura—where the route from
Petra joined the coast road—then to Ostracine and the
temple of Zeus Casius, and so through the desert to
Pelusium and Alexandria; sometimes a man would proceed by boat past Mendes up to Nicopolis. The stages of
this route are given very fully by Josephus in his account
of the march of Titus from Egypt into Palestine, and the

average day's journey appears to have been between sixteen
and twenty miles. On the Western side of the Nile caravan
routes led to different oases; the famous temple of Ammon
lay five days from Paraetonium and the Theban oasis seven
days across the desert from Abydos. From Alexandria a
road ran westwards along the coast to Cyrene and to the
province of Africa; it was probably this road which was
torn up by Jewish insurgents and which Hadrian restored.
Under this emperor and his great predecessor much
activity in road-building was displayed. Thus we find
Hadrian laying down a new road—to be called after him—
from Antinoe straight across the desert and down the coast
to Myos Hormos; this was obviously intended to foster
trade by shortening the journey from the Red Sea to the
Nile, while at the same time it tapped the whole extent of
the Mons Porphyrites along which it passed: to ensure the
safety of travellers armed guards were stationed at intervals
and cisterns provided. One exception occurs to prove the
rule of water travel: Strabo says that from Syene to Philae
he travelled by waggon through level country, and a milestone of Trajan has been discovered southwards of
Assouan. The reason is obvious: past Syene come the
cataracts of the Nile rendering all navigation difficult; in
addition, from here to Hierasycaminos was a tract of
debateable land which may have been occupied under
Augustus and was certainly Roman territory by the
days of Domitian. Hence for military purposes quick
communication was an essential and good roads a
necessity.

Upon the question of speed we are not so well informed,
for the notices we have usually only refer to quite exceptional achievements. But the need for a regular and punc-
tual corn supply must have induced the emperors to pay
special attention to the efficiency and safety of the service,
which was entirely under imperial administration. Augustus

assumed the "cura annonae" personally and we find early
emperors helping in times of scarcity by funds from the
fiscus or by offering bounties to ship-captains for winter
sailing. Much depended on the winds. During the first
part of the summer a direct voyage from Alexandria to
Rome could be made, but about mid-July the Etesians,
blowing strongly from the North-West, stopped all direct
westward navigation, while accelerating the eastward passage. The only possible course then for travellers was slow
sailing at night (when the wind dropped) or hugging the
Syrian and Asiatic coasts and taking advantage of local
breezes. For Alexandria was the great centre for those who
wished to sail not only from Egypt but also from Syria and
Judea, and the usual method was to coast down thither and
await the sailing of the corn-convoy, which carried passengers, often in large numbers. Of course navigation in
winter was not absolutely impossible, but the ordinary
merchant would not dream of trusting himself to the
stormy waters save under strong urgency. The quickest
time made from Rome was a voyage of nine days, and
doubtless the recorded seven-day passages from Messana
and Utica were all made during the blowing of the
Etesians. Usually the passage from Crete took three or
four days and that from Rhodes three, and in comparison
with these figures the ordinary voyage from Rome must
have taken eighteen or nineteen days. We find that news
of events in Rome during the spring and early summer
could be known in Egypt in at least twenty days, whereas
in winter it took double that time. For the return from
Alexandria we have even less information, but it would be
probably no exaggeration to place it at twenty-five days
even under favourable circumstances; such a voyage as
that to Massilia in thirteen days must be regarded as something utterly out of the common. Inland, we know that the
voyage up the river to Coptos took twelve days and that it

needed nearly two months for the news of Nero's death to reach Elephantine; from Coptos, Myos Hormos lay seven and Berenice twelve days' journey. Marching up from Alexandria into Palestine Titus took about fourteen days —including a two days' rest—and in later times Bethlehem could be reached from Egypt in sixteen. Once again the exceptional nature of the country is responsible; transport by river or camel is not to be hurried; there was not the bustle and hurry of the western provinces with their well-laid roads, but rather the less ostentatious methods of the East which though slow yet brought a volume of merchandise to Rome in exchange for her specie.

To turn now to the resources of the province. Its wealth came mostly from the river and its fertilising mud, but some portion of it arose also from the vast store of magnificent building material lying in quarries to the East of the Nile, besides the revenue derived from tolls on traffic passing through the land. Far in the South gold and iron were exported from Aethiopia, especially from the mines round about Meroe, while in properly Egyptian territory both these minerals were found near Syene. But veins of copper and iron lay nearer at hand in the mountains of the Sinai peninsula, where they had been worked from very early days, and in addition gold and silver were brought across the peninsula from the land of Nabat. Both at Syene and also in the mountains fringing the Red Sea building stone was accessible; with this the temples of Egypt had been built, and it was also exported to Rome for the decoration of the homes of the wealthy. From Syene was obtained black basalt and a beautiful kind of red granite which had been used for the third pyramid, and which has been found in the ruins of Belgian villas. In the Mons Claudianus lay veined marbles as well as serpentine, granite, and green and red porphyry; all this was exported to Italy and the West. These mines were the property of the emperor and

were either worked by his servants or by contractors. The
opening of such quarries during our period shews how
large a demand there was for building material and the
encouragement given to such working. Near Memphis lay
the quarries from which had been carved the stone used
in the construction of the first two pyramids. Along the
desert road to Berenice amethysts, beryls, and other precious stones could be gathered; and there was an island
just off the harbour called Smaragdinon from the quantity
of emeralds picked up there. In the valleys by Memphis
and along the Canopic branch of the Nile native soda was
dug and the Vallis Nitria was so named from the abundance of that mineral; it was made up and exported to
Rome, though Pliny tells us that it was much adulterated.
Lastly, alum was a product of the land, being used for the
dyeing and tanning of leather, and Egyptian alum was said
to be the best procurable.

We have already mentioned the fertilising waters of the
Nile and their supreme importance for agriculture, but it
is a fact that can never be sufficiently iterated that the river
is the sole explanation of the nature of the country and of
its institutions. The fertility of the land was extraordinary;
three crops a year could be produced and the abundance
of all necessary foodstuffs made it singularly independent
of all outside aid. In the valley various kinds of cereals
were sown, such as wheat, millet, barley, and spelt; flax
was extensively cultivated, together with the byblus and
Egyptian bean, gourds, cucumbers, and lentils, and the
olive and the vine grew in some parts, being specially
tended round Alexandria and the Fay'um, while a good
brand of wine came from Pelusium. The date-palm, though
it grew in the Delta, was not much esteemed there, but that
of Thebes and of the Southern valleys was famous. In the
orchards figs, pomegranates, peaches, cherries, citrons,
melons, and black olives ripened, with other kinds of fruit;

olives, cyprus, castor and the sesame plant were all cultivated for the sake of oil, but corn, dates, and papyrus were
the three most renowned articles of export. In the country
asses, sheep, and oxen were raised, and these provided
wool and hides and cheeses. The old system of administration was taken over by Augustus; though here and there
changes in name and office were introduced, no real
alteration was brought about. Thus not only was the corn
trade—as we might have expected—wholly in the hands
of the imperial agents, from the moment when they delivered seed to the "royal farmers" to the time when the
grain was delivered to the overseer at Alexandria for transport to Rome, but the sowing of flax (for linen production),
of castor and sesame (for oil), was strictly controlled by the
same officials, who determined the area of land to be sown
each year, and doled out the proper amount of seed for the
plots. Again, the sale of the finished products was an
imperial monopoly, and in this way the production and
even the selling-price of linen garments and rough cloth,
of bricks, of papyrus, of glass ware, of perfumes, cosmetics,
ointments, of alum, and even of the indispensable $\zeta \hat{v} \theta o \varsigma$
or beer were all supervised by the emperor's servants, and
the resulting profits went to the imperial exchequer.
Whether some of the other industries such as the tanning
and dyeing of leather, the weaving and dyeing of wool, the
production of purple, the salting and pickling of fish, were
also monopolies it would be hard to say, but we are certainly left with the impression that trade in the Nile valley
was most jealously watched over and very little left to
private enterprise. This, however, had great scope in the
importation of material for the workshops of Alexandria
to use, and large profits could be secured. But it was
only profitable to import those articles which the workmen
of Alexandria and of other towns made into finished products; there was little market for Sidonian glass or for

Western pottery in Egypt. The oil of the Delta was poor,
yet no importation of foreign oil was allowed at all; even
the neighbouring Syrian oil could only be brought into
the country for personal use after payment of a duty of
25 per cent., and its importation for sale was absolutely
forbidden. The making of papyrus into paper, and its
export had been found so profitable that a deliberate
attempt was made to enhance its price by careful restriction upon growing. By such measures the rulers of the
land jealously guarded its resources and secured their own
revenue.

Thanks to recent discoveries of papyrus we are now able
to construct for ourselves a very accurate picture of the
commercial life of Roman Egypt, both in its towns and in
its villages. Easily the most important centre was Alexandria which out-topped all other cities. Indeed it was the
second one of the Empire: in commerce it was the first in
the whole world. It was said that Augustus had originally
meant to build a rival to it, but soon realised the exceptional
opportunities of its site and fostered its trade rather than
diminished it. By day its two large sea-harbours lay open
to all vessels, by night the lofty Pharos pointed out the way
to approaching mariners; inland, there was a third harbour
whither came the wares of Aethiopia, Arabia, and India,
and the bulk of the trade was larger here than in both the
two seaward harbours. For it was here that the raw material from the East—the silk, cotton, ivory, hides, drugs,
and spices—were received into her workshops, to be
despatched from them into every quarter of the Mediterranean world. Yet in return for these she drew few
imports from the North; the merchant vessels which set
sail heavily laden from her havens never returned from the
ports of Italy with an equal freight. To carry on her
diverse trades the city had attracted to herself a population
as mingled then as it is now; native Egyptians jostled Greeks

and Syrians and Arabs in the streets; Italian merchants on business, Romans travelling for pleasure and sight-seeing, Western provincials who came to attend the great medical school or upon some business errand, Sabaeans and even Indians, all helped to swell the motley crowd of the city, while the Jews had settled here in such numbers that they comprised two-fifths of the total population, probably the richest; although they shared in the privileges of citizenship they were apparently segregated from the other citizens under an ethnarch of their own and a separate council. This mingling of races did not tend to peaceful living; continual petty riots took place, even under Roman rule, although, as Strabo confesses, much had been done for the peaceableness and good order of the city. Outbreaks against the Jews seem to have been especially common—possibly owing to their usury—and any occasion was deemed good enough excuse by either party; during nearly every reign an embassy of some sort went to the court of Rome to lay its complaint before the emperor. Indeed the Alexandrian mob had a bad reputation from early times and it is said that the governors dreaded going there.

Though the city needed comparatively little in the way of imports, we find amber and tin being brought in from the North-West, wines coming from Italy, the Greek islands, and Asia, and horses being brought from Syria. Reference is also made to Spanish cloaks and to Narbonese and Arretine pottery; how far this was a regular trade and not a mere importation of household goods by soldiers and their families it would be difficult to say. From the East, on the other hand, she received cinnamon, myrrh, pepper, ginger, Indian incense, drugs, precious stones, ivory and tortoise-shell, Indian steel, cotton and rough cloth, and passed these on to the West. But two of the most famous industries were glass-making and the weaving and preparation of linen cloth and garments. The making of glass had been practised here for nearly two thousand years and had been brought to a high pitch of perfection; among the tribute levied from Alexandria by Augustus was a quantity of glass ware, and the making of it was an imperial monopoly. The products of the Alexandrian workshops soon spread all over the Empire, and we find that during the first century factories began to spring up not only in Campania, Rome, and the North of Italy, but also in Spain and Gaul, along the banks of the Rhine, and even in far-distant Britain; for the establishment of these factories skilled workmen from Alexandria must have been required, if indeed they were independent, and not merely branch agencies of the Egyptian manufacturers. The recent discovery of the method of blowing glass had reduced the price so considerably that instead of its being an article of luxury it could now compete with metal vessels, and quantities of the cheaper sorts of household ware and vases were now being turned out: all over the Western provinces of the Empire are unearthed the brightly-coloured glass beads, the oil-flasks, and perfume bottles which were manufactured here, and competition was so great that the workmen of Alexandria carefully imitated the products of rival shops. Again, no contracts are more frequently met with in the papyri of the period than those of apprenticeship to a weaver; the industry was almost universal and we find Egyptian cloth and woven garments from various centres being exported down the coast into Africa and even into the Indian ports, whither too cheap glass and ornaments were taken. It was this busy trade which filled the workshops of which Strabo speaks, and which made a later historian exclaim that "not an idle person lives in Alexandria. Some manufacture glass, some papyrus, others are linen-workers, while all profess some trade or other." Everything was to be found in the city which the heart of man could desire and it was easy for the weary merchant to find there all the relaxation and pleasure he could wish. Even in the heat of the summer there were always the cool breezes blowing in from the sea and in the evenings the pleasure-boats made their leisurely way along the canals to Lake Mareotis or to Canopus. In spite of the turbulence of the citizens, we may say that the city was at the height of its prosperity during our period; the Bucolic war, however, dealt a severe blow at the industry and commerce of Egypt, and its decline was accelerated by the senseless and tyrannical massacre of the Alexandrians by Caracalla. Trade never recovered its former prosperity; it is only after the time of Constantine that we can trace a gradual improvement, and that is beyond our period.

The corn trade was another imperial monopoly. Some of the supply to the city came in the form of tribute, some was raised by the "royal farmers" upon the emperor's domains. The imperial officials decided how much land was to be sown every year, and how much seed devoted to the purpose. After it had been reaped and threshed it was conveyed to the proper granaries for the district; from these it was taken down to the landing-places upon the river or adjacent canals, and shipped down to Alexandria, where it was handed over to another official; here finally ship-companies or private owners took charge of it for transport to Rome. Thus it was that every year Egypt contributed to the hungry populace of the city some twenty million bushels of corn, besides supplying its own wants. It was of the utmost importance to the emperor that the service should be regular and constant, and that it should be safely conducted; the ships usually arrived in large convoys, and careful provision was made for their reception. Even the mad Caligula had proposed to construct harbours of refuge for storm-tossed convoys by the Sicilian straits, though apparently the scheme fell through. During Claudius' reign the city had once but fifteen days' supply of corn left

and only an exceptionally mild winter and the bounties
offered by the emperor to all merchants who would undertake the voyage tided over the dangerous situation. Ship-
builders were encouraged; a large harbour was built at
Ostia for the reception of the corn-ships, which was enlarged and improved by succeeding emperors, and owners
of ships were allowed to deduct the value of their vessels
from their total property when being assessed for taxes.
One of the main duties of the governor must have been the
supervision of the supply; how absolutely it was controlled
by him is displayed by the fact that Herod, on the occasion
of a famine in Judea, could not import corn privately out of
Egypt, but had to apply for permission to Petronius the
governor. Again, Germanicus was severely rebuked for
entering Egypt—a province over which he had no jurisdiction—during a scarcity, which he relieved by releasing
surplus corn in the imperial granaries; by so doing he
greatly endangered the supply of the capital. At a later
period, by careful conservation in the Italian warehouses,
Trajan was able to relieve a poor year in Egypt by sending
straight back the ships which had just arrived at Ostia. In
the second century, however, wars and various disturbances
appear to have seriously damaged the productive power
of Egypt, and a significant mark of this was the setting-up
of a separate African corn-fleet by Commodus.

In comparison with Alexandria all other cities of the
land appear small and insignificant; yet we can see that
they were full of a thriving commercial activity and our
knowledge of this has been enormously increased since the
publication of the papyri, which throw a vivid light upon
every side of life from early Ptolemaic days down to the
incursion of the Arabs. Glass vases and ware were manufactured at Diospolis; clothing for export to the Eastern
coast of Africa at Arsinoe on the Red Sea; we have an
almost intimate acquaintance with the region of the

Fay'um. Here in the town of Arsinoe, lying in the midst of the most fertile region of the whole land, we know the very names of the roads, the Street of the Linenweavers, the Street of the Fishers, and other streets named after the trades and callings that were practised in them. Here are to be found innumerable small shopkeepers and pedlars, sellers of wine and beer, of salt and fish (for every kind of fish was to be caught in the river), of bread and vegetables and fruit, of wood and furniture, of dyed wool and rugs and garments, of gold and silver and precious stones, and here are the captains who carry the corn down the river and hand it over to the superintendents at Alexandria. And the same tale is told by the papyri coming from other villages; the same prosperity and eager life reigned at such towns as Karanis, Euhemeria, Bacchias, Hermupolis Magna, and in Oxyrhynchus itself, "the glorious and renowned city," as its inhabitants proudly term it. We can discern the villagers in their everyday life, engaged at their common tasks; we can read their letters and reconstruct for ourselves, twenty centuries after, an unrivalled picture of their surroundings. Contracts of apprenticeship, leases of gardens and orchards, undertaking of a monopoly for the sale of some article, all these come before our eyes constantly. We can still read the letters in which the writers beg their friends not to forget to send down the wine or cheese or food they want, or the fine rugs or cloaks from Alexandria that they wish to display: or there are anxious requests for a water-wheel that is long overdue, enquiries as to whether a particular plot of ground is to be flooded, rejoicings over a successful business deal, advice from an elder to a younger partner, and warnings to a young man in financial trouble to "keep away from the Jews." It is a vivid picture that is presented to us and one that speaks much for the security and contentedness brought about under Roman rule.

Although Roman traders are met with in Egypt as early as 100 B.C. and occasionally an enterprising capitalist such as Rabirius, was able to make a good deal in the royal monopolies, we may be reasonably sure that the bulk of the trade lay in the hands of the Greek citizens of Alexandria, and that it was they who ventured out down the Red Sea or up the Nile Valley to Aethiopia. A certain amount of traffic must have been carried on with the latter country by means of the river, and this goes back to very early times, as excavations at Meroe have shewn: some could come by sea, but Strabo expressly states that the Aethiopians did not use the Red Sea much, and so it must have been by the Nile that the gold and bronze and iron of the country together with its ivory, ebony, and precious stones came to Egypt. It was possibly in search of new routes and relations that the exploratory force was despatched up the Nile by Nero, and returned with a map to the Court. But the merchants of Egypt spread far beyond the confines of their country; we know that there was a constant coming and going between it and such places as Gaza or Petra, and we find an Egyptian resident at Palmyra. The bulk of the corn-trade must have been theirs, and a great deal of the carrying traffic between East and West. We have only to remember the Alexandrian ships mentioned in the Acts, the vessel upon which Josephus sailed, and the Alexandrian ship of which Thamus was the pilot, or think of the worship paid to Augustus by Alexandrian sailors, or of the panegyrics of Philo, to realise how largely the Mediterranean must have been studded by their vessels, and how much the peace and security of the Empire meant for their prosperity. But more, they established themselves in Rome itself, to the disgust of the satirists, who viewed with indignation such men as Crispinus growing rich and powerful at Court, and lording it over Roman citizens. So, too, the Red Sea voyagers to India must have been all

Greeks. From the very moment of Augustus' conquest of Egypt, the Indian and Eastern trade took on a new lease of life; merchants in increasing numbers undertook the voyage and the imperial policy fostered this trade by all possible means; Roman warships appear to have operated on occasion in the Red Sea. Nero paid special attention to all the Eastern trade-routes and it is interesting to compare the differing narratives of Strabo, of the author of the *Periplus*, and of Ptolemy and mark the steadily growing geographical knowledge that they display. It was with the Orient that the main bulk of traffic lay, and we shall shortly trace it out, after first considering Syria.

CHAPTER THREE

SYRIA

"Dives et aureis
Mercator exsiccet culullis
Vina Syra reparata merce."

HORACE

"Itidem opimam illam fertilemque
Syriam velut amplexu suo tegebat
Euphrates." MAMERTINUS

CHAPTER THREE

SYRIA

IN the region of the East that province which presented the greatest problems to the Roman government was undoubtedly Syria. It possessed for them a twofold importance arising not only from its position as a centre for trade and industry but also from the fact that, together with Cappadocia, it formed the frontier against Parthia. We might compare its situation with that of Northern Gaul in the West, but the issues were still further complicated here, firstly because the South-Eastern frontiers were only vaguely defined and liable to predatory inroads of Arabs and Nabataeans, and secondly because the province was not uniformly under Roman rule for many years, but during the first century was governed in part directly by imperial officers, in part by petty princes and tetrarchs. It is true that these rulers were supposed to contribute to the Roman forces in time of war, and that they aided—if they were energetic—in stamping out robbery and brigandage, but their ambitions or their suspected ambitions continually gave uneasiness at the capital; the governor had to be on the watch against them, and the princes retaliated by trying to outdo the governors in services and information to the emperor. A king such as Herod the Great or Agrippa I did good by restoring law and order in the mountainous districts, by erecting buildings, by encouraging trade through the construction of new harbours and roads, or by going round—on the pattern of the ancient Jewish kings—to administer justice to the people, as did the tetrarch Philip; but where the rulers were not strong they proved merely a burden to their unfortunate subjects by the taxes which they imposed in order to maintain the splendour of their courts and establishments.

This is not the place to enter into a discussion of the frontier except so far as is necessary to understand the main history of the period. Armenia was the distressful country which played the part of buffer state between the Parthians and the Romans, who placed their rival candidates alternately on the throne of the land. Tiberius had been sent, when a young man, by Augustus to impose a king on the country and to recover from the Parthians the standards lost at Carrhae: when he himself came to the throne he already knew the East well; it is interesting to find him taking steps, which though reversed by his immediate successors, were confirmed by later emperors. Thus his annexation of Cappadocia and Commagene secured to the Empire two highly important crossings of the Euphrates, at Melitene and at Samosata, making defence of the frontier easier, and this policy was confirmed by the shrewd Vespasian. Again Tiberius' orders to dethrone the king of the Nabataeans would have meant the creation of a province of Arabia, with control of the route through Petra to the Red Sea, and the annexation of the Nabataean kingdom was actually carried into effect by Trajan about seventy years later. Indeed the Flavian and later emperors did what their predecessors had hesitated to do, they abolished the troublesome system of client-princes, and one by one Cappadocia, Commagene, Chalcis, Abilene, Batanea, and Judea were quietly annexed. In this way not only was the security of the frontier assured, but one efficient mode of government substituted for the petty rivalries of the former rulers.

In Syria more than in any other province of the Empire we are impressed with the antiquity of the routes followed. From ages past it has formed the medium of communication between East and West and also between Egypt and the North-East, and roads had been marked out long before the Romans set foot in the province. Damascus was situated

at a spot where routes converge from every direction
and where the riches of every land of the old world could
be exchanged, nor must we forget the important part
which such great religious centres as Jerusalem, or such
shrines as those of Doliche or Emesa, play in the building
up of trade. The country is one of lofty mountain-chains
and of deep river-valleys, of which the longest is the great
depression known as the Jordan valley, which is continued
down to the Red Sea in the Wadi-el-Arabah. To the East
of this valley lie the high table-lands of the desert. These
natural features have controlled and determined the roads
which man should follow in intercourse with his fellows.
From Egypt northwards there was only one practicable
route, which kept close to the coastline until it reached
Gaza, where a division occurred, one branch striking across
the sands to Petra and the East, while the others went
North. Of these the most westerly simply hugged the
coast past its numerous harbours, such as Caesarea and
Tyre and Berytus, up to Seleucia, the port for Antioch.
Another way, doubtless much frequented by the Jews
coming up from Egypt for the feasts at Jerusalem, led
straight across the desert to that city, and it was upon this
road that Philip met the eunuch returning to Ethiopia.
But the main trade-route started from Gaza and after
keeping parallel to the coast for some time turned eastwards to surmount the ranges of Carmel and Ephraim by
the passes of Dothan down into the plain of Esdraelon;
thence it followed first the valley of the upper Jordan, then
struck up the stream of the river Litas, past Heliopolis,
and so down the valley of the Orontes to Emesa, Antioch,
and the North: but from Esdraelon an important and frequented route crossed the Jordan and led to Damascus,
which through the ages has been one of the great exchange
marts of East and West. In the South the Jordan valley
and its continuing depression form another natural way

for commerce coming up from the Red Sea; merchandise
could be landed either direct at Aila or at Leuce Come,
whence there was a much-used road to Petra; here it
divided, one way going West to Gaza and the Mediterranean, the other climbing northward among the hills to
the East of the Jordan through Philadelphia and Canatha
to Damascus. From the latter city a caravan track led
through the desert to the rich oasis of Palmyra and the
Euphrates, while another struck directly northward to
Epiphania, whence it was possible to reach all the towns
of the Orontes valley and Antioch itself; or a man might
go through Chalcis and Beroea up to the famous crossing
of the Euphrates at Zeugma, or westward to the passes over
Mount Amanus in Cilicia. Roads radiated from the capital
Antioch in all directions; westwards to Cilicia and so to
Byzantium, eastwards to Palmyra, the Euphrates, and
Babylon, northwards to the important crossings of the
Euphrates at Samosata and Zeugma, and to the iron and
stone quarries of those regions. After Trajan's time five
routes converged on this city and here was the seat for the
exaction of customs-duties and so on; in this district and
near Cyrrhus have been discovered many remains of
Roman roads, and their magnificent bridges still remain
standing where the modern French or Turkish constructions have been swept away. Naturally there were roads
leading from the more important inland towns to the coast;
Antioch was so linked with its port of Seleucia, Apamea
with Laodicea, Hemesa with Aradus, Damascus with
Sidon, and Jerusalem with Caesarea; in the region of Lake
Tiberias too there appear to have been many local roads
and much traffic upon them. But the main currents of
traffic flowed North and South, and just as Thothmes III
defeated the Syrian princes at Megiddo, and Rameses II
routed the Hittites at Kadesh on the Orontes, so in later
ages Allenby crushed the Turkish forces at Armageddon,

all following the same natural and clearly-defined route.

What the actual state of the roads was at the beginning of the period it is difficult to say with any certainty, but in many parts of the country a paved track was not needed, for the desert surface was sufficiently firm and hard, and all that was needful was to bridge the rapid torrents and possibly pave those portions of the roadway that led through towns, as was done at Antioch. Doubtless the Hellenistic rulers had done something towards improving communications, and we have already seen that Herod and his family built harbours and warehouses and generally did much for trade, and it seems probable that short spaces of track were paved though the greater part of the roads was not. There is an interesting inscription from Abila, belonging to the time of Tiberius, in which a freedman of the royal house boasts of having erected buildings, and further that he had "paved the road which had been without stone before." We hear also of a spacious roadway cut through the hills to the West of Antioch, but the date of its construction is uncertain, thought it may be assigned to this period. Only in the North of the province where military considerations rendered rapid communication desirable may we be reasonably sure that real Roman roads existed. Usually a hard-beaten track lasted well, though we hear of one being swept away by a mountain torrent in spate. But apart from natural obstructions, so long as most of the land was under native rulers, the country districts were infested by robbers or by the bands that gathered round fanatical prophets; these people made themselves a nuisance to Romans and natives alike, while on the East side of the Jordan the Arabs were always ready to take toll of traders, and their petty officials had to be bribed in proportion to the riches of the caravan. The dangers of a journey through mountainous Judea were not small and a guard had often to be provided against foot-pads and thieves. Yet such kings as Herod certainly did make an effort to put down brigandage, by stationing garrisons in the hilly regions, and the great Agrippa, the friend and general of Augustus, set an example by estab-lishing colonies of veterans at Berytus and at Heliopolis, where they could command and secure the important road that led through the Lebanon and anti-Lebanon from Damascus to Berytus. The presence of Roman armed forces in the land and the orderliness which they pro-duced was the greatest guarantee of security for traders and travellers. In later times when Trajan added the province of Arabia Petraea to the Empire a splendid system of paved roads sprang up East of the Jordan, connecting the more important centres, while along the most easterly was set a line of watch-towers and posts. At the same time the main roads of Syria and Judea were carefully paved and set in order, and garrisons placed at suitable points: so too the long road from Antioch to the East was pro-tected by armed bands which the various municipalities supplied, and the greatest care was taken of it, all holes and erosion being filled up and the road-bed constantly repaired. On the Northern Syrian roads, where miles of track built out of the splendid black basalt of the region have been preserved almost intact, there has been found a softer road-bed not existent in other countries, which would make travelling of every kind much easier. Many authors bear witness to the peace which Roman rule brought to a land formerly harried by robbers, and remark upon the immense improvement which took place.

Traffic by water had been common from the earliest days. There were not many long navigable rivers as in the Western provinces, but Antioch could be reached from its port Seleucia in one day's sail up the Orontes, and other rivers were navigable in short stretches. The sea-coast,

though it contains scarcely any large harbours, afforded
many havens sufficient for the small ships of that time, and
Seleucia, Laodicea, Aradus, Berytus, Ptolemais, Joppa,
Ascalon, and Gaza, not to mention the Phoenician towns,
drove a flourishing trade and were crowded with throngs
of sailors and of loungers, who were always ready to join
in a riot or aid in causing trouble. Tyre and Berytus were
enriched and adorned with buildings by Herod the Great;
to the South he provided a new port for his capital, by
making an artificial harbour at a place called Turris
Stratonis, which he re-named Caesarea Sebaste, in compliment to his suzerain Augustus. This harbour was as
large as that of Athens, gave a depth of twenty fathoms of
water and was protected by an immense mole. Similar
measures were taken by the emperors in many places, and
at Seleucia in Pieria extensive improvements were carried
out by Vespasian; the channel which had silted up was
widened, a new sea-wall built, and quays and warehouses
constructed to foster trade, for this port served far the
greater part of Northern Syria.

Along the whole length of this coast a busy commerce
was kept up, and we find St Paul and others embarking on
vessels which made frequent calls at small havens; sometimes the ships would be Syrian, more often from Alexandria or from a port in Asia Minor. But no attempt was
made to sail direct to Rome: the usual method was to board
a ship bound for Alexandria, and there wait for a boat
sailing to Italy. Thus Agrippa I in the days of his poverty
and misery took a passage on a boat coasting down by
Ptolemais and Anthedon to the Egyptian capital, and thence
—with borrowed money—made his way to Rome; later he
returned by the same route, though this time as king of
Judea. Alternatively the journey could be made up the
coast and round Cyprus, past the havens of Lycia and
Pamphylia, to Rhodes and Samos; in fact the Northern

route seems to have been the favourite one for those who had no pressing calls of business, for it afforded an opportunity of seeing some of the spots most famous in history and legend. And the voyage from Italy or Greece to Syria often followed the same route; we have only to compare the journeys of Herod, of Germanicus, of Piso, and of St Paul (on his return from Ephesus) to see how common it was. Of the Red Sea ports, belonging to the Nabataean kingdom, we shall speak elsewhere in considering the Indian trade-route; here it will suffice to say that the revival of the Far Eastern trade under Augustus, and the interest that he displayed in Egypt and Arabia, would lead us to infer that some action was taken there; there was certainly a Roman centurion stationed at Leuce Come to collect the necessary dues. A century later we find Trajan actually installing a fleet in the Red Sea, probably to put down the Arab pirates, who were a perpetual menace to peaceful merchants and made a permanent police force necessary.

This brings us to another point, the question of speed on land and sea. We have not many indications as to land travel here; Strabo informs us that the journey from Jericho to Petra occupied three to four days, and a very much later author gives twenty-five days for that from Jerusalem to Edessa; we are told that Babylon was considered seventy days' distance from Antioch, from which Beroea could be reached in two days. From Jerusalem to Alexandria took about fifteen or sixteen days. From one or two other notices and from the indications of modern travellers we may take it that foot-passengers would rarely accomplish more than twenty miles in a day, while those on horseback might possibly travel half as far again; thus St Paul appears to have had a conveyance or horses for his two-day journey from Caesarea to Jerusalem. Of course the imperial post-service was much quicker and special

relays of men and horses were provided for it, but we are
here trying to estimate the times of ordinary travellers and
merchants. We cannot give definite figures for the journey
from Rome to Syria by sea or for the speed with which
news of events in the province would reach the capital.
Before the establishment of the Empire we find from
Cicero's correspondence that fifty days was considered
good time from Syria, while the average was nearer one
hundred. But with the Empire greater regularity and
greater efficiency followed; service in summer was good,
but in winter the only sure route would be overland, and
dispatches would almost certainly take at least three months
from the capital. We must not be misled by Pliny's record
of exceptionally good passages, such as that of nine days
from Puteoli to Alexandria; usually the voyage must have
taken nearly twice as long and at least another six days
would be necessary in order to make the coast of Syria.
We have even less definite information as regards the
Northern route; Herod left Samos and reached Caesarea,
with favouring winds, "in a few days," which expression
implies that such a voyage generally took considerably
longer. Unfortunately most of our notices apply to royal
voyages, where special facilities must have been available.
The ordinary merchant would be compelled to use slow
coasting vessels and would think himself lucky if a month's
voyage brought him in sight of Caesarea or hill-crowned
Berytus.

The actual mineral resources of the province were poor
when compared with the riches of the West. True there
was a small quantity of iron in the mountains behind
Berytus, and the iron mines of Germanicia in the North
have been worked even up to the present day, but it can
have been used only for local purposes, since Indian iron
and steel were imported, especially to Damascus, and had
the reputation of being the finest in the world. We also

hear later of copper mines and of an imperial official
placed in charge of them. But the province possessed
great store of limestone and of basalt, which were extensively quarried for the magnificent structures which adorned
its large towns, and from which the splendid Trajanic
roads were paved; there were marble quarries at Sidon,
and the local stone near Enesh was cut out of the hills by
the soldiery there and floated down the river; there was also
an alabaster stone found near Damascus. The abundance
of native material accounts for the great extent and solidity
of the buildings which we meet everywhere in the province; East of the Jordan the lack of timber compelled the
craftsmen to use stone even more extensively and a new
style of architecture grew up; this becomes of special
importance in Christian times, but even before then Syria
may have exerted some influence upon Rome, for one of
Trajan's greatest architects was Apollodorus of Damascus,
who built for him the huge bridge across the Danube, and
subsequently planned the Forum Traianum and the pillar
of Trajan in Rome. But generally speaking Syria had small
store of minerals, though she worked up the raw materials
which were sent to her from other countries; indeed she
was probably the greatest manufacturing centre of the
ancient world. But her agricultural wealth was greater;
the forests of Lebanon and of the surrounding hills, with
their tall cedars, had of old provided for the navies of Tyre
and Sidon, and certain varieties of timber were expressly
reserved for the Roman fleets. Many of the rivers, such as
the Orontes, the Chrysorroas, the Lycus, and the Jordan,
flowed through valleys rich in crops, and the natural fertility of the region was still further strengthened by careful
irrigation and a system of canals and reservoirs. Strabo
tells us that the Chrysorroas was divided into irrigation
conduits and we have an inscription recording the carving
of a reservoir and channel out of the rock, and in many

places come across the remains of such works (as we do also in Africa). Not only were corn and cereals cultivated here, but fruit-trees in abundance, vines, olives, apples, pears, plums, figs, pomegranates, dates, nuts, and many varieties of scented plants such as rushes, nard, and balsam. There was a great export trade in these fruits to Rome, and also in dried fruits; some trees had already been naturalised in Italy, and even transplanted as far West as Spain, by imperial officers or merchants.

To start from the North: Antioch, the metropolis, was a magnificent city, second only to Alexandria in importance, and to none in the wealth and gaiety which it displayed by day, or by night, when its streets were ablaze with artificial light. It lived by transport and had few manufactures of its own; there were market-gardens and orchards outside the city, but it was a place of residence for the opulent merchant shippers of the East, who exchanged the goods of two continents and lived a life of ostentatious luxury. The well-paved streets, the magnificent temples and porticoes, gifts of wealthy princes or public-spirited citizens, and the famous pleasure-gardens of Daphne some miles away, had bred a pleasure-loving and luxurious population whose arrogant temper more than once brought it into conflict with the authorities. But all this wealth depended upon its being a centre of commerce and transport; it lay within one day's sail of its port, Seleucia, and in the Flavian era a canal was dug to improve navigation upon the Orontes, and extensive repairs and alterations carried out in the harbour itself.

Upon the Southern route towards Epiphania and Palmyra lay the thriving town of Apamea, in a well-watered plain of great extent: here horses and oxen were bred in large numbers, and in the Seleucid era it had been the seat of the famous royal stables. Upon the coast nearly opposite to it was situate the port of Laodicea, lying at the foot

of hills, whose slopes were covered with vines in great profusion; it possessed a good harbour and the native wine
was much exported to Alexandria and farther, for we hear
that it was in demand down the Red Sea coast and even
taken to India. The country all round the city was of great
fertility, and it was here that a celebrated kind of linen was
made and garments woven from it; cloaks and cloth from
Laodicea always commanded a good price. Further South
came the port of Aradus, which had been famous from
very early times; long before the imperial era we find their
merchants established in the island of Nisyros and Rhodes
and in the Aegean, and by our period their many traders
and carriers were organised into powerful guilds presided
over by councillors ($\pi\rho\delta\beta ov\lambda ot$).

But probably the most celebrated town of all and one
that lay in the very heart of the Syrian province was that
of Damascus. Nature had so placed it upon the lines of
traffic that it was bound to be the central mart and exchange
for all who traded in those regions. Here from the earliest
times the minerals of the West had been exchanged for the
silks and spices of China and India, and in our period the
city was at the height of its prosperity. It lay in a fertile
plain watered by many rivers and by artificial irrigation
channels; on every side were to be seen orchards and
gardens and vineyards and various kinds of fruit-trees. In
earlier centuries the city had been renowned for a brand
of wine—the Chalybonian—which it was rumoured the
Great King drank at his table; here, too, were grown olives,
apples, pears, pomegranates, dates, figs, plums, nuts, and
pistachios, and a good export trade was carried on; the dry-
ing of fruit alone formed an industry, and the "pruna"
and "cottana" of Damascus made very acceptable presents. Already some varieties of these trees had been
transplanted into Italy and the West and acclimated there;
Vitellius the famous legate of Syria brought back a species

of fig to Italy, while one of his friends took pistachios to Spain, doubtless with a view to starting a rival industry; sometimes we can observe the result, for about a century later Galen remarks that the dried plums of Spain come a good second to those of Damascus. Flax was cultivated in the plains, and the linens of the city, its cloths and cushions, were in good repute. It would be interesting to speculate whether the famous Arab industry of the tempering of steel had its counterpart in Roman days, for Indian steel was certainly shipped to these regions, but we have not sufficient evidence upon which to base a conclusion.

In connection with the Eastern route a word must be said here about Palmyra. It is true that the city probably lay outside the bounds of the Empire during this period, and also that owing to the defectiveness of our literary sources we know little of its history. But even before the establishment of the Empire it had been famous for its wealth and fertility and had attracted the cupidity of Antonius the triumvir; and as early as the first century B.C. many fine buildings existed. When we observe that the vast temple of Ba'al, which was originally constructed in the first century B.C., was undergoing alterations and additions during the reign of Tiberius, when we find Germanicus sending a rescript with regard to the payment of tolls (a precedent followed by the general Corbulo a generation later), and a Palmyrene tribe named after the emperor Claudius, we are forced to conclude that early in the present era the city had already attained considerable prosperity and was greatly influenced by Rome. Still further inferences can be drawn; certainly by the second century, if not before, all dues of more than one denarius had to be paid in Roman coin and the Roman modius was used as a measure of quantity; furthermore, the frequent references to imperial freedmen, such as Statilius, Barbarus, and Cilix, to whom letters were sent by the governors of

Syria, would lead us to think that these freedmen must have
been imperial agents, resident at Palmyra, who looked
after Roman interests; there may even have been some
kind of minor "iuridicus" there to settle disputes between
the merchants and the toll-collectors. The city itself lay in
a fertile oasis of land in the centre of the desert on the
route between Damascus and the Euphrates, and it was to
this position probably more than even to its agricultural
wealth that it owed its prosperity; for this enabled it to take
toll of the caravans continually passing along the route.
We still possess many inscriptions set up by merchants who
had made the journey from the city, down the Euphrates,
to Charax Spasinu, the port at the mouth of the river. They
always travelled in large caravans and one merchant was
always chosen as leader and commander and received the
compliment of a dedication upon the safe completion of the
passage. The purpose of the tariff-list which was drawn up
in the second century was to put an end to the continual
disputes between collectors and merchants; from it we can
gather an interesting idea of the trade that passed through
the city. In this document are mentioned slaves, wool
(both dyed and undyed), purple garments, perfumes and
ointment in alabaster cases, spices, corn and wine, salt and
pickled fish, and dried goods such as prunes and pine-
kernels, nuts and almonds, and so on. We also find notice
of itinerant clothes-vendors (doubtless merchants with the
products of the looms of the Phoenician coast), and of hide-
sellers, of guilds of goldsmiths and silversmiths, and lastly
of the highly-organised corporations of merchants who
travelled the Euphrates route. The busy traffic that passed
up and down the river is reflected in an itinerary of the
first century, wherein a merchant of Charax details the
various stations between Antioch and Seleucia and even
beyond to the East. All this gives us a very fair impression
of the extent of the trade which supported Palmyra and

raised it in the third century to be for a short time a rival
even of imperial Rome.

Nearly opposite Damascus on the coast lay the important
harbour of Berytus; work was being done early in the first
century upon the road which connected the two towns.
The vineyards and the flax plantations of the district produced the sweet wine and the linen for which it was famous;
along with the other coastal towns of the region Berytus
sent its linen cloths into the whole world, but the city was
celebrated as well for its silken stuffs which were made out
of the raw material which came to it *viâ* Damascus from
China. Indeed throughout this whole region and in
Galilee weaving was the main industry; linen was woven
at Laodicea, Byblus, and Tyre, and Clement of Alexandria
informs us that much was exported from the land of the
Hebrews. A very important centre was the town of
Scythopolis, commanding one of the keys of the overland
route, the crossing of the Jordan (at the modern Beth-
Shean); it was here that the bulk of the linen was made
and under the later empire its importance was such that
it became one of the large imperial Houses of Weaving
(Linypheia). The whole of this region must have formed
one of the most active industrial centres of the Empire, for
both Tyre and Sidon were famous for the manufacture of
silk and silken garments as well as for their linen, and as a
late chronicler tells us "Tyre seethes with every kind of
business." During the times of Augustus these towns
must have been especially prosperous, since silken garments had been much in fashion and were worn by men
and women alike; in the reign of Tiberius some attempt
was made to limit its use, whether successfully or not we
cannot say, and perhaps the economies of the Flavian era
may have diminished their output somewhat. The immense
distances that the silk had to come upon the overland route
from China must have raised the price to a height at which

few but the very rich or those of the emperor's family could afford to buy it, though it is noteworthy that apparently its quality was good enough to drive out of the market the Coan silks which were so much worn during the times of Augustus; these simply vanish from notice, no reference being made to them after the elder Pliny.

Mention of the famous old cities of Tyre and Sidon leads us to speak of two other industries for which they were celebrated. The murex, the shellfish from which the purple dye is extracted, was to be found in quantities all round the Phoenician coast, and hence these cities sent out robes of purple and other dyed cloths to all quarters of the world for the ornament of the rich and luxurious. Some of the other cities of the region exported a different kind of purple, as did Sarepta and Caesarea, but the products of Tyre and Sidon were always considered the superior. They were also renowned for another industry, that of glass-making, and to Sidonian merchants legend ascribed the invention of the process. We cannot, in the light of modern investigation, give our assent to this assertion; glass had been known in Egypt for centuries, and we may believe that the making of it was not introduced into Syria until at least the middle of the first century before our era. But about the time of the Caesarean civil wars a discovery was made, that of glass-blowing, which revolutionised the art, and possibly that discovery occurred at Sidon. The consequences were important: whereas formerly glass had been an instrument of luxury and used for ornament and for ostentation, now the most ordinary kind of household vessels could be made in hundreds and produced at a price much lower than that of metal ones. That is why the industry made so sudden and so enormous an advance in the period immediately following the establishment of the Augustan peace. All over Palestine great quantities of glass belonging to this era have been unearthed, which bear witness to a surprising activity on the part of the Phoenician manufacturers; the wares of these cities are scattered all over the Empire. Signed vases of such Syrian Greeks as Artas, Eirenaios, Ennion and others are to be found not only at Rome, but also in Africa, Gaul, and Germany, where on the banks of the Rhine vessels with Sidonian reliefs upon them have been discovered. But just as the Western provinces had soon learnt the secret of pottery-making, so now they quickly mastered the methods of Syrian and Alexandrian craftsmen, and after a brief period of imitation actually outsold their Eastern competitors in the end. In the reign of Tiberius a factory for making glass was started close to the Porta Capena, and though the legends about the invention of "unbreakable glass" are absurd and untrue, there can be little doubt that they faithfully reflect the amazing progress which the manufacture of glass made in this period.

The inland regions of Galilee and Judea were famous for their fertility in palms, olives, and vines, and the district was dotted with small cities and the more pretentious foundations of the tetrarchs and rulers. Places such as Tiberias—with its salubrious waters—or Livias, Genesara, Julias, Hippo, Archelais, and Phaselis, were all extremely pleasant to live in and traders passed constantly on the roads between them. The sea of Tiberias yielded all kinds of fish in abundance, and the pickling of them must have been a great industry since we find a town named after it, Taricheia. In the region around Jericho, which was celebrated for its palm-trees and streams, lay some of the most productive soil in Judea, and parts of the country round Jamneia had been bequeathed to the imperial family by grateful vassals. Of Jerusalem itself and of the immense trade it drove, in providing for the annual pilgrims and their needs, it is superfluous to speak. It was from this region that came the jujube-trees and the truffles which so delighted Rome and had been acclimated to Italian soil. Towards the South the land grew more rugged and barren but was not without activity, for the Dead Sea supplied bitumen which was exported to Egypt, and in the East lay the great route to Petra and to Arabia; on the coast stood the ports of Gaza and Ascalon, both celebrated for their wine, and the latter city was also famous for onions. These were all exported into Egypt and even farther, for the cities lay upon the great Southern route of which we have already spoken. Altogether this land must have been one of the most busy and fertile corners of the Empire and a delightful one for residence as well, while the foundation of so many towns by the local rulers must have contributed in no small degree to promoting commercial activity.

So much for the coast-land. East of the Jordan lay cities which after the first century increased hugely in prosperity; they were those which sprang up upon the already mentioned route from the Red Sea towards Damascus and the North. When Trajan annexed Arabia Petraea a new era opened for Bostra, Canatha, Philadelphia and other towns, and the former was proud to call itself "the New Bostra of Trajan." At this time a land that is even now little more than desert was fertile and prosperous, owing to the careful irrigation, to the means taken to conserve the scanty water supply, and the vast and far-stretching aqueducts which were built by the governors of the land, remains of which still greet us, constructed of massive blocks hewn from the native stone, wherewith the roads too were made. In their desolation these ruins stand as melancholy testimonials to the civilising power of the Roman.

To the South and East extended the rugged and mountainous lands of Idumaea and of Nabataea, sparsely inhabited and devoid of importance, were it not for the trade-route which ran through them. This made all the

difference, and that is why many Romans and foreigners
were to be found in residence at Petra, where their presence entailed continual law-suits, more in fact than those
of the natives themselves. So large were the caravans that
moved along this route with bales of spices, gums, and
perfumes, from Arabia Sabaea and the South, that they
were compared to an army by Strabo. A century later they
were able to pass securely upon the colossal "New Road"
which Trajan constructed, through his legates, from the
boundaries of Syria to the Red Sea itself: there is left to us
an inscription of this time recording the erection of a gateway at Petra by some rich caravan-master. The country
itself was fruitful in corn and vines, though not in olive, in
place of which the oil of sesame was used; flocks of sheep
and herds of large cattle supplied the inhabitants with
clothing and hides, and many kinds of spices grew in the
land; gold and silver also were mined but not in such large
quantities as the Romans supposed, and the import of
these metals was very carefully controlled, as was the sale
of several of the native products. But the purple of Tyre
and the saffron of Cilicia had to be admitted for the court
of the king, as had also the sculpture and painting of
Hellenic artists for the adornment of his palace, and
doubtless, as at Iol Caesarea, many merchants congregated at Petra to satisfy the royal needs.

Few races shewed such an instinct for trade as the
Syrians; from the earliest times they had been the carriers
and shippers of the Eastern Mediterranean basin, and
though they had sometimes to endure keen competition
they were never ousted. Inscriptions reveal them in the
most outlying parts of the Empire, sometimes as adventurous individuals, sometimes joined together in influential
corporations as at Puteoli and the Italian ports. Merchants
from Aradus and from Tyre and Berytus had settled at
Aegean towns, especially at Delos, as early as the second

century before Christ. Later there was a corresponding
movement of Italians eastward and many merchants of
Rome are met with in Syria, and especially at Antioch,
Jerusalem, and at Petra. But during the first century of
the Empire the provincials grew more and more enterprising and began to outrival the Italians; finally, they beat
them even in Italy and flocked in hundreds to the capital.
Greeks and Syrians were as ubiquitous in Rome as Jews
and Irish in New York; a satirist complains that the
"Syrian Orontes has poured its waters into the Tiber"
and can find no words strong enough to express his abhor-
rence of these Levantines. But nothing availed to stop
their expansion; they are found of course in Alexandria,
which must have been one of the great export-centres for
their wares, and doubtless the Sidonians whom Dio
Chrysostom saw there had come on some business connected with glass. Italy itself they overflowed, especially
in Rome and the region round the Padus valley; they are
met with at Luna, at Ravenna, and at Verona, and hail
from Berytus, Heliopolis, Damascus, Caesarea, and Ascalon. Some had settled at Malaca in Spain; in Gaul we find
one from Germanicia, and another at Lugdunum (he
appears to have travelled between that town and Aquitania), not to mention the many traces which they have
left on the banks of the Rhine. They are found too at
Sirmium and at Celeia, and even penetrated to the Northern
wilds of Dacia; in Sicily we encounter one keeping an inn.
Men of Berytus are found at Palmyra, and it is interesting
to discover a Greco-Nabataean carrying on business near
Miletus. One very fascinating document left to us is a
letter from one of the Tyrian agencies in Puteoli to their
head office in Tyre; they complain that their "statio" is
getting poorer and poorer, owing to falling off of trade;
that they can no longer afford to pay the high ground-rate
demanded, although their "statio" in Rome is flourishing;

doubtless this was due to Trajan's energetic measures at Ostia, where he had enlarged and greatly deepened the former Claudian port. But in spite of this pathetic letter we have no reason to believe that the Syrians got the worst in trade transactions; they were better liars, more unscrupulous, and probably less proud than the average Italian. Yet it was due to Roman tolerance and to Roman good government that they enjoyed this prosperity, though the average Roman opinion is probably best represented by the disgusted inscription of some soldier serving in Syria; he scratched upon a rock, for all to read, his sentence: "the Syrians are a rotten race."

CHAPTER FOUR

THE SEA-ROUTE TO INDIA AND CEYLON

"Two days sail, or three, beyond Malao, is the market-town of Mundus....The traders living here are more quarrelsome."
Periplus Maris Erythraei

THE SEA-ROUTE TO INDIA AND CEYLON

WHEN Rome first came into contact with the Hellenised Orient she not only adopted for her convenience Hellenised and Oriental forms of government but took over, to her profit, the bulk of the Eastern trade as well. Under the last years of the Republic little was done to improve existing conditions, but with the establishment of the Empire Augustus perceived that it was to his own interest to encourage commerce in every possible way, especially the profitable traffic in the goods of Arabia and India. Three routes lay open to the Far East: firstly, that by the Black Sea, along the river valleys of the Caucasian country, across the Caspian, up the Oxus, and so by Northern Bactria into China or India; secondly, that which led from Syria down the Euphrates to the Parthian capital, and across Persia; thirdly, that by the Red Sea and the Indian Ocean. Of the first comparatively little can be known, and the second was under the disadvantage of leading directly through the Parthian territory; it is not surprising therefore if we find the emperors concentrating their efforts upon fostering trade by the sea-route and encouraging it in various ways.

Of the antiquity of the trade between India and Egypt there can be no doubt. But a great impetus was given to it, as also to the East African commerce, by the advent of the Lagids to the throne of Egypt at the end of the fourth century B.C. These rulers, especially Ptolemy II, paid great attention to the African coast, founding colonies along it and even out as far as the island of Socotra; it was from East Africa that they obtained not only ivory and tortoise-shell and slaves, but also elephants, which were a most important branch of the Hellenistic armies. For this reason they carefully restored the old canal which led from the easternmost branch of the Nile delta into the Red Sea near Arsinoe, and repaired the road from Coptos to Berenice, a port on the Red Sea coast. Communication between Egypt and India was quite possible, though not very frequent, and probably depended much upon the intermediary Arabs who bordered the Eastern side of the Red Sea. Thus we may explain the fact that the great Buddhist emperor of India, Açoka, could boast of having sent missionaries and embassies to the kings of the West (Egypt, Syria, Macedonia, and Epirus), and it will be remembered that an ambassador had been sent to his father, Vindusara, by a king of Egypt. But a further degree of intercourse is perhaps indicated by a curious farce which has come down to us in papyri fragments, in which some Greek mariners have been wrecked upon a barbarian coast and are being hospitably entertained by the king of the country. He speaks an almost unintelligible language, but as all his phrases are interpreted by one of the Greeks as invitations to drink, the party proceeds merrily. Recently it has been shewn by an Oriental scholar that this language is Canarese, a dialect of Southern India, and we may safely assume that some rough knowledge of these tongues had been picked up by the Greek captains of Alexandria in the course of their voyages. Lastly, in the temple at Redesîya, lying on the desert-route to the Red Sea, was discovered a dedication by an Indian to Pan, pointing to a real and direct intercourse between the two peoples.

But the strong rule of the early Ptolemies declined; weak kings and wastrels sat upon the throne of Egypt; Rome began to extend her conquering arm over the countries of the East. The canals gradually silted up, the desert roads were beset by brigands and the seas by pirates; the rioting and wastefulness of Cleopatra brought the country low, and but few merchants ventured on the Southern voyage. When, after years of strife, Augustus finally brought peace to the Western civilised world, a thorough reconstruction was necessary. Expeditions were undertaken against the Arabs of the Red Sea coast in order to check their raiding, the Aethiopians of the South were driven back and compelled to live as peaceable neighbours, and the irrigation and navigable canals were again cleaned out and put in working order. As a consequence of these measures trade began to flourish once more and Strabo at Myos Hormos was assured that one hundred and twenty vessels now sailed to India in a year and that many essayed the formerly dangerous passage. From Myos Hormos merchandise was taken by camel across land to Coptos and so down the Nile to Alexandria.

A few decades later a most important change took place. Hitherto mariners had been content to make the long voyage to India by feeling their way cautiously along the coast after passing Aden. Thus the towns at the Southern tip of the peninsula, Ocelis and Arabia Eudaimon, naturally acquired great importance as exchange centres where Indians and Greeks met, under the supervision of Arabs, and exchanged their wares; the mastery of the commerce was really held by Arabs. But about the middle of the first century of our era an otherwise unknown sea-captain, of the name of Hippalus, observing the periodicity of the monsoons, ventured to trust himself to the winds and so made the passage direct across to India. This meant a great deal to the Roman traders. Firstly, as regards speed; a man could now leave Egypt in July and reach the Indian ports by the end of September; after getting rid of his cargo and re-stocking his vessel with the Oriental luxuries so much in demand at Rome, he would set sail about the end of November and, wafted by the North-East monsoon, put in at Aden and so up the Red Sea to Alexandria where he would arrive about February; the return voyage became easily possible within the year. Secondly, the Arab towns

now saw their monopoly spoilt and made themselves
troublesome in every way; but their efforts were useless.
Eudaimon was taken and sacked, and the West definitely
set itself up as a trader to the East without intermediary.
A huge increase in trade followed which lasted well into
Hadrianic times. Pliny bewails the vast amount spent upon
Eastern luxuries, and though the economical policy of
Vespasian and the cutting down of extravagance may have
made some difference, the commerce in cotton and industrial goods went on strongly. In Southern India, where
the pearls and spices were sold, great quantities of coins
of the early emperors have been discovered; after the reign
of Nero, however, they diminish in number and more are
found in the Northern regions, where the cotton was
raised; in the third century there comes a distinct falling
off in the quantity of the coins which seems to indicate a
real decline of commerce. Both Ptolemy and the unknown
author of the *Periplus* bear witness to the number of merchants engaged in the Indian trade, and the former draws
much of his information about India from men who had
voyaged there and even resided for long in that country.

In pursuance of the general policy of the Empire to give
security to trading, we find efforts made not only to improve existing facilities and make known ways safer, but
also some attempt to gain control of those parts of the
routes which were not already in Roman hands. Thus the
road across the Egyptian desert from Coptos to Myos
Hormos was carefully marked out into stages, depôts made
for storage, reservoirs for water constructed, and armed
guards for the protection of travellers provided. The
Aethiopians of the Southern frontier were put down, while
the abortive expedition of Gallus in Arabia and the projected one of Gaius, Augustus' grandson, were intended
not only to secure the rumoured wealth of the region, but
also to win control of the route from Gerrha across the

centre of Arabia, to establish a sphere of influence along the Eastern coast of the Red Sea from Leuce Come downwards, and to assert law and order among the piratical tribes there. Certainly a fleet was stationed in the Red Sea at that period, and we hear of the merchant vessels going armed to protect themselves against raiders. Several embassies came to Augustus from India, and rights of penetration up country seem to have been secured. Tiberius had intended to convert the client-kingdom of Nabataea into a province, and thus control the overland trade from Leuce Come and Aila to Petra and Gaza as well as the Central Arabian route from Gerrha; his death prevented the annexation, but it was carried out seventy-five years later by Trajan. During the reign of Claudius, when Hippalus discovered the direct route, the tribes of the Southern tip of Arabia, seeing their prosperity vanishing, gave trouble; an expedition was sent against them and the town of Arabia Eudaimon reduced to unimportance. Later still Trajan cleaned out afresh the Nile-Red Sea canal, which was henceforth called "Trajan's River," and set a fleet in the sea to give protection to traffic; his successor Hadrian built an entirely new road to the Red Sea, through level country, and furnished it with stations, reservoirs and garrisons. The impetus which these measures gave to the trade is shewn in various ways. Thus we find on a census-list of the time of Vespasian that an Egyptian is registered as being absent in India; Dio Chrysostom remarks upon the number of Arabs and Indians to be met with in the streets of Alexandria; Pausanias refers to merchants to India and tells of the parrots and marvellous creatures they bring back, and Ptolemy speaks of numerous merchants resident there; Tamil poems sing of the ships of the Yavana arriving at their ports laden with wine and wares. A late map shews us a temple of Augustus existing at Muziris (in the region of Mysore), which is by no means improbable. The *Periplus of the Erythraean Sea* is a practical handbook written by a merchant for the aid of other merchants, and contains such items as the nature of the people along the coast, harbours, tides, prevailing winds, where good anchorages are to be found, what sort of cargo to take, imports and exports of various places and so on. Lastly the increase in trade is attested for us by the wider knowledge of Africa and India which Pliny shews as compared with Strabo, and still more in the superiority of Ptolemy's information, which is often surprisingly correct, though misinterpreted by him in order to fit a preconceived system of latitude and longitude. We are left with the impression that the emperors deliberately fostered the sea-voyage to India because it meant that all tolls and harbour dues would fall into Roman hands instead of going to enrich the Parthian and Arab officials.

The voyage might be undertaken either from the Egyptian or Nabataean side; the former was more usual. Here there were three ports from which ships could start; the first was Arsinoe, at the head of the Gulf of Suez and at the point of issue of the canal; the second was Myos Hormos, half-way down the coast of Egypt, and distant seven days from Coptos; the third was Berenice, at the extreme limit of the province, and distant eleven days from the Nile valley. But both at Arsinoe and at Berenice winds and shoals and rough water proved troublous to shipping, so that Myos Hormos gradually became the principal harbour. On the other side the main ports were Aila and Leuce Come, frequented however by smaller sailing-vessels. Merchandise landed here was taken on camel-back up to Petra and the Mediterranean: this was a very crowded route, and Strabo describes the immense caravans which used to move to and fro, comparable to armies in size, and we hear also of the great number of Romans who were wont to reside at Petra for the purposes of business. Leuce

Come itself was a large harbour filled with the small Arabian craft; so great was the volume of traffic that there was stationed here a Roman centurion to receive the dues, with a small garrison at his command. Doubt has sometimes been thrown upon this statement, but the matter should be beyond dispute. The kingdom of Nabataea was a vassal kingdom; Augustus arbitrated between its ruler and Herod the Great, and arrogated to himself the right of appointing the successor to the throne; we find these kings supplying their regular contingent to the Roman armies, doing homage to the Roman representatives, and sending the customary presents. When we remember Annius Plocamus, who was farming the Red Sea dues in the time of Claudius, when we think of Palmyra or of the arrangements in the Cottian kingdom (and there appears to have been some representative of Augustus at the Nabataean court), we cannot doubt that the emperors had reserved to themselves the collection of the dues from so profitable a region.

In sailing down the Red Sea it was advisable to keep to the middle of the channel, for not only was the Arabian side poorly provided with anchorages, but it swarmed with uncivilised tribes and pirates. At first it had been necessary to equip merchant vessels sailing there with armed guards, but such precautions were relaxed later. On the African side the most important harbour was that of Adulis, which served as a depôt for the trade of the newly-risen kingdom of the Axumites (Abyssinia), which had its capital eight days' journey inland. This was the main centre for the ivory trade, the best coming from here, but rhinoceros horn, hides, tortoise-shell and slaves were also exported. The main body of this trade went by sea, though it appears probable that some came down the Nile valley and through Nubia into Egypt. Dues were high, for the kingdom had only recently been established. It is interesting to note the articles of import here. They included undressed cloth, robes and garments from the Egyptian factories, various kinds of glass vessels of the same provenance, olive oil and wine (both from Syria and Italy), swords and axes, brass, copper, and iron, and a certain amount of coin for the purposes of trading. To this town also came goods from India, which we shall note later. Further still down the coast, in the region which corresponds roughly to British Somaliland, were various trading towns and small factories, such as Malao, Mundus, Mosyllum, and Opone. From these towns the exports were much the same; mostly myrrh, frankincense, and fragrant gums; cinnamon was shipped in bulk from Mundus, while from Opone the better kind of tortoise-shell was taken, and our author notes that slaves of a superior sort could be obtained there and were being taken in increasing numbers to Egypt. Into these towns were imported glass of various kinds, garments and dyed cloth from Arsinoe, grape-juice, wheat and wine, iron and some tin, and a small quantity of gold and silver coin, in fact a typical cargo for natives, wherein the Europeans endeavoured to exchange the cheaper but gaudy and pretty-looking cloaks and glass of the West for the raw products of the East. Here, too, Indian ships were met bringing rice, ghee, sesame-oil, cotton and sugar.

Yet men penetrated even farther in search of profit, as far South as the modern Uganda. Here there lay a large town called Rhapta, which was the last port known to our author, for he notes that "beyond these places the unexplored ocean curves away to the West." The usual ivory and tortoise-shell were to be found, though not of the quality of that of Adulis. The whole region lay under the control of the king of the Homerite and Sabaean Arabs, who had established a nominal suzerainty there, and sent tools and the products of Arabian craftsmen to these towns. It is significant that he was not allowed to retain or gain any hold over the towns immediately opposite Ocelis or Eudaimon which might have hindered the Roman-Indian trade; the Arab domination of the African coast was comparatively unimportant, though their shipowners and traders came into competition with the Romans. It is particularly worth notice here that the geographer Ptolemy, scarcely more than seventy years after our author, has far more information not only about the Southern coast of Africa, but also about the towns, lakes, and rivers of the Axumite kingdom and about the Southern coast of the Arabian peninsula, and this increase of knowledge can scarcely be due to anything but greater mercantile activity and in consequence better and more reliable reports. It is probable that during this period, roughly contemporary with Hadrian, trade with the East was at its height.

The opposite coast of Arabia from Leuce Come to the South was rough, dangerous, and uninviting, and the shores were infested by savage and piratical tribes. But towards the straits the country became less rugged and more fertile, and the nomad Arabs had been gathered together into a vague kingdom under the sway of a ruler who had his residence at Saphar and held dominion over the tribes of the Homeritae and the Sabaei. Near by was the port of Muza; this was filled by Arab merchants and shipowners and busy with all kinds of commerce; the land produced wine and wheat, and the craftsmen of the city made daggers and knives and hatchets and various tools for export to the Southern coast of Africa. Hither came traders in quest of that incense and those spices for which the land of the Sabaeans was famous, and for the $\zeta\iota\gamma\gamma\iota\beta\epsilon\rho\iota$ (ginger) which, Dioscorides informs us, was imported to Italy in jars. The king, to whom handsome presents had to be offered, was in friendly relations with the emperors, and trade was good. Various kinds of myrrh and spices were obtainable here, which Pliny enumerates at his usual length. Directly upon the straits lay another Arab town, called Ocelis, where there was a convenient anchorage and watering-place and this is mentioned by Pliny as being the best port for India. Not far round the corner lay the shrunken town of Eudaimon Arabia. The voyage now lay straight across the ocean, unless a merchant was seeking the ports at the foot of the Persian Gulf, such as Charax Spasini; some trade was also carried on with the island of Dioscorida (Socotra), where dwelt a mingled population of Arabs, Indians, and Greeks—the latter originally planted there by Ptolemy Philadelphus. Cinnabar and tortoise-shell were exported and also a certain quantity of aloes and myrrh. The island was subject to the adjacent Arabian kingdom and occupied by a native garrison: hence Arabian traders were frequent.

Although the direct track to India across the ocean was followed we must not imagine that there was not a large coasting trade around the shores of Arabia and the Persian Gulf. A considerable traffic flourished there, and we shall see later that the silks and products of China were often brought to Syria by this route, instead of going overland through the disturbed upper country. In this region there were the great mercantile towns of Gerrha, Ommana, and Charax Spasini, to which the Indian vessels came regularly bringing cargoes of timber, such as teak, blackwood and ebony, while Arabia sent the frankincense and spices of Cana. In return for these goods the region yielded pearls from its fisheries, though these were not of the same quality as the renowned Indian ones. From the town of Charax a route ran up the Euphrates to the North-West and joined the famous inland Eastern route near Seleucia. Trade conditions here were not good, and our authors have a poor opinion of the civilisation of the natives along the coasts. But a considerable amount of commerce was certainly carried on with this part of the Persian Gulf, though probably the Romans bent their efforts more towards India.

The two most important towns to which their vessels were directed were Barygaza, in the North, and Muziris, on the Malabar coast. It is interesting to read that the huge tides experienced there and the number of ships putting in had made a regular pilot service imperative; the incoming vessels were met by fishermen in the pay of the king of the country and towed up the river by them, thus indicating an advanced state of commerce. From this town were exported the usual Indian products; ivory, silk, cotton and coarser sorts of cloth, rice, ghee, and of course pepper, which was so highly prized. In return for these the merchants brought the tin and lead of the western countries (minerals which India did not possess), a fair quantity of wine, Asiatic and Italian (of which the latter was preferred), coral and glass and brightly-coloured girdles—a characteristic touch. Special presents had to be brought for the king, but doubtless the royal families were made to pay high prices for the silver vessels, the singing boys, and maidens for the harem, and the fine wines which were imported. We also notice that gold and silver coin was carried hither, and could be exchanged for a good profit at the tables of the money-changers. Indeed, we have signs that in those days the integrity and purity of standard of the Roman money was admired by the Eastern potentates and accepted everywhere. The emperors had not yet started their fatal policy of debasing the coinage which reached such a dreadful height in the third century

The other large port was that of Muziris, in the district of Malabar, and probably on the site of the modern Cranganore. This had been from early times an ancient depôt for trade, and at this period it must have been at the height of its fortune. It is interesting to note that a colony

of Jews is said to have taken refuge here after the fall of
Jerusalem; such a legend, whether true or not, reflects
faithfully the importance of that part of the coast. For it
was here alone, practically, that those beryls and pearls for
which Rome was prepared to pay so much could be found;
the beryl-mines of Cranganore were famous. It was from
here, too, that the pepper was taken away in such quantities
that ships of the largest burden anchored in the harbour,
which was crowded with Greek and Arabian vessels. Into
this town our merchants would bring clothing, figured
linens, coral, glass, copper, tin, and lead, together with
some wine and a great quantity of coin; in return they
took away pepper in bulk, and great store of fine pearls,
ivory, silk cloth, spikenard, malabathrum, diamonds and
sapphires and other precious stones. Of these products it
is curious to reflect how great a value was set by the Romans
upon pepper; Pliny tells us what a high price it fetched,
and we can judge what a favourite luxury it was with the
men of the West from the fact that Alaric, when he sacked
the imperial city, took away as part of his booty over five
thousand pounds of the precious condiment. Coins have
been found in numbers over this region; we can see that
intercourse chiefly took place on the South coast and with
the Tamils; the Coimbatore district contained the great
beryl-mines, and it is here and in the South that the greater
part of the coins have been discovered. In the tombs of
the Nilghiri hills lamps and vases and coins of this period
have been unearthed, which point to a thriving trade, and
Tamil poems speak of the "cool and fragrant wine brought
by the Yavana in their good ships," and of the Yavana
soldiers and mercenaries in the service of the king, who
guard his tent at night and by their stern looks strike terror
into the heart of the beholder. Yet another speaks of the
"thriving town of Muchiri, whither the beautiful large
ships of the Yavana come, bearing gold, making the water

white with foam, and return laden with pepper," and tells of the huge sacks of pepper which are brought down into the marts of the town. Nor was the commerce confined to Greek or Arabian vessels; these poems shew us that shipping was carefully controlled by the king there (as the pilot-system at Barygaza might lead us to suppose), and upon the Andhra coins of the period large two-masted Indian ships are figured. There must have been a large body of residents of Roman and Greek origin here; our authorities speak of merchants who had made the voyage frequently, and Ptolemy implies that he had information from men who had resided there for some considerable time; and there is still further evidence for this in that the Tabula Peutingerana marks a "Templum Augusti" as existing at Muziris, a fact inherently probable wherever any large number of citizens of the Empire were gathered together. In addition, it may be noted that the Greek terms for rice, ginger, and pepper are derived from the Tamil words, that Galen knows of drugs imported from India and even speaks of the recipe of an Indian physician, and that Dioscorides, in his treatise on drugs, mentions especially the nard of the Ganges and the Indian pepper. From coins found we can discern some of the fluctuations through which this trade passed; the greatest number of them belong to the period between Augustus and Nero and these have been discovered principally round Coimbatore and Madura. After Nero's reign fewer occur, and those that do seem to be shifting North towards the modern Surat and the cotton-growing districts, as we might expect in accordance with Vespasian's policy of retrenchment. Finally there comes a distinct falling off about the period of Marcus Aurelius and after, which faithfully reflects, we may be sure, the decline in trade resulting from the weakness and internal wars of the Empire. In later days, indeed, trade was restored and we hear of Roman merchants triumphantly proving the superiority of their Empire by demonstrating the purity of their gold coins to an Indian king, but it is safe to assert that after the reign of Marcus Aurelius or at any rate towards the close of the second century various causes contributed to kill commerce between the Eastern and Western lands.

Traffic appears to have extended still farther, at least down to Cape Comorin and the island of Ceylon; from all along this coast came pearls, muslin, and tortoise-shell in great quantities, and our author notes that the pearl-fisheries were worked by condemned criminals, doubtless because of the danger of the task. In this region lay the harbours of Camara, Poduca, and Sopatma, where were to be met the boats of the Tamils and of the dwellers round the Ganges, and even from the Malay peninsula. Tamil poems, too, tell of Camara with its wharves and raised platforms and its warehouses for the storage of goods. Lighthouses had been set at various points of the coast to guide merchants, and in the town were settlements of Yavana who exposed attractive wares for sale in the bazaar; we hear also of Yavana carpenters being sent for, and it would be interesting to speculate whether these Western artisans had any influence upon the development of Indian architecture. It will be remembered that, according to legend, St Thomas was induced to go to India through meeting a merchant who had been sent by king Gudnaphar, "that he might bring to him a skilful carpenter." Yet few had penetrated beyond Cape Comorin, in the time of our author, though he knows of the country round the Ganges and also of the land of This, from which the raw silk is brought through Bactria to Barygaza. It is instructive, therefore, to notice that Ptolemy, about fifty years later, knows and is able to describe the whole sea coast from the Cape to the Ganges, and mentions many towns lying along it, and also displays an increased knowledge of the Malay peninsula. The merchants of the Empire were steadily working their way eastwards and finally about A.D. 160 what might have been expected happened. Some daring navigator passed the Straits of Malacca and found himself in through communication with China, which had never happened before by sea. We are told by the Chinese Annals that Rome had always desired to enter into trade relations with China, but the Parthians had prevented them, since they wished to control the silk trade; but in the ninth year of the Yen-hsi period the emperor Marcus Aurelius sent an embassy which from the frontier of Annam offered to the Chinese king ivory, rhinoceros horns, and tortoise-shell. "From that time," the chronicle continues, "dates the direct intercourse with this country." It is only natural that national pride should have transformed the visit of an adventurous merchant into a formal embassy, and the presents offered to the king into a "tribute"; the same thing was done to merchants of Western nations not so many years ago. But from this time onward we have frequent mention in the Chinese records of the country of Ta-tsin (Syria) and an appreciation of the honesty and integrity of the Roman traders, as surprising as it is gratifying.

The discovery of direct intercourse with China was, however, made at a time when trade was beginning to languish, when the Empire itself was suffering from the rule of incompetent or weak princes and from the menace of civil wars, when Parthia and the Middle East were undergoing a series of great and important changes. In consequence the oversea trade with China, which might have developed into a considerable business, and might have brought far-reaching discoveries in geography and general knowledge, which might have led to the "opening-up" of China centuries earlier, and the inter-penetration of two civilisations, never had a chance and died of inanition. On the other hand, overland intercourse with the Eastern

Empire lasted for some time, and in spite of frequent interruptions was in regular use by the reign of Justinian, and it was by this route that such men as Marco Polo made their travels and brought modern geography to birth. But this development, fascinating and instructive though it be, would take us far out of our period and task. We have merely endeavoured to shew of what nature was the trade carried on between Egypt and the Indian countries, what were the products exchanged, and what the development of the commerce. It will be obvious that it was the policy of the Empire to encourage trading by the sea, so as to control the rich revenues arising from it, and prevent them falling into the hands of the Parthians; besides this, whereas the sea-route was comparatively secure (and we have seen the Romans making resolute efforts to protect commerce and put down piracy in these seas), the land road through Parthia was long, infested by robbers that dwelt among the hills, and liable to interruption from the civil discords that prevailed throughout the land. Here, as elsewhere, the instinct of the Romans was for sound and orderly trading with peaceable and law-abiding neighbours, and that is why we have dwelt at greater length upon this sea-route whereon they tried to carry out these principles.

CHAPTER FIVE
ASIA MINOR

"An pingues Asiae campi collesque
morantur?" HORACE

ASIA MINOR

IN spite of the fact that the peninsula known to us as Asia Minor embraced under the Empire a large number of different states and provinces, yet owing to the general geographical and climatic unity of the whole region it has seemed better to treat it as one in considering the resources of the land and the routes that led through it. Speaking roughly, the peninsula may be said to consist of a central high and arid tableland from which rivers make their way to the sea coast, and in doing so have carved out valleys of great fertility: the western coast especially, with its exceptionally favourable climate and its rich plains, has been from very early times a seat of civilisation and of agricultural wealth. But in addition it serves as a natural connecting link between the distant background of the Eastern lands with their civilisations—such as Babylonia and Persia—and the islands of the Aegean, which in their turn lead on to the countries of the West. It is a land-bridge which leads travellers by routes either of the South or North to the centre where now stands Constantinople. This fact, combined with its fertility and mineral wealth, lent it importance in ancient days and later made it one of the richest regions in the Empire.

Long before the Romans officially occupied any part of the peninsula, their merchants and traders had shewn great activity in Greece and the Cyclades, and the region swarmed with business men, whose centre was Delos, at that time the busiest port of the ancient world. When the strange whim of a half-insane king led him to bequeath his kingdom to the Romans, and a province of Asia had been created, merchants, dealers and traders of all kinds, finding a profitable field open for their labours, flocked in and overran the province, and gradually extended their operations over the lands to the South and North. It is from this date that some historians see traces of mercantile influence at work in shaping the policy of Rome. Certainly, as the numbers of business men increased, it became more and more necessary to afford them proper protection, and it is probably owing to their complaints and entreaties that various efforts were made early in the first century B.C. to put down piracy in the Aegean. Inscriptions disclose the steady increase of trade, and when the self-styled deliverer Mithradates issued his order for the massacre of all Italians resident in the province the figure reached the appalling total of 80,000. Yet in spite of this, once Mithradates had been overcome, and as new provinces were carved out of his realm by the irresistible Pompey, the Italians flocked back again, and one high authority gives it as his opinion that the first century before our era was the highwater mark of their prosperity. Indeed, the very fact that Pompey was in command was almost certainly due to the support of the influential moneyed class at Rome, who looked to him to provide, as he did, fresh opportunities for them. These were found not only in the newly-created provinces but also in the numerous client-kingdoms, where money-lending to the impecunious native rulers proved a very lucrative pursuit. But these kingdoms scarcely served the purpose for which they had been created—the defence of the frontiers—being continually occupied in petty bickerings with one another or suspected of conspiracy, and so the emperors made it a deliberate policy to get rid of them altogether and reduce their domains to the status of provinces. This was usually greatly to the advantage of the provincials themselves, who were thereby relieved of the heavy burden of royal taxation, but still more so to the emperors since they secured through communication between the Eastern frontiers and Rome.

In the East the peninsula was separated from the Asian continent by the lofty and difficult uplands of Armenia and by the hill country of Cappadocia and Commagene, save where the Euphrates in its upper course approaches the sources of the Halys and the Lycus. Towards the South, though the country is very mountainous, practicable passes had early been established at the famous "Gates" of Cilicia and Syria. All communication was bound to follow the two obvious routes left open, that of the South and that of the Northern uplands. In the North, two large rivers, the Halys and the Sangarius, of considerable length and flowing through valleys of great fertility, have marked out definite lines for trade-penetration: the only other really important rivers are the Hermus, Caicus, and Cayster, which run West into the Aegean and by which men can find their way from Phrygia and Galatia down to the coast. The cold and bare uplands of Lycaonia, with the central salt plains around Lake Tatta, and the range of the Taurus in the South effectually bar communication, even the river Sarus being forced in one place to tunnel underground in its passage to the sea. In Roman times Asia was famous not only for its agricultural wealth, in crops and fruit harvests, but also for its flocks and herds, its stores of timber and its rich mineral resources. And these must have been even greater in bygone days: throughout Strabo's description (and the geographer knew Asia intimately and accurately) we hear of abandoned mines and deserted workings, of cities once flourishing and now desolate. It was a self-contained region well fitted to be under one ruler, and it is not surprising that in our earliest records we find it under the sway of princes whose seat of empire was centrally situated near Pteria on the Northern Halys. This accounts for the fact that the Northern route seems to have been more used then, leading through Melitene up northwards through Mazaca and down the Halys valley to Pteria. From here the road took a south-westerly turn along the Sangarius valley over the mountains to the valley of the Hermus and to Sardis, where later was the seat of the Lydian kings. But after the overthrow of Lydia, as the cities of Miletus and Ephesus rose to greater importance, the road which communicated with the far-distant Persian capital ran up the Maeander valley past Laodicea and Apamea, Synnada and Pessinus, to Ancyra and so to Melitene, and this was the famous "Royal Road" which Herodotus describes. Besides the main artery the route which led from Ancyra by way of the Sangarius to the Bosporus must always have been of importance, since the trade across the strait was at all times considerable; in addition, there was a very ancient and frequented crossroad which led from the North coast, by Sinope and Amisus, down to Mazaca, and then through Tyana and the Cilician Gates to Tarsus. In this part of Asia there were many old religious centres, and such places with their annual gatherings and fairs have always been the natural points by which trade passes. Thus certainly by the fifth century there were two great ways in existence, that from Ephesus to the Euphrates, and that from Sinope to Tarsus. The conquests of Alexander and the policy of the Hellenistic kingdoms soon produced another route; the northern declined in importance, and Southern Asia Minor became part of the realm of the Seleucids; hence a new way arose which, leaving the old road at Apamea, went by way of Seleucid foundations (such as Antiochia and Laodicea Catacecaumene) to Iconium, and then skirted the salt desert as far as Tyana, where it joined the old Northern route through the Cilician Gates to Tarsus, and so on to Antioch in Syria or the Euphrates; this rapidly became the most important of all the routes.

Thus when the Romans began to take control of Asia and slowly to add province to province, there was a well-defined system of roads already existent by which a considerable body of traffic came and went East and West. One of the earliest measures taken by the proconsul M'. Aquillius was the improvement and repair of the old Royal Road, from Ephesus through Tralles to Laodicea and Apamea: and some efforts were made to put down the pirates and robbers of Isauria and Cilicia, who infested land and sea, such as the ineffectual expedition of Antonius and the more successful ones of Servilius Isauricus and Sulla in Cilicia. Pompey, during his pursuit of Mithradates in the North-West region of Pontus, penetrated into the Caucasus and saw the Caspian Sea, where he learnt of the trade that was brought from India down the Oxus valley. There was an old route which led from the Armenian uplands along the valley of the Lycus to the big religious centre of Comana and also along the Halys valley; in this region he planted five of his many foundations, in order to protect and secure the trade passing into Pontus by way of Amasea. In the South we find that Cicero used the Hellenistic road in order to visit his province; his route lay through Tralles and Laodicea, past Apamea and Philomelium to Iconium, where his army was encamped; after this he apparently went by Laranda and Cybistra through the famous Gates to Tarsus. But it will be remembered that one of the objects for which he used his army was the subjugation of the brigand chiefs of Pindenissus, and doubtless during the ensuing period of the Civil War matters went from bad to worse in the hilly interior. Antony bade Amyntas, whom he made ruler of Galatia and Pisidia, pacify the country, but once again it was Augustus who laid the foundation of peace and prosperity. Colonies and garrisons were placed in various parts of Pisidia and Isauria in order to protect Galatia and the Southern road, and a network of military ways was constructed to link these posts to each other and to the sea; Strabo speaks of bridges in the country round Selge, and it must have been by these

roads that St Paul travelled; Iconium was joined with
Lystra and Laranda and the seaports of Side and Apamea
were connected with Selge and Cremna, as milestones of
Augustus prove. Henceforth the country was well governed,
and occasional outbreaks, such as those of the Lycians, or
of the Homonadenses and Clitae, did little more than create
a momentary disturbance. But so long as the system of
protecting the frontier by buffer-states ruled by client-
princes remained in force little was likely to be done in the
matter of roads, since it was easier to move troops up from
Northern Syria, and quicker to coast from Ephesus by way
of Cyprus to Seleucia on the Orontes than to make the land-
journey. But after some years' trouble with the native
princes, the need for a properly guarded frontier, the wax-
ing power of Parthia, and the increasing volume of trade
which came from the Caucasus region, determined the
Flavian emperors to convert the kingdoms into provinces
and to control all approaches to the Euphrates with Roman
garrisons. Pontus and Lesser Armenia came under direct
Roman rule and the inland parts of Cilicia were united with
the rest of the province and Cappadocia; a strong garrison
was established at Satala and at Melitene, and the two
places were connected by a road built under Vespasian;
the control of this upper region taken with the possession
of the crossings at Samosata and Zeugma meant that the
whole Euphrates was under Roman surveillance. It was
the Flavian dynasty which first took in hand the thorough
organisation of the Northern roads: milestones of Vespasian are found over this region, while Domitian repaired
and set in order all the Asian roads; an inscription of his
testifies to the reorganisation of all the roads of Galatia,
Cappadocia, Pontus, Pisidia, Paphlagonia, Lycaonia, and
Armenia Minor. Nerva and his successors continued the
work, especially on the Northern route: Pannonia and the
Danubian lands had now become the chief Western

military centres, and this route was essential for rapid communication with the Eastern frontiers. Nerva also laid down a road between the two important centres of Tavium and Amasea, and a massive bridge of this date over the Halys is evidence of the importance attached to this route. In Lycaonia we find Titus relaying the road between Derbe and Lystra and repairing bridges; Hadrian appears to have devoted special attention to the maintenance of the roadways; we find milestones of his near Apollonia and Iconium, and also upon the roads which centred in Ancyra from Gangra, Tavium, and Juliopolis, the two latter being upon the main road to Byzantium and Pannonia. Thus the necessities of frontier defence again brought into prominence the old neglected Northern route.

We may now give a rough sketch of those roads which were most in use; it will be understood that it is impossible to give all with certainty and many smaller ones must be omitted; our effort will be to trace out the main lines which assumed most importance for trade. To begin from the South: Ephesus was the starting-point for all going East, its large harbour and docks giving ample room for shipping; receiving as it did the goods of the overland route it was the largest and most prosperous mart in all Asia. From here the road ran past Tralles, "a city full of rich men," and up the Maeander valley to Laodicea, whence came the famous soft dyed wool which brought its inhabitants wealth, thence to Apamea, which was accounted the second largest market in Asia—and into which the wares of Italy came—and up to Antioch in Pisidia with its Roman colony. At Philomelium it turned South and, traversing the plains of Lycaonia, which afforded good grazing for coarse-fleeced sheep and herds of wild asses, reached Iconium, thence by way of Laranda and the Cilician Gates past Tarsus either down to Antioch in Syria or across the mountains to the Euphrates at Zeugma. Thus the whole Southern route ran through country rich in opportunities for trading. Next to this there was a road which we may term the Central Route, which ran up the Hermus valley past Sardis, with its wealth and its excellent land, and through the agricultural country of Philadelphia to Synnada, famous for its quarries of marble, which was exported in great quantities to Rome itself. From here the road turned North-East to Pessinus, which was the most important market-town of all Galatia and situated on the navigable Sangarius: thence it passed to Ancyra and Tavium, both thriving towns, and on to the road-centre of Megalopolis, where the way divided, one branch going South to Melitene, the other North to Nicopolis and Satala to receive the trade of Armenia and the lands beyond. Lastly, there was the important Northern route which started from Nicomedia and forked almost immediately, the lower branch going by Juliopolis (a town so crowded with travellers and passing tradesmen that Pliny could ask the emperor to install a centurion there for collection of dues and guarding of merchants) to join the Central Route at Ancyra, while the upper passed by Claudiopolis and Crateia to Amasea, one of the chief towns of Pontus and in close connection with Sinope, where there was a good market for horses and timber and the produce of the country round; from here it stretched by way of Comana —the centre for merchandise from Armenia—through Nicopolis to Satala. While these were the main Eastern and Western routes there were several cross-roads which linked them up. For instance, the route between Sinope and Tarsus was certainly an ancient one, and gave rise to the curious notion that at this point Asia Minor was considerably narrower; Amasea was the first important station on it; here came a division, the left-hand branch going by way of Tavium, the right-hand—presumably the older—by

way of the religious centre of Comana and the later Megalopolis. Of course there were connecting roads between
such considerable towns as Ephesus, Sardis, Smyrna,
Thyateira, and Pergamum, while in Pisidia the Augustan
colonies were all bound together, and the interest shown
by Claudius in Iconium and other towns of the same region
must have resulted in better communication.

In regard to this we must bear in mind too that it was
nearly as convenient to go by sea as by land, and certainly
cheaper. Though there were few navigable rivers in the
peninsula the whole coastline was dotted with harbours and
anchorages. There were not only the many Greek colonies
and their foundations, but the cities planted or rebuilt by
the Macedonian and Seleucid monarchies, and by the
kings of Pergamum—a dynasty founded upon trade if there
ever was one. On the North coast alone, to mention only
the principal ones, there were the harbours of Trapezus,
Pharnacia, and Sinope, all in a region where ship-timber
was plentiful, and where there was wood, fish, grain, and
fleeces to export in abundance: further West came Amastris,
famous for its boxwood, and Heracleia with its good harbour, while the Sangarius was navigable the whole way
through Bithynia. On the Western coast there was a long
line of harbours and prosperous cities: Parion, Lampsacus,
Cyzicus, Adramyttion, Pitane (with a double harbour),
Mitylene, Antissa, Myrina, Elaia, and then the three large
cities of Chios, Ephesus, and Smyrna, of which the two
latter were easily the most important towns in Asia and
enjoyed great prosperity during the imperial age. Along
the Southern coast lay such harbours as Myra, Attaleia,
Side, Celenderis, and Tarsus, and numberless other small
towns, and above all the populous and great island-city of
Rhodes, which had not yet lost all its glory. There was a
constant stream of traffic between these coastal towns:
small merchant ships passed to and fro bearing Corycian

saffron of Cilicia, the wine and resinous gums of Pamphylia, the oysters of Ephesus, the wool of Miletus, the
tunnies of Byzantium, the timber, wax, and alum of
Pontus, and the wines of the Aegean islands and of Italy.
We can trace this in Strabo's account, where he measures
distance by voyaging, contrasts the direct passage and the
πλοῦς παρὰ γῆν, and speaks of the voyage South from
Byzantium past Sestos and Abydos and down the coast of
Caria. Furthermore, the Southern and Western coast of
Asia lay on the route from Egypt to Rome, and along
this coast ships passed during those months when the
blowing of the Etesians hindered direct sailing. The line
lay from Egypt and Syria along the coasts of Cilicia, Pamphylia, and Lycia, and either up by the islands of the
Aegean to Philippi and so overland along the Via Egnatia,
or past Crete and Cythera and so round into the Adriatic.
It will be remembered that the centurion in charge of
St Paul, when he embarked at Caesarea, found a ship of
Adramyttion bound for Ephesus and the North, and that
after putting in at Myra he transhipped into an Alexandrian
vessel destined for Italy, and went by way of Crete. Herod
sailed from Palestine by way of Rhodes, Cos, and Lesbos
to Mytilene and Byzantium in order to meet Agrippa in
the Black Sea. We have many instances of the opposite
passage: Pompey in his flight from Pharsalia called at
Lesbos and then coasted past Ephesus and Colophon, by
Rhodes and along the shores of Pamphylia to the small
town of Celenderis; after a council of war here, he put to
sea again and after rounding the Eastern corner of Cyprus
cut straight across to Egypt. Similarly, both Antipater and
Piso, coming from the West, coasted along the Southern
shores and put in at Celenderis before making for Seleucia
in Syria. The evidence found in the Acts is perhaps most
valuable of all because it indicates the ordinary voyages and
the conditions that the plain civilian or merchant would

have to face: Herod and the imperial legates had far more resources at their command both in ships and in money. But of the activity of the coastal and Western traffic we need have no doubt; the very fact that "merchants and ship-owners" were among those injured by a rising of the Clitae shews that even in that rough region commerce flourished.

Of the time liable to be occupied in the transmission of news from Rome to the provinces it is hard to give any reliable figures. We learn that in the age of Cicero forty-seven days was considered a quick passage for a mail; a letter which reached him at Cybistra took fifty days. But conditions had almost certainly improved under the Empire and the time must have been reduced by at least one-fifth; thus the death of Gaius Caesar at Limyra was known at Pisae in thirty-six days. The overland route through Mace-donia was constantly used, especially by the imperial posts and couriers, since winter would make no difference in the regularity of transmission. But picked soldiers and runners were chosen for this service; the ordinary merchant could not avail himself of these privileges and had to be content with the slower course of the coasting vessel. On land the journey from Ephesus to Tralles occupied a day; in two more Laodicea could be reached, in another four or five Philomelium sighted, and three days later Iconium; from here to the Euphrates by way of Mazaca and Melitene would take about eighteen days more. To complete the whole journey a man driving or on horseback would require about thirty days, and on foot over thirty-five, while the more speedy imperial messengers might do the distance in about twenty-one days, which would be exceptionally fast. Journeying by the Southern route to Zeugma would take even longer. We know definitely that from Sagalassus to Apamea was a day's march, and Strabo reckons the time from Mazaca to the Cilician Gates at six days, but beyond this and the fact that the voyage from Sinope to Phasis took three full days, we lack any precise information. At sea so much depended upon the class of ship taken; a coastal voyage meant putting into many small havens, while in travelling Northward voyagers were apt to be held up for a long period by the strong winds off the Troad, of which the younger Pliny complains. But of the frequency of the voyages, of the large number of ships employed, and of the busy traffic, there can be no doubt. Upon his tomb-stone a certain merchant of Hierapolis in Phrygia boasts of having rounded Cape Malea seventy-two times, and his was probably not an exceptional record.

We may now turn to consider what were the resources of the provinces; they may be divided under two heads, mineral and agricultural. In ancient times Western Asia had been famous for the wealth it brought its kings; the sands of the Pactolus were said to be rich in gold, and the vast treasures of the kings of Lydia were proverbial. Nearly every mineral which the ancient world needed was to be found in one part or other of the peninsula. It is true that some of the famous veins and old-established workings were by now exhausted, but many mines still proved very profitable. In the client-kingdoms these mines appear to have belonged to the rulers; Strabo tells us of certain mining engineers of King Archelaus who discovered an onyx-like stone in Galatia, and it is reasonable to suppose that the emperors took control of them; still, definite information is lacking, and we may presume that imperial ownership was not widely spread until the second century of our era. It will be convenient to start with the island of Cyprus, which stands in close relationship to the main-land and for the purposes of our survey may be treated as part of it. It was said that originally copper was first found there and took its name from the island. There is abundant evidence for the antiquity of the workings there, and for the wide area over which the metal was exported. There were mines at Amathus, Soli, and Curion, and Strabo declares that those of Tamassos were inexhaustible. As well as the copper a certain amount of silver was also found on the island, and some lead and white-lead. But the great industry was the making of bronze, which was greatly helped by the quantity of timber on the island; we have many references to the busy workshops there, and to the various by-products manufactured. It is important to remember that Cyprus was one of the few places in the Mediterranean where copper was obtained in any quantity, and that as the Romans now controlled both Gallaecia and Cornwall—the main source of the tin supply—they had a practical monopoly of the manufacture of bronze. Both this metal and also lead were exported in bulk to India —which possessed neither—and in this manner Rome was enabled to pay for the precious stones and costly spices which she drew from the East. Hence it was indeed a princely gift when Caesar gave to Herod half the revenue of the mines in Cyprus. Precious stones, too, were found on the island, but none of any great value.

To pass on to the mainland, we find that at the period which we are studying there was practically no gold to be mined in those portions under Roman rule. The region had been only too well exploited, but on the other hand there were rumours of gold-mines in Armenia, near Caballa, and of gold and silver to be found among the Suani in Colchis, and it is tempting to explain the continual warfare for the control of Armenia as directed not only at establishing a satisfactory frontier, but also at tapping new sources of wealth, and dominating the famed route across the Caspian to India. Again there had formerly been mines of silver near Pharnacia, but by Strabo's time they were exhausted, only iron remaining, and in consequence the natural aim of the business men would be to push inland into the mountainous North-East towards unexploited territory; we can under-

stand better, bearing this in mind, the meaning of Nero's
projected expedition to the Caucasus. As for other minerals,
there seems to have been copper near Cisthene in Mysia,
but from the notice given by Strabo it cannot have been
of much importance. Iron, however, was still procurable
in Cappadocia, near the river Cerasus, and also in the hills
above Pharnacia, while near Andeira there was iron ore;
the off-smelting of this, mixed with copper, was made into
the substance known as "oreichalcos," which was highly
prized throughout the Empire; the district round Cibyra
was famous for its beaten iron-work. Sulphide of lead was
found near Zephyrium in Cilicia, and was exported, for
medicinal and other purposes; near Pompeiopolis red
sulphide of arsenic (realgar) was dug out of a hill, and we
have a very interesting description by Strabo of the condition of the workers, which appears to have been deplorable. So dangerous was the work that only men who
had been condemned to slavery for some criminal offence
could be used; the atmosphere was noxious in the extreme
and the unrelenting toil told heavily upon the workers, over
two hundred in number, who were diminished by disease
and death to such an extent that the working of the mine
had often proved unprofitable. It is instructive to compare
this notice with similar ones in Diodorus, and then passing
on a century observe the change which had been effected
by the more humanitarian policy of the Flavians and their
successors, as exemplified in the Lex Metalli Vipascensis
of Spain.

The quarrying of stone in Cappadocia was easy, for the
towering mass of Mount Argaeus provided an inexhaustible
supply; from it much of the neighbouring city of Mazaca
had been built. In Phrygia the white marble of Synnada
was very famous, and had been quarried for some time;
Strabo expressly tells us that the greater resources in the
hands of the Romans enabled them to cut far larger blocks

than formerly, and that whole pillars were quarried out
and, in spite of the distance to the sea, were transported to
Ephesus and shipped to Rome; we have many references
to it in the poets of the era, shewing the esteem in which it
was held. There was also marble to be found on the island
of Ariusia, and in Proconnesus, which was highly prized;
the nearby town of Cyzicus had been built in great measure
from it, but it was exported over a wide area, and has
actually been found in a villa of Northern Gaul. There
were marble quarries in Caria, and there was a legend that
the Carians had invented the cutting of marble. Beside
that kind of onyx which the miners of Archelaus found in
Cappadocia, on the borders of Galatia, there was also a
white stone of an ivory-like surface which was used for
dagger handles and for ornamentation. In Cappadocia,
too, was discovered the most prized kind of red earth, to
which was sometimes given the name of "Sinopic earth,"
because that had formerly been the port for its trading;
but by now the route through Ephesus was used, and the
earth was exported widely, being famed for its medicinal
properties: an inferior quality was also found in Pontus.
There was mica, too ("specularis lapis"), in great quantities; it was inferior only to the Spanish, and only so on
account of its being rather more opaque: in the same province, during Nero's reign, a peculiarly translucent kind of
stone was discovered (apparently crystallised gypsum),
which was called Phengites, and this must have been exported in large quantities; we are told that Domitian used
it for the walls of a portico. Near Ephesus there was red
lead, the best in the whole Empire, though that of Sisapo
in Spain was nearly comparable to it; that exported from
Colchis was spoilt by adulteration. Whetstones were
traded from Cilicia, and in some of the provinces there
were some of the less precious stones to be found, though
their value was small.

But besides the riches that lay concealed beneath the earth the agricultural wealth of the region was immense. Along the southern coast of the Black Sea, in Pontus and Bithynia, were vast forests of oak, fir, maple, and larch, which provided excellent timber for shipping, and finer kinds of wood which were used for furniture, and especially for tables to grace the houses of the rich. In the South, too, there was good store of ship-timber for the small light boats, in which the Cilician pirates had once scoured the seas, and a certain kind of vessel—the "phaselus"—is said to have taken its name from a town on the Lycian coast. Boxwood came from the region around Cytorus and Amastris, and Strabo dwells on the abundance of timber that flourished on the hilly slopes of the Euxine. Pitya had its pines, and on the hillsides of Ida much wood-cutting was done, and there was timber on Mycale. In fact the only place where wood was not to be had in quantity was on the plains of Lycaonia and in Cappadocia, which was practically treeless save for some miles round Mount Argaeus. The climate of the peninsula was well suited to the cultivation of the olive; it is almost unnecessary to name the river valleys of Western Asia as being the home of its cultivation from before the days of the settlements of the Greeks, but it grew also in Melitene, and in the district round Phanaroea, in Pisidia on the hills above Side and Aspendus, and flourished exceedingly in the country round Selge, whence it was exported. Finally, the plain of Synnada produced a good olive. We have records of the "olearii" or merchants and dealers in oil, who passed by way of the Cyclades to Rome in their trading.

Nearly every district produced a wine of its own. Easily the most renowned was that of the South-West coast and the islands near by; the small island of Ariusia was said to produce the best, and the products of Metropolis, Tmolos, Cnidos, and Smyrna were all admired; curiously enough the island of Samos produced no wine, that of Ephesus was not considered good, and as for the wine of Mesogis which Strabo mentions, Pliny dismisses it with the curt remark that it produces a headache. But in the agricultural country of Mysia, by Philadelphia, and in the good soil of Sardis vines were planted, and those of Priapus and of Lampsacus were famous. In Pisidia the wine of Ambleda was exported as being good for invalids, and the treeless plains of Laodicea Catacecaumene yet furnished an excellent wine. All the Northern district of Pontus, the country around Sinope and Themiscyra, was a great fruit-producing district, and the vine of course flourished there, and was found further East in Phanaroea and Melitene.

Of all districts probably that which in Asia was the most valuable was the province of Pontus, with its famous ports Sinope and Trapezus; the former town had been a renowned trade-centre for hundreds of years past. It drew great wealth from the fisheries along the shore; tunny was pickled there, as at Byzantium, and various delicacies made from it. Besides its ship-timber nearly every kind of fruit-tree grew there; vines and olives in profusion, grapes and apples and pears and cherries, which latter were transplanted by the epicure Lucullus to grow on Italian soil; all these, and various kinds of nuts, grew in such quantities that in some cases they were allowed to hang neglected on the trees, and the casual traveller could pick them freely. In fact, the fertility of the sea-coast had always made it a tempting land for invaders and been the cause of frequent migrations and wars. In the country round Sinope were sheep with soft fleeces such as were rare throughout the rest of Cappadocia and Pontus, and herds of cattle; its ducks and geese were also famous. The art of bee-keeping was practised there and the Pontic wax was exported for various uses; a neighbouring tribe paid a portion of their tribute in wax, as some of the tribes of Spain did in coccus. Various resinous plants and gums, such as wild spikenard and mastic, which were needed for medical purposes, were gathered there. Finally, apart from its own produce all the trade of Armenia and Colchis passed along the coast or by the overland route.

In the South in Cilicia lay great forests which had once furnished the pirates with timber for their ships, and now afforded excellent hunting after boar and deer. But the most famous product of the district was undoubtedly the saffron, which grew principally round Mount Corycus; it was largely exported to Rome and Italy, not only for seasoning and medicinal purposes, but also for making into scent. Various kinds of corn and spelt found favourable soil there; figs and olives, dates and vines, all grew well, and the Cilician lettuce was highly praised and had been transplanted to Italy. Along the rocky and indented coastline merchant ships wound in and out in great number; their chief cargoes were undoubtedly the ointments and gums which could be made from the resinous plants of the district; such were the styrax and the iris-gum of Pisidia and of Cilicia, while there also grew here coccus, which was used in purple-dyeing, and the small town of Phaselis was renowned for a rose-perfume which was manufactured in it. The country around Selge was celebrated for its fertility, the oil being especially good, and the ointment made from its iris plant being greatly esteemed. The hills suited goats well, and many were the articles which could be made from goats-hair, such as socks and leggings and a special kind of warm cloak, called a "cilicium," which was much imported to Italy in the time of Augustus. Tarsus was a noted centre for tentmaking, and it will be remembered that St Paul was by profession a tentmaker.

But that which was properly known as the province of Asia was one of the most renowned parts of the Empire: the antiquity of its civilisation, its many ancient and still thriving towns, its agricultural wealth, its industries, its rich population, all these gave it a claim to fame and consideration. Few provinces were more proud of having the cult of the Emperor, and the opulent cities rivalled one another in producing candidates who could be worthy of the honour of being "Chief Priest of the whole of Asia." The sea-coast possessed good fisheries; the shellfish coming from a region called Linon were known as the best in the world, and the oysters of Ephesus held a high place in the estimation of connoisseurs; and again there were the famous purple fisheries of the Anatolian coast. Around Sardis the plains were very fruitful, and Strabo refers frequently to the excellence of the soil. Besides, these plains and the hillsides provided magnificent grazing for flocks and herds, and from of old the wool and fleeces of the Milesian sheep had been sought after: it now only held the third place, since that of Laodicea was regarded as the best. It is interesting to find that this town, famous for its manufacture of woollens, had later to compete with the products of the North Gallic weavers, and sent out from its looms "imitation Nervian cloaks." Where the wool was so good we might expect to see the dyeing industry flourishing; this was so; certain roots were used for refining the wool and the coccus dye applied; the water of Hierapolis had so excellent an action that wool upon which vegetable dyes had been employed, if treated with it, emerged equal in lustre to that on which coccus or murex had been used. Thyateira, whence came Lydia, the purple-seller, whom St Paul met in Greece, was renowned for its purple-dyeworks. Pliny tells us that the very finest truffles came from Asia, especially in the region around Mytilene and Lampsacus. The province was also well supplied with resin-bearing trees, and some of the kings of Pergamum had endeavoured to plant the incense-tree there. So, too, the aloes and apples of the country were much esteemed and huge jars of Asiatic figs and of other fruits, dried and preserved, were imported into Italy.

Finally, a few words may be said about the shifting population. The people of the coast had possessed for many centuries an unusual aptitude for trade, and under the Empire they had an exceptional opportunity to exercise it. Quick-witted and adaptable, well-educated and well-spoken, they made their way rapidly in the cosmopolitan society of Rome. As physicians they were unequalled; it is astonishing how often the name of a doctor shews him to have been a Greek freedman. And their qualities enabled them to hold high places; we have only to think of the Greek physicians of the imperial court, or the indispensable freedmen of the Early Empire, to realise the truth of this statement. Josephus declares that there was a large body of Jews settled in Asia Minor and especially in Ionia, and his remark is confirmed if we think for a moment of Lydia of Thyateira or Aquila of Pontus—both of whom were travelling on business—while from the narrative of the Acts we can see that almost every town had its synagogue. In so rich a province, thickly studded with prosperous cities, the guilds of craftsmen were a very important factor in local politics, and we may recollect the disturbance which was caused by Demetrius, the silversmith, and his fellows. It has been remarked by Hatzfeld, in his brilliant essay, that during the first century of our era the Italian merchants resident in Asia either disappear under stress of competition from native elements or else coalesce with them. But that must not be taken to mean that trade was declining. It is perfectly true that when Pliny was sent out to Bithynia he found the province in a bad way financially, but that was owing to reckless and extravagant expenditure on the part of the municipal authorities rather than to any real unsoundness in the region itself. Towards the close of the first century a gradual change was coming over the Eastern half of the Empire; in place of the Italians, native merchants in increasing quantities began to carry the trade and even to settle in Italy and in Rome itself; having a greater adaptability and less pride of race than the Italians it is not surprising if they succeeded better; satirists complain in bitter tones of their ubiquitousness. With the same wind that brought prunes and figs and damsons to Rome they came, and where they settled they throve. But they advanced even beyond the capital, penetrating the valleys of the North-West with their jewels and ornaments and fine work and with their luxury trades. We find a Bithynian from Nicomedia at Moguntiacum, and Bithynians are mentioned in other inscriptions; one turns up at Burdigala; among the Helvetii we find a Lydian goldsmith, and in other parts of the country a Cappadocian and a Carian. They even ventured as far as Britain, and at Lindum the inscription of an Asiatic Greek has been unearthed. Their physicians, too, were in every city. It was the turn of the tide: no longer were the provinces to be exploited by the Romans, but the Empire had actually taught the provincials how to exploit Rome. Conquered Greece took her conqueror captive in more than literature.

CHAPTER SIX
THE OVERLAND
ROUTE TO CHINA
AND INDIA

"The regions beyond these places
are either difficult of access because of their excessive winters
and great cold, or else cannot be
sought out because of some divine
influence of the gods"

The Periplus

CHAPTER SIX

THE OVERLAND ROUTE TO CHINA AND INDIA

THE establishment of peace and good government throughout the Roman Empire by Augustus and the consequent prosperity led to a great increase in the numbers of those who wanted luxury articles and were ready to pay for them highly. For many of these Rome had recourse to the East, which could supply them abundantly, especially silk, spices and gums, and jewels and precious stones. These commodities were conveyed overland or by sea, through Bactria and Parthia or across the Indian Ocean and up the Red Sea, to the great central depôts of the Syrian region, Antioch, Damascus, Palmyra, Petra, and the like. We have already described in another chapter the route followed by those who sailed from the Red Sea ports and the efforts made by Rome to secure control of it and so diminish the Parthian trade. We shall see later that an attempt was made, probably with success, to set up another route which would also avoid Parthian territory by going northwards through the Caucasus and across the Caspian Sea, but during the first century we may be certain that the route through Mesopotamia was the most frequented.

For those travelling eastward from the sea-coast of Asia Minor to the North Syrian markets a great barrier was presented by the ranges of Taurus and Amanus. The former was crossed by the famous pass of the Cilician Gates, while the latter could be overcome in three places. The most northerly way left the road along the Cilician coast and turned eastward up a tributary of the Pyramus to the Pylae Amani (the modern Bogtche Pass, the route used by the present-day railway) and then straight across to the Euphrates at Zeugma or down to the plains of Chalybon. The second followed the coast-road, as far as Myriandros, where it turned up into the mountains which it crossed by the Pylae Syriae, and so down into the plain. The third followed the coast all the way to Seleucia and then used the Orontes valley to reach Antioch. From these three centres the common meeting-place for all those who were travelling through Mesopotamia down to the Persian Gulf was Zeugma, "renowned for its crossing of the Euphrates"; from here the left bank of the river was followed down to Seleucia and Ctesiphon. Sometimes however caravans from the Central Syrian towns and from Damascus preferred to strike right across the desert to Palmyra and then join the river much lower down at Circesium, and so to the Parthian towns and ports, and we possess many inscriptions set up in honour of the merchants whose duty it was to lead and guide these large companies through the desert. Sometimes the journey was made entirely overland, as was done by the men of Gerrha on the Persian Gulf, who had attained immense wealth by the transportation of the Eastern spices and gums and perfumes across the Arabian desert to Petra. For there was a most profitable traffic in these Eastern goods; moralists and satirists might bewail the amount squandered on luxuries and inveigh against men wearing silken clothing, but the pursuit of these things went on merrily; a great lady like Lollia Paulina could appear at banquets wearing pearls worth millions of sesterces, Nero in his theatrical grief over his victim Poppaea could consume at her pyre more spices than Arabia produced in a year, and silk and silk garments were in constant demand. We have already had occasion to mention the map-makers, the explorers, and the geographers employed by Augustus, especially in regard to the Eastern lands, and among the most interesting documents of his time is a brief itinerary compiled by one Isidore of Charax, recording the stations between Zeugma and Bactria, upon the silk route. Wars and expeditions, and the enterprise of private merchants had considerably increased the knowledge of the Central Asian lands, as Strabo testifies, and resulted in renewed efforts by the Romans to discover and control a more northerly land-way which would not touch the Parthian kingdom.

In addition to questions of trade there were problems of frontier defence to be considered. So long as Rome depended on small kingdoms to carry out this task, it was difficult to take strong action upon an united front. In the first years of the Empire, while Commagene and Cappadocia were still client states, Rome only controlled one crossing of the Euphrates, that of Zeugma, and this was guarded by a legionary camp stationed at Cyrrhus, a well-chosen spot, since it was a centre from which ways radiated to the pass over Amanus, to Doliche and Zeugma, to Chalybon (Beroea), and to Antioch. But Tiberius wisely abolished these client-states along the border, and though his measures were repealed by his successor, under Vespasian these lands became finally incorporated in the Empire; control was thus established of all three crossings of the Euphrates, both in the South, and also at Samosata and more northerly still at Melitene. Zeugma was the starting-point for journeys down into Mesopotamia, through which many laden caravans passed; a customs-station was set up, and as early as Claudius' reign a legionary camp had been established there. The route which is given us by Isidore as usually followed, did not cling closely to the Euphrates, which here makes a large semi-circular bend, but struck out across country to Anthemusias, from which point it ran nearly parallel to the course of the Bilechas, through Ichnae to Nicephorium, where it joined the river again. Still keeping to the left bank it went on to Phaliga (Circesium), where another route came in from across the desert and from distant Palmyra; it was also a point where the Parthian armies, in their raids upon Roman territory,

often crossed the river. Hence it followed the Euphrates
to the thriving Greek town of Seleucia, which was only a
few miles distant from the Parthian capital at Ctesiphon.

It must be remembered that many deviations from this
route occurred; the Euphrates valley was not ideal for
travelling, and the tribes dwelling along the river could not
lose an opportunity of levying profitable tolls; very often,
therefore, the caravans made a northerly circuit through
the desert, crossing the country of the Scenite Arabs,
whose rulers were less grasping, at a distance of three days'
march from the river. And in the hot summer weather
trade clung to an even more Northerly route of great
antiquity, through a belt of country where there was a more
abundant rainfall, and much greater chance of water and
herbage. This route, which strikes out North after crossing
the river, ran through Carrhae and Resaina to Nisibis and
Singara, then joined the Tigris valley near Nineveh and
followed its course down to Ctesiphon; a variant went even
further North, through Edessa and by Marde to Nisibis,
and it was here that Tigranes (with great penetration) set
his ambitious foundation of Tigranocerta; it was no freak
of vanity that led him to place it there, but sound commercial sense. This route was as old as history itself, and
provided an excellent way for large armies or bodies of
men; Alexander followed it in his triumphal progress
through the land, as did Trajan four centuries later in his
war against Parthia, when Nisibis became a permanent
Roman fortress.

But all these routes, however varied, met finally at
Seleucia on the Tigris, a thriving market-town, and one
with an interesting history; originally a Greek foundation
it had preserved much of its Hellenism and usually was
able to hold itself independent of Parthia. Its power and
wealth were very great, doubtless owing to its extremely
favourable situation, and it was inhabited by a mingled

population of Macedonians, Greeks, and Syrians, to which was added later a party of Jews, and the town was busy with continual traffic. A few miles away lay Ctesiphon, which the kings of Parthia had chosen to make their winter capital; Strabo testifies to the large population gathered there, the trade that went on and proved so profitable to the inhabitants, and the magnificence of the buildings erected by the Parthian rulers. A little down the river a new depôt had been founded by king Vologeses, and named after him Vologesias, which was one of the trading-stations frequented by the Palmyrene merchants. The country beyond this, towards the mouth of the river, was under the sway of the Arab king of Charax, and included the town of Phorath. Charax had once lain at the mouth of the river itself, and as late as Strabo's time appears to have been the principal station for shipping, but the deposits brought down by the water accumulated so rapidly that by the end of the first century it was already twelve miles away (a fate which the earlier port of Teredon had also suffered), and the harbour of Apologus had taken its place. Here there used to arrive at regular intervals large vessels from India laden with timber, sandalwood and teakwood, blackwood and ebony, which returned bearing in exchange the pearls of the Persian fisheries, the purples of the Mediterranean, wine and dates and slaves. And it was from this port, as we shall see later, that merchants who had come from Bactria often shipped for Petra and the West.

But to return to Ctesiphon; those who were journeying eastward from this town had to climb the steep ascent up the Zagros mountains that led to the Iranian plateau, and on by the modern Kermanshah route, past the great rock of Behistun, to the wealthy city of Ecbatana, the summer residence of the Parthian kings. From here the road traversed the plains of Media Rhagiana, up to the famous pass of the Caspian Gates, one of the principal strategic

points of ancient history. Then past the far-distant Greek
city of Apamea, and on through the lonely wastes of
Hyrcania to another great Parthian city at Heçatompylos.
Hence the road continued due East to Antiochia Margiana,
the modern Merv; at this point the route described by
Isidore makes a curious detour South to Alexandropolis
(Kandahar), where apparently his agents had met the
Chinese merchants or their intermediaries, and ends there;
but we are fortunately able to supplement his information.

For it so happened that after the time of Isidore a
wealthy Macedonian, named Maes Titianus, of a mercantile family, who was presumably interested in the silk trade,
sent out agents to explore the route carefully and bring
back news of the distances and of the time occupied. (He
must have been one of the Macedonian Greeks settled in
Syria, and it whets our curiosity to find a merchant thus
financing an expedition; doubtless it happened often, but
the only other instance known to us is the despatch of a
Roman knight by an Italian contractor to search for the
route and depôts of the Baltic amber trade.) As far as
Merv their journey was much the same as that outlined by
Isidore; but after leaving that city, instead of turning South,
the agents struck out for Bactra (the modern Balkh), traversed the mountainous country of the Comedi, and through
the territory of the Sacae, until they reached ultimately a
station called the "Stone Tower," where they met the
Chinese traders. This place is almost certainly Tashkurgan,
in Sarikol, a fortified town upon a desolate crag over-
hanging the Upper Yarkand river. This route had been
opened over two centuries ago by the enterprise of the
Bactrian monarchs, Demetrius and Menander, and from
Tashkurgan it continued down the Yarkand valley Eastwards into China to the capital town of Singanfu. From
Bactria there was another route which led over the Hindu
Kush and along the valley of the Kabul river through the

famous Khyber Pass to Taxila and the Indus valley: by this route Alexander approached the Punjab after conquering Bactria. Thus in this lonely region three civilisations, those of China, of India, and of the Hellenised Orient, met and gave in exchange their products, their wares, and their painting and art. What was the effect of all this interchange we cannot say fully as yet; further explorations round Lop Nor (such as those of Sir Aurel Stein) and in a little-explored region may bring forth fascinating discoveries.

But there is another region yet to be considered before we come to our final conclusion. From the time of Lucullus onwards one of the most arresting features of Roman history is the constant struggle to repel Parthia and obtain dominance over Armenia, or at any rate make it a sphere of influence. Now Armenia and Caucasia, the district North of it, were fertile and productive countries; the forests of the Caucasus provided excellent timber, the Phasis ran through a valley fertile in flax, and the linen-making of the district was renowned; wax and pitch too were to be obtained near by, and explain the maritime prosperity of such towns as Sinope, Amisos, and Trapezus. Gold was found in the rivers, and there were mines of red ochre and of gold near Caballa. It was certainly a region worth annexing, yet that motive does not seem the only key to the history of this period. For our purpose we must go back a little and examine previous events in the district.

Early in the first century Pompey after his defeat of Mithradates turned Northward to chastise the plundering tribes of the Iberi and Albani, and we are told that he used the pass of the Cyrus river (near Harmozica) in order to penetrate into the country of the Iberi. From this tribe he learnt about the Indian trade that came down the Oxus valley and across the Caspian, and we may surmise that this information, when carried to Rome, made a great impression among the mercantile classes. Not many years later, Canidius, an officer of Antony, also made an expedition upon the Iberi (using the same pass), defeated them and persuaded them to become allies ("socii"). During the Augustan period we have various attempts to place upon the throne of Armenia a vassal of Rome, or one who would acknowledge some vague kind of allegiance, as in the expeditions of Tiberius, of Gaius Caesar, of Germanicus, of Corbulo and the rest. What is more interesting is that the kings of the Albani and Iberi appear as seeking the friendship of Rome and sending embassies; during the reign of Tiberius we hear that Albania and Iberia are among the small states "protected by the might of Rome against foreign empires"; they appreciated this privilege so far as to send contingents to the help of Rome, which Corbulo promptly used for the more unpleasant tasks. In Nero's reign there was already a garrison at Gorneae, in Armenia, and both Pontus and Lesser Armenia were annexed by that ruler in order to have full control of the frontier line; it is also related that he meditated sending an expedition to the Caspian Gates—almost certainly an error for Caucasian Gates, though the result is much the same in the long run. Cappadocia was finally annexed by Vespasian and legions placed there for defence of the river, presumably at Samosata and Melitene, while at the same time a Roman garrison suddenly made its appearance at Harmozica, in Iberia itself. Among the new roads which Domitian had laid in Eastern Asia Minor we may be certain that the route connecting Samosata-Melitene-Satala and Trapezus was one, and doubtless another was that from Satala to Elegia along which Trajan marched in his Parthian campaigns.

Now if we ask what is the meaning of all this manœuvring, the usual explanation—that it was for frontier defence against the Parthians—is scarcely satisfactory. We know of no Parthian army which came through Northern

Armenia to attack Rome or found it necessary to mount the Cyrus valley and launch upon the Black Sea; their raids were nearly always delivered from the crossings of the Euphrates and centred upon the region of Zeugma and Antioch. The truth seems to be that the Romans were attempting to get control of the trade route which ran through Iberia and thus circumvent Parthia by holding both the Northern and the Southern ways of trade. Already in the third century before Christ Seleucid officers had explored the Caspian route, and we have seen how knowledge of it, preserved by Greek writers, reached Pompey's ears. Phasis, a town upon the river of that name, within two days' sail from Amisus, was the starting-point; the river was large and navigable as far as a fortress called Sarapana, past which cargo had to be transferred to waggons; from here the Phasis wound away into the hills, but the waggon-road was good and within four or five days brought one in sight of the valley of the Cyrus. It was in this district that lay the famous Caucasian Gates, the modern Dariel Pass, through which all traffic coming from the North has to go. From this point not only the Cyrus but other navigable rivers were available to make the journey to the Caspian; thus one could travel down the Alazonius and then by a stone-paved road through the mountains of Albania; one wonders who built such a road in that wild part of the world. An alternative route ran from the port of Trapezus to Satala, and from thence through Elegia to the Araxes valley, which gave into the Caspian not far South of the mouth of the Cyrus; we learn from Tacitus that provisions for Corbulo's army in Armenia were brought by this route, and the gorge of the Araxes was commanded by the important Armenian town of Artaxata, a town which figures not a little in Roman history.

We cannot doubt that it was over the more Northerly of these two routes that Roman policy consistently strove to gain control. That by the Araxes valley might have been subject to Parthian incursions, but the route of the Cyrus and the Caspian, and so up by the Oxus valley—for there is no doubt that the Oxus was in some way connected with the Caspian—to Samarcand was never at any point threatened by Parthian domination. And it seems probable that this policy was fairly successful; we can perceive this from the report which Arrian, in his capacity as consular legate, forwarded to the emperor Hadrian. Along the whole Eastern side of the Black Sea, in the district of Phasis, we hear of many small forts and garrisons, as at Hyssou Limen and at Apsarus. At Phasis itself there was stationed a large force of four hundred picked soldiers, which was admirably placed "with regard to the safety of all those who sail there." Outside the fort itself there had grown up a settlement of veterans and of other men engaged in trade, and Arrian saw to the digging of a fosse for their protection; a little further up the coast at Dioscurias there was another garrison. In addition the small tribes of the mountains had nearly all been given kings by Rome and owed her allegiance; against the Sanni, who had been dilatory in the payment of tribute, Arrian proceeded with a strong hand. Thus the whole of this region was under Roman control, and the garrison which had been posted at Harmozica by Vespasian in A.D. 75 overlooked the Dariel Pass and guarded against the incursions of any barbarians who might molest travellers proceeding to the Caspian. We may be sure that Rome would not have taken such trouble over an outlying district unless the amount of trade pouring through it had made the task worth while.

Beyond Tashkurgan the Chinese merchants awaited the agents of the Westerners, and laid on the river bank the raw silk, silk yarn, and silken garments which they exchanged for the precious stones, amber, and coral that the Romans brought. It is said that they were very honest in their dealings, withdrawing from the spot until the purchasers had made their choice; no word was exchanged during the whole transaction. Of course all the silk exported to Rome did not necessarily come by Parthia; a fair quantity was sent down the Indus to Barygaza and thence transferred to Rome; some even went down the valley of the Ganges to the populous mart of Palibothra, and Ptolemy shews a knowledge of this traffic. Yet in spite of the trade relations established the Romans never evinced much curiosity about the far-distant people who supplied them with silk, and almost to the end they remained enwrapped in an atmosphere of mystery and legend. The Chinese, on the contrary, shewed an enquiring spirit; during the latter part of the first century a celebrated general, by name Pan Chao, was despatched to conquer Chinese Turkestan and secure the routes down the Tarim valley; from here he sent out an ambassador to collect information about the state of Parthia and about the more distant Ta-ts'in (Syria). The ambassador, Kan Ying, brought back a report which must have proved interesting reading: thus he declared that "when a severe calamity visits the country, or untimely rain-storms, the king is deposed or replaced by another. The one relieved from his duties submits to his degradation without a murmur." But he noted the post-stations and the accurate measurement of distances along the roads; reported that the country contained gold and precious stones, gums and spices in abundance; "they are honest in their dealings and there are no double prices." Furthermore "their kings always desired to send embassies to China, but the An-hsi (Parthians) wished to carry on trade with them in Chinese silks, and it is for this reason that they were cut off from communication." He was also informed of the sea-voyage round Arabia that it was necessary to make in order to reach Rome, and in connection with this we may reproduce another passage from a later record which perhaps explains why Kan Ying did not see Italy. It runs as follows: "In the ninth year of Yung-yuan of Ho-ti (A.D. 97) the general Pan Chao sent Kan-ying as an ambassador to Ta-ts'in, who tarried in T'iao-chih, on the coast of the great sea. When about to take his passage across the sea, the sailors of the western frontier of Parthia told Kan-ying: 'The sea is vast and great; with favourable winds it is possible to cross within three months; but if you meet slow winds, it may also take you two years. It is for this reason that those who go to sea take on board a supply of three years' provisions. There is something in the sea which is apt to make a man homesick, and several have thus lost their lives.' When Kan-ying heard this, he stopped...." Finally, as has been already recounted, an embassy from Marcus Aurelius reached China from the frontier of Annam, offering ivory, rhinoceros horns, and tortoise-shell. "From that time," continues the chronicle, "dates the direct intercourse with this country."

It appears likely that silk came into greater use at Rome about the period of the civil wars; it was woven at Tyre and Berytus and also at Cos, and poets of the time are full of references to the "Coae vestes" and their exquisite tissue. Vergil knows the legendary account of its origin, imagining that it is plucked in the form of threads from a tree. The cost of transport enormously enhanced the price, and only the very richest or members of princely families could afford to wear it; Lucan tells how Cleopatra appeared at a banquet resplendent in silken vestments woven by the skilful workmen of Tyre; the moralists, however, were shocked by these thin-spun and delicate garments, which "while they cover a woman, at the same time reveal her naked charms," and inveigh against its use generally. So fashionable did it become that even men took to wearing it, but this practice was repressed by an edict in the reign of Tiberius, as being too effeminate. But the trade in it went on in spite of edicts; Pliny includes silk among his list of most expensive and precious products, and from Martial we gather that it was to be found only in the houses of the very wealthy or of the imperial family and was sold in one of the most fashionable shopping quarters of Rome. The new era inaugurated by Trajan and Hadrian, though it may have stopped some of the more senseless extravagances, did not curb the silk trade, since it is during their time that we find the most active measures being taken to secure the Caspian route.

For many years the production of silk garments flourished in the Syrian towns, especially at Berytus and at Tyre. At the former city an inscription was discovered commemorating a silk-merchant, but as might be expected even more are found in Italy, whither many found it profitable to migrate and carry on their business in the centre of demand; thus one Heliodorus of Antioch in Syria is found plying his trade at Naples, and at Gabii there is an inscription of a rich Syrian Greek, by name Epaphroditus, who having attained enormous wealth by his trade spent it in the most lavish manner upon his adopted town; we find other merchants at Tibur, and there was even a woman carrying on business at Rome.

The literary evidence for this trade and intercourse is, as we have seen, tantalisingly small, and when we consider the absolute chance that appears to preside over archaeological or epigraphical discoveries, any testimony that we can gain from these should be allowed its fullest weight. It is worth noting, for instance, that the gold coins of North India in the first century are of the same weight as the Roman aurei of that period, and very often display an imitation of their design; the Roman gold coinage was a standard and was accepted over a very wide area. So, too, the word "denarius" persists for long in Indian literature, and some think that faint traces of Roman law and procedure can be found in texts of the time. But perhaps most astounding of all were the discoveries made by Sir Aurel Stein at Miran in the Tarim valley; in this deserted fort that lay upon the ancient silk-route frescoes and paintings were dug up revealing that strange mixture of Indian and Greek art that might have been expected from the region; more surprising was the fact that some of the figures shewed distinctly Roman poses and attitudes and the faces displayed features of a Roman type. Not far away in the sand-covered ruins of Lop Nor were found many traces of this trade and in one house a small bale of silk perfectly preserved. When conditions admit and these regions are once more thrown open to exploration we may surely hope for much in the way of fresh discoveries.

CHAPTER SEVEN
GREECE

"ἐπεὶ καὶ νῦν...σχεδόν τι τὰ δύο
μέρη τῆς χώρας ἡμῶν ἔρημά ἐστι δι'
ἀμέλειάν τε καὶ ὀλιγανθρωπίαν·
κἀγὼ πολλὰ κέκτημαι πλέθρα...ἃ εἴ
τις ἐθέλοι γεωργεῖν, οὐ μόνον ἂν
προῖκα δοίην, ἀλλὰ καὶ ἀργύριον
ἡδέως προστελέσαιμι."

DIO CHRYSOSTOM

At present practically two-thirds
of our country (Euboea) is lying
waste through neglect and lack
of men. I too possess many acres
of land...if someone will only till
it for me, I shall not only allow
him to do so freely, but gladly
pay him money as well.

GREECE

IT is worthy of remark that the occasion of Rome's first intervention in the affairs of Greece was the damage done to shipping and commerce in the Adriatic by the piracy of the Illyrians. Our accounts differ slightly as to the exact pretext: patriotic writers were ready to believe that Rome chivalrously took up the cause of the people of Issa, who had been attacked by the pirates; other authors told of the ill-treatment which was meted out to the Roman ambassadors by Teuta, the Illyrian queen; but in spite of slight divergencies there can be no doubt that the main reason was the damage done to merchants from Brundisium by the Illyrians, and especially by the Ardiaei, who were the most powerful. From this time onward Rome's relations with the Greek states grew in extent and complexity; Macedonia had to be conquered, the independence of the Leagues crushed; insensibly this led on to wider schemes in Asia Minor and the East. The Northern frontier of Macedonia and the tribes adjacent were somewhat neglected under the Republic, though Marcus Lucullus subdued the Thracians and so secured the coast road to Byzantium and the Bosporus. Under Augustus Illyria and the neighbouring lands were pacified, and the Danube became the Northern frontier of Roman power, while the settlement of Moesia was reserved for Tiberius; these frontier districts were placed under imperial legates. Yet trade was not forgotten in the midst of conquest: after the capture of Ambracia Rome demanded freedom from customs-duties both for herself and for her allies, and later in the century Delos was turned into a free port. It is not necessary to see in this merely a selfish encouragement of Roman commerce; those who profited most were the Asiatics and Syrians and the natives of

Magna Graecia. The destruction of Corinth, which is usually viewed as an instance of mercantile influence upon policy, was meant to be an example and a warning to other Greek states not to behave foolishly. It is only in the first century B.C. that Italian and Roman traders really established themselves firmly in the Aegean.

Macedonia was of far more importance to the Romans than Achaea: we shall see later that there was little activity in the latter province. Through Macedonia ran the highway of communication between Rome and the East, which had to be kept open at all costs. This road—the Via Egnatia—had been laid down between Apollonia and Thessalonica as early as 148 B.C., when distances were carefully measured and milestones placed; later it was extended as far as the Hebrus. It became the great highway for all going Eastward, and the towns situated at either end, Apollonia and Dyrrhachium and Thessalonica, enjoyed a flourishing trade. By this route Cicero made his melancholy way into exile; by it Pompey meant to fall back on Asia, and along it later came Antony and Octavian to avenge Caesar's murder at Philippi. Under the Empire new roads were built and old ones improved, but very few milestones of the imperial age have so far been unearthed, and none in Achaea of an earlier date than 400, which tends to confirm the view grounded upon literary sources, that there was little trading activity in that province. Curiously enough we find roads being repaired in the islands; thus Claudius and Vespasian did work in Crete, and the latter built roads in Cyprus. But the greatest benefactor was the philhellene Hadrian; one of his milestones has been found near Hypata, on the main route between Athens and Thessalonica, and instead of the old narrow and dangerous road between Corinth and Athens, of which Strabo complains, he carved out a new way along the precipitous cliffs of the Corinthian Gulf. Otherwise our epigraphic evidence is sadly lacking.

In literary sources, on the other hand, we have plenty of information as to the existence of roads, but very little about their nature or state. The whole of the Peloponnese was intersected by them, but in many places they can have been little more than mule-tracks. Thus although both Strabo and Pausanias mention innumerable local roads, the latter says that a certain pass was called "the ladder" on account of steps cut in it, notices that the road to Titane is too narrow for vehicles, and remarks upon that from Tegea to Argos as being an excellent carriage road. But the roads were not good or solidly laid for the simple reason that very little trade went on within the Peloponnese; the only really important towns, Patrae and Corinth, were upon its extreme borders. Still there were country tracks and lanes running through the valleys and up over the mountains that divided the states from one another. Corinth was their chief starting-point: from here roads struck out to Epidaurus and Troezen, to Cleonae and Argos, and to Sicyon and Phlius, and Northward a road led along the coast to Megara and Athens and Boeotia. From Argos there was one leading to Mantinea, which lay in a long narrow plain, and was a great centre, and so on to Sparta and the South. From Mantinea ways led Southward to Messenia and Westward to Olympia and Elis. Along the Northern coast ran a road from Corinth, through Pellene and Aegae to the busy port of Patrae; hence it was continued to Dyme and so round to Elis. Thus the Peloponnese was completely encircled by its roads and in good communication with the central uplands of Arcadia. Yet there was little heavy traffic passing upon them and transport by sea was often easier and more convenient. Great festival centres such as Olympia or Nemea attracted crowds during the games, but these were only held at stated intervals. And in that mountainous country there were few rivers which were navigable over any length; the Alpheus

would admit ships for a short distance, and the Pamisus,
in Messenia, for about a mile. Again, in the South, the
Cape of Malea had an ill repute on account of its storms.
But there were plenty of small ports and harbours along the
coast, though they would not admit vessels of large draught.
From Aegium a ferry crossed the Corinthian Gulf to
Cirrha, and at Patrae, Dyme, and Cyllene (which latter
was the port for Elis) there were good harbours which
received the sea-trade coming from Italy. On the South
coast there were numerous small harbours of refuge and
roadsteads where ships could lie, when detained by the
strong winds off Malea, or which they could make in case
of a storm. On the Eastern coast there lay the harbours of
Troezen, Prasiae, and Epidaurus. But by far the most
important maritime city was Corinth: through it journeyed merchants both to and from the Peloponnese and it
controlled the East and West trade as well, since it was far
more convenient to have vessels drawn across the roller-
way that spanned the narrow isthmus, and pay the necessary dues, than to have to battle with adverse winds off
Malea. Both Julius Caesar and the emperor Nero had
thoughts of cutting through the isthmus, but their plans
were never carried out. In the nineteenth century, when the
use of steam for shipping made it no longer necessary, the
scheme was duly put into execution, and during the excavations traces of the Neronian undertaking were discovered.

Outside of the Peloponnese the road-system was rather
different. There was one great triangle, the base of which
was formed by the Apollonia-Thessalonica route; the one
side of this ran from Apollonia down the coast to the
flourishing town of Nicopolis, and then turned to follow
the Northern side of the Corinthian Gulf through the
deserted territory of Aetolia to Thebes, Athens and
Corinth; the other side was formed by a road which started
from Athens, passed through Thebes, and up by the pass

of Thermopylae, into the plains of Thessaly, through Larisa and down the valley of the Peneus, and so along the shore of the Thermaic Gulf to join the overland route at Thessalonica. Within this district the usual local roads were to be found; from Athens along the shore of the Saronic Gulf to Megara and Corinth, from Thebes by way of the Chaeronea pass into Phocis and so to Delphi, and from Thebes also to the seaport towns of Chalcis and Anthedon. But the overland route between Apollonia and Thessalonica was far the most considerable, and its stages must be given in greater detail. Its importance lay in the fact that during the winter, when all navigation was closed, it gave the only secure means of communication with the Eastern provinces. The two ports of Dyrrhachium and Apollonia could be reached after a short sea-passage from Brundisium, or by the longer route overland through Illyria. The two branches of the road met at Clodiana, and proceeded up the valley of the Genusos and crossed the river to the town of Candavia; from here it skirted the North-Eastern side of Lake Lychnitis to Lychnidos, and thence across the mountains to the important centre of Heraclea in Lyncestis, where a branch turned Northward up the valley of the Axius into Moesia. From Heraclea the road proceeded to Edessa, and so down the valley of the Ludias, and across the Axius into Thessalonica. If the entire journey was to be accomplished by land, the traveller would continue along the Thracian coast by way of Philippi and on through to Perinthus and eventually reach Byzantium. This town, situated at a spot where routes from two continents and from North and South all met, was a populous trade-centre during the Early Empire, and merchants flowed into it from all parts so that a centurion with a small force of soldiers was stationed there to help the local police in the preservation of order. It was eminently suited by its position to be the capital of a

Mediterranean Empire; both Caesar and Augustus had thought of moving the capital to such a region, and the change was actually made under Constantine. But the overland route was a lengthy one and if the weather permitted the traveller would usually embark at Neapolis, the port of Philippi, and sailing across to the Troad would follow the Western coast of Asia Minor. This was the route taken by St Paul when he visited Macedonia and Northern Greece.

As in the Peloponnese there were few navigable rivers here save in the regions of Thrace and Macedonia, where the Hebrus was navigable as far as Cypsela, and the Ludias as far as Pella. But in the Southern region there was a great number of harbours, mostly small, though the larger one of Athens still retained something of its ancient importance; yet this was difficult of access save when a South-East wind was blowing. Boeotia possessed a great many small harbours, and an important one at Aulis. In Euboea the chief harbour was that of Chalcis, and going further North, in Thessaly there was Pyrasos, and in Macedonia Thessalonica and Neapolis.

For further communication with the lands between Macedonia and the Danube—which became increasingly necessary as the provinces of Moesia were pacified and when Trajan added the rich regions of Dacia to the Empire—there was a route which left Thessalonica and struck up the valley of the Axius past Stobi as far as Scupi (the modern Uskub), and then forced its way over a difficult mountain pass to find the valley of the Morava near Naissus, and so down to the Danube at Viminacium. At Naissus it was joined by a road which ran through Thrace from Byzantium passing through Philippopolis and Serdica. The emperor Nero appears to have had this road properly laid out and provided with camps and places where travellers could rest or buy necessaries. This route, as has

been shewn in the chapter on Asia, became of great importance in the second century, as being the connecting link
between the armies upon the Danube and those of the
East, and the attention which later emperors paid to this
region is shewn by the foundation of Hadrianopolis upon
the Naissus-Byzantium road, and that of Traianopolis
upon the coast-road from Philippi to Byzantium. While
Trajan, too, completed the chain of roads between the
Black Sea and the Atlantic, Hadrian saw to the laying out
of one along the Western shores of the Black Sea, which
would link up such ports as Mesembria and Odessus and
even the far-distant Tomi with Byzantium.

Throughout its history Greece was never a country
noted for agricultural wealth; save for one or two patches
of fertile plain, the rest of the land was hillside and shallow
soil. This explains in early times the constant wars for the
possession of plains, the Lelantine plain, the level land of
Tegea, and the rich plain of Messenia. Now after centuries of habitation and cultivation much of the goodness
in the soil had gone, and land was everywhere being given
over to pasturage. When we compare it with any other of
the provinces we see at once how exiguous its resources
were. In the Peloponnese the region of Messenia was well
watered by such rivers as the Pamisus and Nedon, and the
land was well tilled and fruitful; so, too, in the West the
land of Elis was famous for the growing of flax, as delicate
and fine as that grown in Judaea, but not of such a yellow
colour, while the valley of neighbouring Triphylia was also
very fertile, though liable to occasional blights. Arcadia
provided good pasturage for horses and asses, and was
renowned for a good breed of the former. The plain of
Argos was watered by many small rivers, and carefully
cultivated, and such towns as Sicyon and Phelloë were
celebrated for their olives or their vines. But after this
enumeration there is very little left; the soil of the

Peloponnese as a whole was rough and poor, and Strabo expressly tells us that Laconia was but poorly inhabited in comparison with its former glories; the land was going to waste for sheer lack of men to cultivate it. And in consequence crops were being given up, land was bought by wealthy men and turned to pasturage or grazing, and became the property of a few rich proprietors, men such as Eurycles of Sparta, or Herodes of Athens, or the unknown capitalist who owned nearly all the land in Euboea. And throughout the pages of Strabo and Pausanias, and in other writers of our period, we meet a mournful list of cities that had dwindled into villages, of lands once cultivated and now lying deserted, and of towns that had vanished and left no trace.

The same picture of depopulation and of neglect meets our eyes when we look Northward, though there were some districts that still retained a vestige of prosperity. True there was still the olive-oil for which Attica had been so famous, and the honey of Hymettus was exported in large quantities; but the land produced no other crops. The soil of Boeotia was fertile and well watered by lakes and rivers; among the benefits which a rich Boeotian, Epaminondas by name, conferred upon his countrymen, was the reopening of the old tunnels which drained the Copaic Lake and prevented its over-flooding the land. Hence it was a region of great productivity; at Aulis were grown dates far superior to those of Ionia, though not so good as the Palestinian, and at Chaeronea were immense gardens of roses, narcissi, and other flowers, from which fragrant unguents were distilled and exported. In the North-Western districts, beyond Boeotia, good hellebore was to be found upon the slopes of Mount Oeta, but that of Anticyra though inferior in quality was better compounded and so commanded a higher price. At Ambrosus grew the coccus plant from which dye was made, and the plain of Crisa was noted for its fertility. By the town of Tithorea olives grew plentifully; though less was produced than at Athens, the oil was of the finest quality, and sweeter than the Spanish; it was an important article of export, and was sent to the emperor's table. It is interesting to note that this industry was of recent growth, since Plutarch tells us that in Sulla's time the town was of little importance. Yet Strabo enumerates many cities of Boeotia that were completely deserted, and according to Pausanias only the acropolis of Thebes was inhabited, while towns such as Scolus and Ascra lay in ruins. The land of Aetolia and Acarnania had sunk into neglect and desolation; continual wars had ravaged and impoverished it. Even along the Western coast the same tale held good: on the island of Cephallenia cities had vanished leaving scarcely a trace, the town of Lysimachia on the mainland had fallen into ruin, and Strabo tells us of statues being carried away to Italy because of the decay of the buildings wherein they had been erected. Zacynthus was well-wooded and fertile, but the most prosperous place in the region was a new Roman foundation, established by Augustus in commemoration of his victory, and called Nicopolis. Yet it is significant that this town was partly formed by bringing together such population as still remained in the dwindling cities of the district, and its prosperity does not appear to have been long-lived.

Upon the Eastern islands conditions were probably little better. Strabo mentions flocks in Euboea, and we are given an interesting glimpse into the state of the island towards the end of the first century, in a speech of Dio Chrysostom. The account he gives has been sometimes rejected as imaginary or overdrawn, but from other evidence it seems only too certain that the details are correct. The greater part of the island had been owned by one rich man during the reign of Nero, but he had been put to death and his property confiscated. Two-thirds of the town territory was completely deserted owing to carelessness and lack of men. A great deal of this was in the hands of a large proprietor, who was only too ready to pay if anyone could be found to work; the land outside the city gates looked like a wilderness rather than a suburb. The one thing necessary was to get men to work on the land.

But to one travelling Northward a better aspect of things presented itself. The plains of Thessaly, watered by the Peneus and its tributaries, were famous not only for the crops which they yielded, but also for the good breed of horses they produced. It was indeed a fortunate country, save for its liability to sudden flooding from the swollen river. Larisa was still a prosperous country town and lay in the midst of a fertile plain. The whole country was famous for its horses, which were among the best of the Empire. Further North in Macedonia a man would find mountainous but well-wooded country; from the whole of this district good timber was to be had in abundance. Strabo specially mentions the country round Datum for its productiveness, and Pliny speaks in high terms of the timber of Macedonia.

Though there was an almost complete lack of precious metals, Greece was exceptionally rich in marble and stone for building. The quarries had been worked for many years but were not exhausted; indeed new veins were sometimes discovered. Laconia was renowned for its marbles; a particularly beautiful veined stone was found near Croceae; though hard to work and demanding skilled labour, it was much in demand for more ornate temples or buildings. Recently too new quarries had been opened on Mount Taygetus; we are told that it was Roman capital that enabled them to be worked, and that they were large and profitable. The marble was of a greenish hue, and was exported to Italy; it is mentioned by many writers of the

period. There were old quarries near Taenarus too, but
these had been worked out. Otherwise the Peloponnese
lacked stone, though there were local marbles, such as that
of Sicyon, and Laconia itself supplied excellent whetstones.

North of the Peloponnese stone was to be found in
various centres. In Attica there were stone-quarries at
Amphiale, on the road to Eleusis, but the most famous
were those on Hymettus and Pentelicus, whence came the
splendid marble which the Athenian sculptors had used.
Numberless dedications had been made from this marble,
and that the quarries were still workable is shewn by the
fact that Herodes Atticus used Pentelic marble for many
of the buildings with which he adorned Athens; it was not
now such an article of export as formerly, owing to the
discovery in Italy of the Luna (Carrara) marbles. In the
neighbouring island of Euboea there were good quarries
near Carystus: the marble was variegated, as was that of
Scyros, which was exported in immense blocks to Rome
to be worked there. And there was also the stone of Thasos,
and most renowned of all the marble from the island of
Paros, which was the finest obtainable. Naturally there
were many varieties of local stone; here it is only possible
to mention the more important.

Save for stone and marble, however, Greece was
deficient in minerals. It seems to have had no metals of
its own by this time; such mines as had existed before
appear to have been exhausted. We hear nothing of the
iron of Laconia during this period; so, too, the copper
and iron mines of the Lelantine plain were worked to a
finish; most notable of all, the mines of Laurion, which had
been the mainstay of Athenian greatness, were completely
exhausted, as all our authors witness. For wealth in
minerals we must look to Macedonia: there the mines
which had once supplied Philip with his wealth were still

worked and yielded a good return. Gold was found near
Datum, in Crenides, and on Mount Pangaeus, where silver
also was mined. Copper-green was found among the hills.
As late as the fourth century we have mention of the Macedonian mines and they must have been an important source
of revenue to the imperial treasury.

In industry Greece was not as thriving as the other
provinces. In the Peloponnese there was indeed the purple-
fishing of Cythera, and dyeing was extensively practised;
a great deal was also carried out at Amyclae, and the
Spartan purple was the best in Europe, according to Pliny.
A certain amount of weaving and clothes-making went on
at Sparta, but probably the most important industrial
centre was the town of Patrae. It lay on the very route
from Brundisium to Corinth, and so had large shipping
interests; but the main business there was the weaving of
the flax which was brought to it from the fields of Elis,
and we hear that all the women of the district were employed on the work. Yet in later centuries we do not find
it included among the great imperial Houses of Weaving,
and compared with a town such as Scythopolis or Ravenna
its importance would have appeared small. In Athens,
besides the exportation of oil, honey, and marble, the
manufacture of statuary held a prominent position. Every
Roman of wealth or distinction was bound to have copies
of the famous statues of old to adorn his villa, and the
making of these copies on a large scale became a profitable
trade. In the more Northern parts we have mention of the
distillation of perfumes, and of the making of ointments
and salves at Chaeronea and at Tithorea (the latter town
supplied the emperor with oil), and Aulis manufactured a
good deal of pottery. In Phocis practically half the population of the little town of Bulis was employed upon purple-
fishing, in connection with Corinth, where the actual dyeing was carried out. In the same way, Thessalonica in the

North received the produce of the purple-fisheries of the region. But after this short enumeration there comes an end.

It may be contended that too gloomy a view is here presented of the condition of Greece. Yet it is drawn from contemporary authors, from Strabo and Pausanias and Dio Chrysostom, who are all in substantial agreement, and what Plutarch says corroborates them. The sole exception is Apuleius, who gives a glowing description of certain Thessalian towns, among them Hypata. But the whole book of Apuleius is of the fairy-tale type and not to be taken at its face value; the town is not known to any of the authors mentioned above, and Pliny notices it solely to record the curative values of its hellebore. Unless, therefore, we postulate a large population of lunatics we cannot imagine any very great activity in this inland Thessalian town. When two writers a century apart, as are Strabo and Pausanias, give the same mournful account of the state of Greece, telling of cities once famous but now vanished, of once prosperous towns reduced to villages, when both lay stress on the lack of men to till the land or engage in industry, and when these two are supported by the utterances of Plutarch and Dio Chrysostom, we cannot but believe that such an account is true, and must discredit the fabulous narrative of Apuleius. There were only two towns in Greece which could compare at all with the great cities of the Empire: both owed their prosperity to their fortunate situation upon frequented routes rather than to any resources of their own; these towns were Thessalonica and Corinth. The former was a great port for those travelling between Rome and the Eastern provinces: it lay midway between Apollonia and Byzantium, and received as well the traffic that came down the Axius valley from the regions of the Danube. It was also the dyeing centre for the purple-fisheries of the district. Corinth, too, owed its prosperity to its unique situation: lying between two seas and between two land masses it not only controlled and received the trade between Rome and the Aegean, but all such merchandise and traffic as went on between the Peloponnese and Northern Greece. In contrast to the other cities of Greece Strabo calls it "rich and prosperous." Its restoration by Julius Caesar had revived much of its former greatness and the new citizens were proud of the past glories of their city. A century later Dio could call it the head of Greece, and congratulate the citizens upon their opulence and good fortune; merchants and sightseers and ambassadors, men passing through bent on business or pleasure, were a common sight within the city.

Towards the close of our period an effort was made to revive the activity of Greece; it would be difficult to determine whether it met with any degree of success. The emperor Hadrian, the enthusiastic Hellenist, justified his honourable title of "Restitutor" (which appears frequently upon his coins) by the numbers of temples, buildings, and works of public utility that he lavished upon the Grecian cities. Thus—to mention but a few of his great gifts—he brought water to Corinth by a new aqueduct; he improved the road that ran along the Scironian cliffs between Corinth and Athens; he restored many buildings at Athens, and especially the famous temple of Olympian Zeus which had been begun seven centuries before by the tyrant Pisistratus. Pausanias declares that he "made the Greek people thrive," and we can well understand how the Greeks raised statues to him in gratitude as "the saviour, who has rescued and given life to his own Greece." His example was followed by a remarkable man of immense wealth, known as Herodes Atticus, who made princely gifts to Athens and to other cities both in Greece proper and in Asia Minor. Yet these efforts proved of little avail; the canker had eaten in too far to be arrested by the beneficence or the public spirit of a few men.

The causes for this failing of power were two: first, long years of cultivation, extending back through centuries, had exhausted a soil not originally rich or deep, and in consequence the birth-rate had declined and there were not enough men to do the work that was necessary. Grazing took the place of sowing; Italy was not the only land that was ruined by "latifundia." Second, a much more profitable career lay open to the Greek in foreign lands than in his own; Italy and the Western provinces would greet him with admiration and compete for his services. Just as English or French men of letters find it lucrative to cross the Atlantic and win the applause of Middle Western cities, so in those days the finest prospect a Greek ever saw was the Appian way which conducted him to Rome. In art or science, in society or business he was equally at home. In the service of the emperor he could rise to positions of extraordinary power and influence: hence the number of Greek confidential freedmen whom Augustus or Claudius possessed. Tiberius took Greek mathematicians and savants to live with him on Capreae. Pallas and Narcissus, the two most powerful freedmen of Claudius, were reputed to be men richer than their master: Xenophon, his physician, gained immunity from tribute for his native island of Cos, and was rewarded by inscriptions and dedications without number from his grateful fellow-countrymen.

When such careers lay open to a Greek outside his own land it is scarcely surprising that he fared abroad. Yet those who stayed at home appreciated the benefits that Roman rule had brought them. The gentle Plutarch declares that "every Greek and every barbarian war has departed from us and clean vanished," while Epictetus exclaims "Caesar has procured us a profound peace: there are neither wars nor battles, nor great robberies nor piracies, but we may travel at all hours, and sail from East to West."

Thus Greece, too, enjoyed to the full the tranquillity, if not the prosperity, which the Empire brought. Though she did not play the part we would fain have seen her playing, she yet retained some small commercial importance, until years later in the time of Justinian Christian monks succeeded in bringing back from China the eggs of the silkworm and thus started the silk industry in Greece and in the Levant.

CHAPTER EIGHT

AFRICA

"Ager frugum fertilis, bonus
pecori, arbori infecundus."

SALLUST

AFRICA

IN the Roman world the term Africa was capable of
two distinct meanings; it was sometimes employed in
a broad sense to designate the whole strip of coast
stretching from the Lesser Syrtes to the Pillars of Hercules
and beyond, but more usually it was applied to the roughly
triangular section of land lying between the mouth of the
Ampsaga and the Lesser Syrtes and having its apex in the
Hermaean promontory. The latter region comprised a
coastline of great, indeed of exceptional fertility, plentifully
watered by good rivers, and thickly inhabited, especially
in the parts around Carthage; "the soil of Africa," as one
ancient geographer declares, "was wholly devoted to
Ceres." More Westerly, although the soil was not so rich,
there were broad plains fit for the breeding of horses and
raising of cattle, and the slopes of the hills and mountains
were thickly wooded. Behind this line of coast rose a mass
of hills, high and forbidding, though not impenetrable,
infested by savage tribes and nomads, who in their desire
for pasture and corn land made continual raids on the
coast. They preyed, too, upon the caravans that passed
through the gaps in the mountain chain across the desert
to trade with the savages there, and to receive the gems,
wood, and ivory, which they could offer. It was not surprising that the wild tribes were attracted by the corn and
oil and wealth of the Carthaginian territory; for many years
the soil had been worked and the land farmed scientific-
ally, so as to secure the greatest possible productivity. A
careful system of irrigation and sparing conservation of the
water-supply in tanks and reservoirs had provided miles
of corn and vine land, with orchards and gardens, while
along the banks of the rivers cattle grazed and on the slopes
of the hills sheep pastured. When Agathocles and his

Sicilians landed on Carthaginian territory and marched towards the capital city they passed through vast areas of fruit and corn and oil, and were amazed by the extent and the richness of the estates and farms.

Yet strange to say when the Roman Senate took over the governance of this realm from defeated Carthage it would have nothing to do with the development of the land. Frankly it did not want to be bothered, and so it contented itself with appropriating the smallest portion of land possible in the circumstances and graciously allotting the rest of the territory to cities or client kings. These latter, while owning a doubtful allegiance to the Senate, were fully occupied in trying to restrain the rebelliousness of their wild tribes, who owned a still more doubtful allegiance to them. The younger Gracchus indeed saw the opportunity Africa presented for the development of trade, but his schemes were fated to come to nought. Nearly a hundred years later they were put into execution by Caesar, who had been in Africa himself and fully realised—possibly from the amount of booty in corn and oil that he brought back— the potentialities of the province.

But, as usual, it was reserved for his great successor, Augustus, to carry out a complete scheme of pacification and organisation, and to provide for the security of trade and the safety of merchants, by the construction of roads, the foundation of colonies, and the provision of police forces. One great problem that confronted him was that of Mauretania and the Western lands; instead of giving them as an insecure heritage to some barbarian prince, he solved the question by putting over the tribes at once a ruler and a civiliser; Juba, who had for a short time been king of Numidia, was raised to the throne of Mauretania —his former kingdom being annexed to the province— and while he guarded the land from the incursions of such tribes as the Autolules or the Baquates, he also made his capital the centre of art and literature. He was a hellenising prince, whose learning and whose charm of character won the praise of all who met him. Some colonies also were founded in Western Mauretania, even beyond the Pillars of Hercules; they were placed, however, under the jurisdiction of the governor of Baetica, and seem to have been empowered to raise local militia to meet raids from the desert. In the province of Africa itself, though it had been granted to the Senate, Augustus made an exception to his general rule, and allowed the proconsul to hold an army at his disposal. By such means peace was safeguarded. It is true that during the early years of the Empire occasional disturbances arose, border tribes had to be put down with a stern hand, as in the expedition of Cossus, and the revolt of Tacfarinas and the patriotic rising of Aedemon caused serious and prolonged fighting. But this warfare all took place on the borders of the province; the army was well situated and could strike quickly and effectually; the towns themselves, the merchants and traders, were little affected by the rebellions, and during the first two centuries of our era Africa steadily grew in importance as a granary of the Empire.

Our information as regards the road-system of the province until the closing years of the first century is unfortunately very defective; there are no milestones to help us, and we have to rely upon much older notices and occasional references in various authors. In general, we may well believe that the most used routes followed the lines of river-valleys and made for the gaps in the hill-chain or hugged the coast. From our evidence, however, we can reasonably assume that there was a road from Carthage to Utica and on to Hippo Diarrhytus which crossed the Bagradas by a bridge near its mouth; another cut through the hills that encircled Carthage and led probably up the valley of the Bagradas through the rich corn-bearing region, known as the Great Plains, to Sicca Veneria; it is not unreasonable to suppose that it also led ultimately to Theveste, for that city was situate in a singularly fertile district and was one of the principal towns of Africa and of great renown in ancient times. Another road led from Carthage direct to Neapolis, thereby saving the dangerous sea-passage round Cape Bon, and since we hear of an elaborate causeway built to the East of Leptis Magna, it is possible that the road ran the whole length of the coast; this possibility becomes a certainty when we reflect upon the great riches of this stretch of land, the district of Byzacium, which was called Emporia in ancient times, owing to the wealth it brought its masters. Under Roman rule we may be sure that the existing system was kept up, even if not developed; the campaigns of Marius would suggest a road running up at least as far as Sicca Veneria, and that of Caesar shews that communication between Hadrumetum and Thapsus was swift and easy.

We can only be sure of the most obvious and natural roads for the time of the Republic; with the advent of the Empire the usual development came. Augustus founded many colonies in Africa, and though no milestones of his have as yet come to light, we may be certain—to take only one typical instance—that the new colony of Simitthu, lying near the fruitful Bagradas valley and possessing valuable marble quarries, was properly connected by a paved road with Carthage; more especially so, when we consider that it lay on the way to Theveste, which was the headquarters of the Legio Tertia Augusta, since easy communication between camp and coast was essential. Indeed, during the principate of Augustus several military operations had to be undertaken, to put down revolting tribesmen or to check the raids of the desert hordes; the Musulamii and the Gaetuli rose in rebellion, and in the year 6 Cossus quelled an attempt at revolt. Thus we may be certain that at this period there were one or two paved roads in the province, among which we may include the route from Carthage to Hippo Regius, which is of great antiquity and crosses the Bagradas by a bridge which Tissot conjectured to be Punic. But during the reign of Tiberius a more serious rising took place, under Tacfarinas, and it gradually began to be understood that in order to protect the province the camp of the legions must be pushed further forward and better connection with the sea-coast established. At the very beginning of his reign the proconsul and his soldiery had been occupied in constructing a road from their headquarters to the coast of the Lesser Syrtis at Tacape, thereby providing a second route for provisions and reinforcements and securing a good base-line for striking against the desert tribes. After the war with Tacfarinas we have indications of an enlargement of the bounds of the province, and from that time onward through the century we find the legionary camp steadily advanced towards the South-West and the hills that encircle the province. Under Vespasian a road was built connecting Theveste with Hippo Regius and the camp thus received a third outlet towards the sea; the emperors of the next hundred years, however, especially Trajan, did most towards completing the system. Vespasian repaired the old road between Carthage and Hippo Regius, and rebuilt the bridge over the Bagradas; the extent to which this highway was used by traffic can be gauged from the fact that less than forty years after Trajan found it necessary to relay the road and strengthen the bridge, employing soldiers upon the work. Under this emperor the camp of the legion was moved successively westward, first to Thamugadi, and later to Lambaesis; here in Numidia not far from the frowning massif of the Mons Aurasius the army occupied a central position, and could strike quickly out against the desert. Trajan, of course, provided the roads between Theveste and Thamugadi, and between the latter town and the camp at Lambaesis, while we also find him at work improving the road that ran up the Bagradas valley to Theveste, as would be necessary upon so busy a highway. But so intense was the traffic that traversed the valley that only thirty years afterward Hadrian had to repair the whole road, while at the same time we find him connecting Cirta with Rusicade, and developing the Western part of the province by a road between Sitifis and Djemila. Apart from this there was the important trans-continental highway which ran from Carthage down the Eastern coast through Hadrumetum and Syllecte to Tacape, and thence past Sabrata and Oea and the wastes of the Greater Syrtis to Cyrenaica, and so utimately to Egypt; portions of this road were torn up by insurgents during the Jewish Rebellion and we find Hadrian repairing it thoroughly.

We may conclude, then, that the road-system of the province was governed by two main considerations; firstly, the need for providing communication between the great agricultural districts and the capital (as witness the roads up the Bagradas valley and along the coast down to the Lesser Syrtis), secondly, the need for protecting this rich triangle of land by a well-placed military force, moving upon inner lines, and always ready to strike against any part of the surrounding hill-country. To make this force effective roads were needed to all parts of the province, but those constructed by the government for military purposes served equally well to attract trade, and we have only to observe the prosperity and size of such towns as Theveste, Thamugadi, or Lambaesis to see the truth of this. As well as the government roads there were of course many that had been constructed by the municipalities or by the generosity and prudence of private citizens, for example, at Theveste and at Cirta, where we read that a highway was constructed by the citizens at their own cost.

So far no word has been said of roads in the Western parts, as Mauretania. The reason is that our information is scanty and tantalising; we may assume that the colonies which Augustus founded in Western Mauretania were connected with the sea, and possibly with each other; in later times beyond our period we know that roads existed between such points as Tingis, Sala, and ad Mercurios, and between Tingis and Volubilis, but these Western towns were really far more closely related to the neighbouring coast of Spain than to the rest of the province, and at no time was communication by land continuous. Even in the third and fourth centuries, when the network of roads had been developed to its fullest extent, we learn from the itineraries that the only means of transport between Portus Magnus and Tingis was by sea; the land gap was never spanned. It was indeed impossible properly to garrison the whole vast expanse of the Western country, and just as the municipalities had the right of raising and leading out emergency troops, so we find some of the large estates fortified and capable of being formed into small garrisons of their own against raids from the hills; like the early settlers in Canada and the United States the farmers had to be prepared to defend themselves at all times from the incursions of savage tribes, who swooped down without warning and vanished into the desert as swiftly as they had come.

This break in the continuity of the road-system is also to be explained by the fact that transport by sea was easier and quite as common as by land. There were plenty of navigable rivers, to connect inland towns with the sea, and authors tell us of the immense traffic that went to and fro along the Northern coast of Africa, and even past the Straits down the Western shores in search of fish and of purple. We have some figures which afford an idea of the time occupied in making passages between various points in the province and also from Carthage to Italy. A heavy transport took two days and a night to cross from Neapolis to Selinus; Caesar spent four days on a voyage between Lilybaeum and Hadrumetum, when his ships were harassed by the wind, and Curio with his transports took three days and two nights from a point in Sicily to Clupea. It is also said that a voyage from Carthage to the Straits of Gibraltar would occupy, under favourable conditions, seven days and seven nights, but probably this notice means as far as Gades. The isle of Ebusus, off the Spanish coast, was distant one day and one night from Africa; but all these figures relate to transports or heavy cargo-ships: when necessary, quicker passages could certainly be made. On his return from Africa Caesar reached the harbour of Carales in Sardinia in three days; Marius, under good conditions, accomplished the voyage between Utica and Rome in four, and the famous figs which Cato produced in the Senate are said to have been plucked only three days before in the Carthaginian territory. Apart from the ships occupied with the corn-traffic, the number of which was very large, we shall find evidence as the chapter proceeds for great maritime activity and the exchange of goods between province and province. Less could scarcely be expected; seafaring trade had been the source of Carthaginian greatness and the *raison d'être* of the cities planted along the coast; when Carthage lost her position as capital and mistress, the other cities, especially Utica, assumed a new importance and derived a fresh life from the volume of trade which had formerly gone to enrich the mother-city; thus they kept up the tradition of maritime commerce, and as the needs of Italy increased, so their enterprise grew greater, until in the first century the line of coast from the mouth of the Bagradas to the Lesser Syrtis was dotted with thriving ports and harbours.

We have already related how Juba was chosen by Augustus to rule over and civilise the region of Mauretania. The task set was not easy; he had to govern a tract of country containing few towns save on the coast, with little settled life inland; the population was nomadic, living by its flocks and scouring the plains on horseback. Yet the land, in spite of some desert patches, was productive, being well supplied with rivers and lakes; the slopes of the hills were covered with forests, while upon the plains flocks of sheep wandered the year round needing little attention, and there was a breed of small but wiry horses. Vines grew well, but above all the country was famed for the quantity of big game and wild animals to be found in its borders, and the export of these to Rome for the games was a profitable business. Pitch and bitumen were to be found near Siga, and at that town the copper of the mines near Cartenna and of the neighbouring district was worked. Precious stones and gems were also discovered in the country or brought in by the desert tribes. But its most famous exports have yet to be mentioned; ebony and citrus woods were hewn on the hills and conveyed to Rome where they commanded a high price; sometimes so large were the trees that the tables were carved from single blocks; every forest was eagerly searched for the precious trees. At this period, too, purple was much in demand, and Juba, in spite of his scholarly proclivities, was able to derive profit from it; off the Moorish coast the purple murex was found in large quantities and the king seems to have established dye-works upon some of the islands opposite Mogador. Here the wool of the country was dipped and dyed and doubtless the king had a monopoly of the business; Horace speaks of robes "twice dyed in African purple" as an article of luxury. Voyages down the Western African coast were now frequent; there were the fishing-boats of the men of Gades and of the natives, and the fleet of Juba ventured some way into the Atlantic waters, and returned with tales of puzzling tides and currents and of the Fortunate Isles lying far to the South; they also brought hunting dogs from the Canaries.

As part of his civilising policy this shrewd monarch also founded a town in a sheltered position on the coast which he named Iol Caesarea in honour of his suzerain; whether it was the shellfish of the district (which Pliny pronounces excellent) or the good harbour, which influenced him, we do not know, but his foundation rapidly increased and became a centre of thriving commerce. To it were attracted all those luxury craftsmen and artists which a court supports; silversmiths and goldsmiths, embossers, sculptors, and painters filled the palace with their work and have left us their inscriptions. Hither came some of the best statuary of Greece, among which we may enumerate the recently discovered Apollo of Cherchel, and heads of Bacchus, Apollo, and of Juba himself, while there are also fine mosaics of the Judgment of Paris and of hunting scenes; we may wonder whether the wrecked ship off Mahdia was not conveying statuary and works of art from Athens or some such centre intended for the royal galleries. In this town also there existed a factory, apparently of one Sempronius, which made lamps of a peculiar design; its products have been discovered in Baetica and as far as Sardinia.

The other towns of the country were not of any great significance, though colonies had been placed on the Western shores by Augustus. One fact about them stands out very clearly, how closely they were related in trade and commerce to the towns of the Spanish coast. Thus Tingis had a ferry service with Belo, the crossing being only thirty miles; Lixus faced Gades and had also its ferry service; we are reminded too of the fact that Columella's uncle obtained rams from Africa on the boats of certain "munerarii"—companies of men who shipped wild beasts for the games. Siga lay opposite Malaca, which was, as Strabo declares, "a mart for the nomads of the other side." This closeness is also proved by the number of inscriptions commemorating Spaniards in Africa, or Africans in Spain; we meet a citizen of Iol at Tarraco, and can read the epitaph of a Baetican who was buried at Iol; the dedications which some Spanish cities made to Juba, and the finding of African lamps in Baetica itself all point the same way, nor must we forget that at least one colony in Africa was under the jurisdiction of the governor of Baetica.

Numidia, which had been originally granted to Juba, was a few years later taken away from him (when he received the throne of Mauretania) and incorporated in the province of Africa. Thus it resembled a ring of less fertile land surrounding and guarding the more productive soil of the province. In comparison with Mauretania it was cultivated, and during the first two centuries more soil was irrigated and put under the plough, more cities sprang up to be dowered with magnificent buildings by patriotic citizens, and its prosperity increased in every way; the ruins of its countless towns now being excavated bear witness to the wealth and energy of the country. But in earlier years this cultivation had not proceeded far; Pliny declares scornfully that it had nothing but its wild beasts and its marbles; these wild beasts were of course exported for the games at Rome, as were those of Mauretania. The marbles of Simitthu and of other local quarries were justly famous and greatly in demand for building at Rome, and we have many references in contemporary poets to their use and export; they were much used in the province too, as we can see from a temple raised at Bulla Regia (from the marble of Chem-Tou) and from buildings in other towns at this period. Indeed, there are many constructions and dedications dating from this era which serve to shew the steady growth of prosperity in these parts and how public-spirited citizens met the demand for buildings; Cirta and Bulla Regia were considerable cities and filled with mer-chants who provided porticoes, gymnasia, baths, shelters, and the like. The flocks of sheep which roamed the plains gave wool for garments, and we find a guild of "vestiarii" mentioned at Cuicul. Though Spain was more distant, even from this part of Africa communication was kept up, and we find a Spaniard at Cirta, and a wealthy citizen of Madaura resident in Emerita.

In the senatorial province of Africa proper a different state of things meets our eye. Though on the South-West and on the boundaries there lay mountains or bare deserts, yet nearer to the coastline and especially along the river-valleys the productivity of the soil was extraordinary. Here were fields of corn and wheat and barley, groves of vines and olives, gardens of figs, cherries, pomegranates, and other fruit-trees, of almonds and walnuts. The country swarmed with horses and asses and mules, with herds of cattle and flocks of sheep. Its natural fertility had even been increased by irrigation and allotment of the water-supply. Centuries afterwards when barbarian raids had done much to destroy prosperity and break down the aqueducts, the Arabs entering the province found them-selves in what they described as a paradise. At the present time, when the country is being restored to its former state, the French engineers often find that they are merely following the line of much earlier Roman works and have even been able to use some of them.

The fertility of the land is referred to by many writers and by contemporary poets; Ceres had claimed the soil of Africa as her own, and Columella declares that the country abounds in corn. Of all this rich district the rich-est far was that of Byzacium; it had been called by the

Carthaginians the "Land of Markets," because of the purchases and profits made there. It is said that one of the emperor's procurators sent to Rome more than four hundred grains of wheat grown out of one, and though such stories have doubtless lost nothing in the telling, yet the productiveness of the country was phenomenal. We hear, too, of olive-trees with a yield of from one hundred to one hundred and fifty per cent.; such trees were termed "milliariae" because of the rich crop they produced. So good was the system, so scientific the technique of the Carthaginian farming, that the Senate had ordered a translation of Mago's works to be made for the instruction of their countrymen. The corn, when harvested, was stored in underground chambers, as a precaution against damp and also against the raids of the nomads. Caesar took an enormous amount of corn to Rome as booty; Plutarch says it equalled twenty thousand Attic medimni. In later years its despatch to feed the hungry populace of the capital was regularised; we are informed that as much as forty million modii of wheat was annually transported. It was this cornland that the nomads above all desired, as we can discern in the demands made by Tacfarinas, and some merchants were accused of supplying the enemy with wheat.

Vines and olives grew equally well in the delightful climate; on the Eastern coast, in the region of Byzacium, the groves stretched for miles; quantities of oil were demanded from the district by the victorious Caesar, and Leptis had to pay heavily. In addition, the oil from the cedrus was much used for preserving wood and timber from decay, and was exported. The figs and pomegranates of the country were alike excellent, and foremost among the delicacies which Africa shipped to Rome in spring were the truffles, which were joyously acclaimed by connoisseurs, as also were the African cucumbers. The coccus plant was available for the dyeing of wool, as was also the murex of the coast of the Syrtes; many towns are mentioned as living by the purple-dyeing industry, and the African purple had a repute only second to the Tyrian.

There were quarries of stone at Tunis, but the most famous were those of Simitthu and of the Bagradas valley; much of this marble was shipped to Rome or used by the wealthier at Carthage; the poor had to put up with the rough tufa of the surrounding hills. Mica, which was taken in large quantities from Spain, was discovered in Africa during the first century, and trade in it doubtless tried to rival that of the neighbouring province. Another industry of the coast was fishing and the pickling of fish and the preparation of that sauce or "garum" which was so popular in antiquity; we have already mentioned the shell-fish of Iol Caesarea. There was a city, named from the industry, Taricheia, near Thapsus, and the fisheries of Leptis were well known. Strabo tells us that in the Lesser Syrtis there were many small towns which owed their existence to fishing, and mentions the pickling and curing industry which was carried on at Zuchis.

Amid this region of intense economic activity Carthage stood as the natural receiving and shipping depôt for the produce, and also as the administrative centre of the province. The Republic, with its bitter memories of warfare, had never allowed a great city to grow up on the site of its former rival; but Caesar and Augustus were wiser and perceiving the unexampled advantages of the situation planted colonists there and fostered its trade. The result was soon seen; Strabo says it was the best inhabited of all the African cities, and half a century later Mela declares that it has regained its former wealth. Doubtless it had its local industries, its fisheries, its potteries and image-making, and its manufacture of glass; in the latter it must have excelled, since Lugdunum in Gaul sent to Carthage for a young and expert glass-blower to supervise production there; but we may say with some certainty that most attention was paid to its marine commerce and especially to the traffic in corn. Shipowners and captains of Carthaginian ships are met with at Ostia, and also a kind of agent, whose business seems to have been to look after all Carthaginian ships putting into this port. This corn was grown partly on imperial domains and partly on private estates. It was the concentration of the land in the hands of a few owners and of the emperor that ultimately led to the ruin of the agricultural system of Africa. Already even in the first half of the first century six magnates owned half of Africa between them; when their estates were confiscated by Nero the imperial domains steadily increased, till the revenues accruing from these estates and the corn transported must have formed no inconsiderable part of the emperor's treasury. But we must not imagine that Africa stood on anything like the same footing that Egypt enjoyed in regard to the transport of corn; it only acquired importance slowly. So long as Egypt remained prosperous Africa played only a subsidiary rôle in the corn supply; it was only late in the second century, after the troubles and shortages resulting from the Bucolic war, that Commodus established an African corn-fleet as an emergency measure.

Carthage herself was only first among equals; many other cities, such as Theveste, Utica, Hippo Regius, Hadrumetum, Leptis, Tacape, Sabrata, and Oea, were as busily occupied with the transport of corn and oil and of agricultural produce, and with the raising of stock. Pliny supplies us with a lengthy list of cities in the province, detailing which were colonies, which municipalities, and which free. These cities were so wealthy and arrogant that in disturbed times their rivalries might easily lead to something very like war. Thus in the year of the Four Emperors, A.D. 70, an affair arose between the states of Leptis and Oea, which commencing with the usual border raids upon herds and crops ended by needing the armed intervention of the legate of the province.

Some notion of the trade that went on in the country may also be obtained from a tariff-list preserved from the town of Zarai. Here among the regular articles of sale are mentioned slaves (doubtless prisoners of the desert), beasts (and their hides), clothing of various kinds, leather and furs, wine, pickles, and fruit; in exchange for these articles the town imported salt, iron, copper, and flax. Thus we see that in general the province sent out its agricultural produce and received in return those minerals which it lacked. Oil was exported from the region round Leptis; we have mentioned Caesar's requisitions, and at Rome there have been found casks and jars coming from the town, as also amphorae from the Numidian city of Tubusuctu, which once carried the produce of its fruitful fields. We find wine-merchants and wine-sellers at Carthage, but it is doubtful whether wine was much exported. In Rome we have inscriptions of those men who brought to the city the ebony wood and the citrus tables which were so highly prized; and we hear of one exiled noble who eked out a miserable livelihood by trading and peddling between Africa and Sicily. But the corn-traffic was of the most importance and was the staple of African prosperity; though Carthage was the main centre for despatch, yet there were large granaries at Rusicade, and doubtless at other cities. So, too, there were receiving warehouses at the Italian ports, such as Puteoli, and we meet with a merchant from Oea there. But the efforts of such emperors as Claudius and Trajan to give Rome a near and deep harbour resulted in bringing Ostia into a prominence that outdid all the other Italian ports: in consequence all merchants and shippers used it and we have been enabled to see this more clearly in recent years, since Ostia has been excavated. Here amid the numerous warehouses, storage-depôts, and offices we find many belonging to Africans or to African companies; in the office of some rich merchant prince there was a mosaic representing the four provinces from which he had obtained his wealth; each province is represented by some pictorial emblem, that of Spain being the olive, and Africa being depicted by wheat-sheaves. Here, too, we find mention of the measurers of corn and of various officials of the port, but most interesting for our present purpose is the fact that several towns of the province appear as having agencies here. Thus we find inscriptions set up by the shipowners of Misua and of Diarrhytus; at another point stood the factory and office of the merchants of Sabrata; it is interesting to recall, in connection with this last town, that the shrewd Vespasian married the daughter of a wealthy Roman knight from there, who had doubtless made his money in the corn-trade. In another quarter we meet with inscriptions of shipowners of the town of Gummi and also from Carthage itself (we have already had occasion to remark the "curator navium Carthaginiensium"), and the list is closed by ship-owners from Syllecte and merchants from the town of Curubis. Many of the towns here named are scarcely noticed in our literary sources, and it gives us a wonderful idea of the widespread business activity of the whole province that these almost unknown places should have had their own agencies and depôts at Ostia: doubtless as excavation continues we shall gain even more information. There still remain ruins of cities and buildings, of bridges and aqueducts, in regions now desolate, which bear silent witness to the former prosperity and energy of the country; and we may find yet another proof of this if we recollect that during the century between A.D. 150 and 250 indisputably the greatest names in Latin literature are those of three Africans: Fronto, Apuleius, Tertullian.

CHAPTER NINE

SPAIN

"Hispania...viris equis ferro plumbo aere argento auroque etiam abundans, et adeo fertilis ut sicubi ob penuriam aquarum effeta et sui dissimilis est, linum tamen aut spartam alat."

MELA

"Adde tot egregias civitates, adde culta incultaque omnia vel fructibus plena vel gregibus, adde auriferorum opes fluminum, adde radiantium metalla gemmarum."

PACATUS

SPAIN

WHEN the Romans undertook the government of
Spain they entered into the inheritance of their
former foes the Carthaginians; these had for
many years past trained the tribes and worked the mines
of the Eastern half. But the West and North-West had
never been properly subdued, and although the rest of the
country was more or less Romanised by Cicero's time,
these regions offered stubborn opposition to the process;
it was Augustus and his great lieutenant Agrippa who
finally pacified the country after many years of guerilla
warfare among the hills. From henceforward Spain proved
herself one of the most loyal and devoted of all the provinces, and gave her wealth and genius unsparingly to the
Empire. In the South there lay the agricultural district
of Baetica and the mines of the Sierra Morena; in the
North-West region were gold- and lead-mines of vast
value to the revenue, and it is not surprising that Augustus
fought so obstinately to bring this part under control, nor
that subsequent emperors provided it so abundantly with
roads. The towns were large and prosperous, the municipal
life active, and trade brisk; in contrast with Gaul its mines
appear to have gone on producing in abundance, though
its industries may not have been so many and various. A
writer of the early principate describes Spain in terms
bordering on panegyric; its moderate climate avoids the
extreme heat of Africa and the cold winds of Gaul; its
harvests feed not only its inhabitants but supply Italy and
Rome as well in abundance; lastly, it has inexhaustible
mineral wealth. The enthusiasm of this writer is echoed by
Pliny and others, and there can be little doubt that, taken
all in all, the peninsula was one of the most valuable of
the Empire's possessions. Save for the ranges of the

Pyrenees its mountains nowhere offered difficult barriers
to traffic; its rivers were navigable for considerable distances, and while their valleys provided corn and fruit
land, the hills enclosing them abounded in mineral ores,
and the slopes afforded grazing for cattle. The building of
roads in this country was certainly much influenced by
trade considerations, since there were no frontiers here to
protect, but rich districts to exploit.

Nature has marked out in an unusually clear manner the
routes which men must follow in the peninsula. There are
two large masses of mountains in the North-West and the
South, and in the centre a high tableland; all the important
rivers have their water-parting from this central plateau,
and flow East, South, and West. By going up the Ebro
or Sucro and their tributaries, from the Eastern coast a
man can soon reach by means of easy passes the sources of
the long rivers, the Tagus, Durius, and Anas, which drain
out in a Western or South-Westerly direction. The river
Baetis practically bisects the province to which it gave its
name, and even the smaller streams are navigable for some
distance. The Eastern coast is comparatively flat and level
and provides an easy passage for those coming down from
the North. While the Carthaginians were in control they
exploited the mineral wealth in many places especially near
Carthago Nova, and doubtless improved communication in
the East. Here the Republic built two main roads; the
first followed the coastline from the Pyrenees through
Saguntum to Carthago Nova, with a branch which diverged
after crossing the Sucro, towards the valley of the Baetis,
to tap the wealth of the province; the second led from
Barcino to Ilerda, and presumably on to the mining district of Osca, upon which Republican milestones have been
found. Doubtless the Southern road was continued down
the valley of the Baetis for some distance, until that river
became navigable for large ships, for we hear of a bridge

at Corduba in pre-Augustan times. But with the complete subjugation of Spain, Augustus determined to lay out a proper system of roads, comparable to that which Agrippa had planned in Gaul, and the outline appears to have been completed in his time. He repaired and relaid the coast road from Tarraco (which was the imperial headquarters), through Valentia to Carthago Nova, and also that through the Baetis valley by way of Corduba and Hispalis to Gades itself, and upon this a great many of his milestones have been found. Our information is somewhat scanty, but there are two points from which we may start; firstly, the numerous Augustan foundations, such as Caesaraugusta, Juliobriga, Asturica Augusta, Lucus Augusti, Emerita Augusta, and the rest, which one would naturally assume to have been connected with the East, and, secondly, the finding of milestones of the emperor in various parts of Spain. These have been discovered along the road from Bracara through Lucus Augusti to Asturica, and also upon that which followed the course of the Ebro from Caesaraugusta to Juliobriga; the road from Emerita to Hispalis (piercing the rich mining district of the Montes Mariani) bears signs of his activity, as does that from Carthago Nova to Castulo (another mineral region); lastly, there was a road built by him from Ilerda to Caesaraugusta, crossing the Ebro near Celas by a wooden bridge—as Strabo informs us—and apparently one from Aesuris to Pax Julia, up the course of the Anas. Thus we should be justified in saying that Augustus had surrounded Spain with a great circle of roads, with one or two branches penetrating inland. In complete contrast to Gaul, where there were four or five roads radiating from a central hub, here we find the periphery of the wheel, and it was left for succeeding emperors to fill in the spokes and make more direct cross-country routes. Tiberius took up the task with energy; in the North he laid a road from Virovesca through Pompaelo

and the Western passes of the Pyrenees to Burdigala, which
bears witness to the growth of the traffic at that port; a
new route was opened to the West from Caesaraugusta
through Turiassio, Clunia, and Ocelodurum to Asturica,
and two new roads constructed between Bracara and the
former town. All this activity in the North-Western district indicates exploitation of the mineral wealth found
there. We have also evidence for a road from Emerita to
Salmantica, which crossed the Tagus by a bridge of eleven
arches; while in A.D. 33 having confiscated the mines of
Sextus Marius, Tiberius built a short road from Corduba
through Castulo into the Montes Mariani and the gold
districts of the Oretani. Finally, in the last years of his
reign he repaired the Via Augusta from Ossigi to Hispalis.
Moreover, he made every effort to induce the Western
tribes to adopt a more settled way of life by bringing them
together in cities, and by the encouragement of agriculture.
Claudius shewed equal energy: he relaid the road between
Carthago Nova and the Pyrenees, and repaired or made
roads in the neighbourhood of Castulo, between Emerita
and Salmantica, and two between Asturica and Bracara.
We find Nero reconstructing the Western route that ran
through Clunia, repairing the Via Augusta, and also attend-
ing to the road between Emerita and Salmantica. We know
that Vespasian took a great deal of trouble over the Spanish
provinces, and we find him relaying a road between
Bracara and Asturica, and remaking the Via Augusta
through Baetica; he also probably undertook the construction of a transverse road, which leaving Emerita
turned up the Tagus valley through Augustobriga, Toletum and Complutum, and down by Segontia to Caesaraugusta, thus providing a second land-route to the mines
of the Montes Mariani and the agricultural wealth of
Western Baetica and the banks of the Anas; this latter
road was repaired by Trajan at the beginning of the second

century. Trajan also remade the road between Emerita and Salmantica and paid attention to the routes round Castulo and in Lusitania. It is noteworthy that the constructive activity of the rulers centred mainly on three districts, the mines of Baetica and of the Montes Mariani, the North-West country, and the district lying between them and watered by the Tagus. The frequency with which roads were relaid or alternative routes constructed bears witness to the volume of traffic coming and going in these parts, and no less to the determination of the emperors to provide full facilities for inter-communication and for the exploitation of the resources of the district. For these roads cannot have been built for any other purpose than that of encouraging trade.

Such were the artificial highways constructed by the Romans which doubtless followed older trade-tracks. But apart from these, Spain—like Gaul—was marvellously supplied with the great natural highways of rivers. To mention only the larger ones: on the Atlantic coast there was the Durius, which had its source in the far-distant hills around Numantia and flowed nearly due West throughout its course; it was deep and navigable by vessels of large draught for nearly one hundred miles. Southward came the Tagus with its gold and its fisheries, a river which could take the largest merchant ships. Two others, the Anas and Baetis, flowed through a rich metalliferous region and one famed for its agricultural wealth as well. The Baetis itself was navigable as far as Hispalis, and even up to Corduba in smaller vessels. It was from the mouth of this river that the greater part of the commerce between Spain and Rome started; here stood a tower as a guide to mariners, and from near-by Gades, the whole year round, merchants and ship-captains set out to trade with Italy, and especially with Ostia and Puteoli. In the South of the peninsula lay Aesuris, and near the extreme tip, Belo,

whence there was a short ferry across to Tingis in Mauretania. Further on came Mellaria, and on the Eastern coast
lay Malaca, another trading-place for the nomad Moors
of the African coast. The harbour of Carthago Nova exported its silver and lead and also the esparto grass which
grew in the plains near by. To the North came the port of
Dianium, with its ironworks, and Scombraria with its
fisheries, and past the mouth of the Ebro was situate the
great city of Tarraco, the seat of the imperial governor.
Last but not least in the North-West came the port of the
Artabri, Brigantium, which was the shipping centre for
the mineral traffic of the district, and was reorganised as
a Latin town by Vespasian; here, too, tin from Britain was
received. But besides the larger harbours and rivers, there
were—especially in the South-West—numberless small
creeks running inland and havens situate upon them, all
of which did a busy trade.

Communication with Rome was quick and easy, the main
ports being Tarraco, Carthago Nova, and Gades. The
first town was the seat of the imperial governor, and it was
hither that reinforcements and all official messengers were
sent, and a regular service must have been ensured. It was
only four days sail from Rome, and from it every part of
Spain could soon be reached by road. In the ordinary way
it took five days to Bilbilis, but an imperial freedman,
travelling with important news and at full speed, managed
to arrive at Clunia (which was further along the road than
Bilbilis) in seven days from Rome, which implies three
days land-journey. From Ostia to Gades took seven days
under favourable conditions, and the average time was
doubtless about ten. Finally we are told that from Gades
to Tarraco the voyage could be made "in a few days."
These are the indications we have as to length of time.

With regard to the road-system; on the East side the
Via Domitia came from Gaul along the coast through

Emporiae and Barcino to Tarraco; on the extreme West a road struck through from Burdigala between the sea and the Pyrenees to Pompaelo and to Virovesca, where it joined another that ran West from Tarraco up the Ebro valley to Juliobriga and Asturica; along this came not only the soldiers intended for the camp at Legio but also the traders and contractors who were occupied in exploiting the North-West region. From Asturica a road went up through Lucus Augusti to Brigantium, the port of that district, while as many as four different ways led to Bracara. Emerita could be reached by a road leading through the linen district of Zoelae, and by Salmantica and the lands of the Tagus valley, while from Asturica and Bracara another way led down the coast to Olisipo, with a branch diverging towards Pax Julia and the Anas valley. Emerita was connected with Hispalis, and the whole of the Northern region of Baetica, from the neighbourhood of Emerita to Castulo, was intersected with roads that ran in among the hills and served the mining region. The course of the Baetis was followed by the Via Augusta, which after leaving Baetica cut across country through Lamnium towards the coast and Tarraco. Then there was what may be termed the longer coast road, which went through Carteia and Malaca to Carthago Nova, and thence up the Eastern coast by Saetabis, Valentia, Saguntum and Dertosa to Tarraco. Finally, there was the cross-road which led from Caesaraugusta to Bilbilis across the mountains and down the Tagus valley by way of Complutum and Toletum to Emerita.

The sea was equally busy; we have literary testimony for the amount of merchandise exported from Spain, and near Rome heaps of broken jars and amphorae in which it was brought have revealed the names of firms, while there exist many inscriptions of traders in wine and oil. Round the coast and in the rivers many species of fish were to be caught, and a great trade was done in them. In the West the oysters of the Douro and Tagus were famous, while on the East coast salted and pickled fish was exported from the city of the Exitani and from Carthago Nova, where inscriptions mention a guild of fishers and fish-sellers; an isle in front of the city was named Scombraria after the fish in which it dealt. The South coast was still better off: the men of Gades were foremost in the trade and their fishing vessels, large and small, used to go out on long voyages down the Western coast of Africa past the river Lixus and far out to sea in search of fish. But other towns made a profit from it as well; Strabo informs us that oysters, shell-fish, narwhals, another kind of whale, conger-eels, lampreys, cuttle-fish and tunny were all to be caught off the Baetic shore-line. Such cities as Gades, Malaca, Mellaria and Belo made a speciality of catching and curing fish and making pickles and sauces from it; at the latter town have been recently discovered the pits and basins in which the garum was prepared. In fact the pickles of the South of Spain were considered in no way inferior to those of Pontus. Sea-salt and river-salt were easily obtainable for making these preparations and for other remedies, such as the eye-salve made of salt and honey which Columella recommends.

In its total mineral wealth Spain was the richest province of the whole Empire, both in the variety and the quantity of the metals it contained. One writer refers to the "abundant richness of its deep-hidden metals," and Pliny declares that "nearly all Spain is full of mines of lead, iron, copper, silver and gold" and then goes on to detail metals peculiar to different regions. And these riches appear to have lasted longer than those of the neighbouring province of France; it is true that Spanish lead may have been ousted by British in the second and later centuries, but Pliny refers not only to mines working but also relates that several that seemed exhausted had suddenly become productive again, and instances a mine in Baetica.

During the course of the first century all the mines were brought under imperial control, if they did not already belong to the royal family; thus in the year 33 Tiberius confiscated the gold and copper mines of a Spaniard who had been put to death by him. The working was done either by the imperial slaves direct or they were let out to companies, such as the "Societas montis argentarii Ilucronensis" or the "Socii Sisapones," which we find in inscriptions. There would appear to have been firstly a general law, a "lex metallis dicta," governing the conditions under which the mines could be let out, the amount of the rent, and so on, and then laws and statutes relating to kinds of mines and finally even to particular mines by themselves; to the former class belong the "Lex ferrariarum" and to the latter the fragments of the famous "Lex Metalli Vipascensis." Enormous bodies of men were sometimes used on the working; the mines at Carthago Nova are said to have given regular employ to forty thousand; mostly these were slaves, and their condition must have been deplorable, working under the lash all day in ill-lighted and ill-ventilated headings. But in later times more humane conditions obtained; a certain number of free labourers seem to have been given work, and in the conditions governing the renting out of the Vipasca mine we see that the government made careful provision for health and proper treatment of the workmen; this humanity towards slaves is a noteworthy feature of the Flavian and succeeding dynasty. Baths and laundries are to be set up by the contractor, and barbers' and cobblers' shops provided; education was encouraged by giving teachers free range of the town; a strict control of all charges was established and the thorough efficiency of all services secured. But whether the condition of the workers was good or not, the splendid engineering and scientific management of the Romans made the mines of Spain far more lucrative than those of Laurion, with which Diodorus contrasts them; the shafts ran far into the hills and the draining arrangements were good. Occasionally foreign labour seems to have been imported; thus at the mines of Baebelo in the North of Spain hundreds of slaves from Aquitania were kept busy day and night draining the headings. The ore was not always smelted or refined on the spot; it was often taken direct to Rome, but we are informed that adulteration was much practised and brought an easy profit to the company; sometimes—as, for instance, at Turiassio or Bilbilis, where the water was exceptionally good for tempering iron—it would be transported many miles to the right spot. The good returns from mining account for the large number of Italians who migrated to Spain and were ready to undertake the contracts for renting and working them.

We may now consider more closely the various districts in which the particular metals were found. Gold was not only mined, but also was obtained by washing from the river deposits; the gold-bearing sands of the Tagus were famous. It would be curious to speculate whether this gold-dust was really the off-scourings of more ancient workers many years ago, whose primitive methods of washing did not allow them to extract the utmost of the precious ore; in Cornwall at the present day there are still workable rich deposits of tin formed by the river bringing down the remains of former washings. There were many gold mines in the region round Calpe and it was also dug in the Montes Mariani, so-called from the owner who had made his fortune there, a fortune which turned to his own ruin. It was also to be found at Corduba, in the mountains among the Oretani, and at Carteia, and generally in the country of the Turdetani, the whole of the rich metalliferous district that lies between the Baetis and the Anas. Another most productive region lay in the mountains of the North-West; both the trade that came through here and also the mineral wealth explain the repeated efforts, culminating in final success, which were made by Augustus and his lieutenants to bring this quarter of the country under control, and account for the many roads and facilities for transport provided. The districts of Lusitania, Asturia, and Gallaecia were notable for their gold mines and produced twenty thousand pounds of the precious metal annually, and in one Gallaecian mine the ore was so pure that there was only an admixture of one-thirtieth of silver. The whole process of extracting the ore was a highly complicated one involving many operations, which are described minutely by Strabo in an interesting passage.

The finest silver in the world was to be found in the province, and it had been famous ever since the days when the Carthaginians worked the mines at Carthago Nova. At the time of their greatest activity these mines had been able to give employment to twenty thousand men; even now, after three centuries continuous output, they were not exhausted, but still yielded good silver to the crowd of Italian contractors and business men who managed them. The depth and extent of the headings here was very great, and the problems presented by difficulties of drainage had been overcome by a system of pumps and gravity channels down which the water flowed away; the pump was the invention of the great Sicilian, Archimedes. As might have been expected silver was also found Southward in the region by Ilipa and Sisapo; there was some at Castulo, but the expense and trouble of extracting the ore was too great for profitable results. It was also mined in the North-West of the peninsula, in the country of the Artabri, and near by there was a hill known as "Silver Mount" from the quantities of the metal lying there. A mine at Ilucro was also profitable, and we have some inscriptions left commemorating the company which had been formed to work it; dyes and stamps have been found both in Spain and at Rome.

The lead of Spain was reputed the finest in the world. One of the most productive mines was at Baebelo in the Northern region; Aquitanian slaves were employed upon drainage here, doubtless because their experience proved useful, for the Aquitani were skilful at all such work; as much as three hundred pounds was often extracted daily from the shafts. It was also obtained in the Ebro valley, at Oretum in Baetica, and as well from one of the Balearic Isles, Capraria by name; the territory of the Madulingenses contained it, and we are told of two places, one a town, Molybdana, and the other the island of Plumbaria, both of which received their name from the masses of metal found there. But the best centre of all was the great city of Carthago Nova; a vast number of lead stamps have been found here, indicating that it was the main port for the export trade, but they decrease in the second century, and it seems likely that lead from Britain was taking its place; Pliny remarks that it was dug with more difficulty in Spain than in Britain, where it could be almost gathered off the ground, and a remarkable feature, which we shall touch on later, is the great advance in trade made by our island during the second century. Lead was one of its main exports, and Pliny says that it was conveyed as far as India, which in return sent her pearls and jewels—a remark which is borne out by the evidence of the author of the *Periplus of the Erythraean Sea*.

The above were the main articles of export, but copper was obtainable near Corduba, in the Montes Mariani, and in some parts of Turdetania. Iron, too, was found in Cantabria; sometimes it was smelted and worked on the spot, but it was occasionally taken over great distances as to Bilbilis or Turiassio where the peculiar quality of the water greatly improved its tempering, although there was no ore to be quarried there. It was also transported down the river-valley of the Ebro to Dianium, a town on the coast, where there were large iron manufactories. Thus the Ebro valley and the Cantabrian highlands were the main centres of manufacture and doubtless it was from here that came the famous Spanish swords, breastplates and armour, to which many writers refer.

Tin was to be obtained in Gallaecia and also in the land of the Artabri; men and women were employed on digging it or washing out the river-deposits. But in addition it came in bulk by ship to the port of the Artabri from the islands of the Cassiterides. During our period, owing to the exceptional richness of the region around the North-West, Brigantium and the harbour towns must have grown and benefited greatly, and we find Vespasian interesting himself much in the cities of the district; this would bear out Pliny's account of the number of vessels that sailed there. It is possible, too, that tin was even brought to Spain from Britain and down the Ebro route to Massilia and Italy, but the conquest of our island probably resulted in such commerce taking the more direct route through France.

As regards other minerals, minium was to be obtained in large quantities from a mine near Sisapo in Baetica; it was not melted there, however, but transported to Rome, where it was dealt with by skilled Ephesian labour. Mica and a transparent stone used in making windows were also got from Spain, and the Spanish mica was preferred to the Cappadocian, though that was the other source of supply. Pliny also speaks of marble quarries that existed in the province, and we possess various inscriptions from stone-quarries and the slaves employed upon them.

Of the fertility of Spain, of its extraordinary agricultural wealth contemporary writers find it hard to speak without exaggeration. It was prolific in all kinds of crops and fruits; so abundant were its harvests, that it was able to supply Italy as well as Rome with its surplus; corn, wine, honey and oil are all mentioned as exports, and these were ferried across the sea in vessels large and small that were continually making the passage between the South of Spain and Ostia or Puteoli. Turdetania was a land especially favoured; apart from its large store of metals underground, its valleys were rich in crops of every kind, and the hills above them were clothed in forests which provided timber for the ships used for exporting; the rivers, too, were navigable for a considerable distance so that many inland towns became easily accessible from the sea. All the trade was with Italy and Rome, Strabo declares, and in it the merchants of Gades took no small part.

Oil was the most important export of the South; though it was not sent out in large quantities its quality was of the best. Although the olive grew in other parts of Spain, and was praised by Pliny, yet Baetica was its real home. The rich full Baetic oil was famous, and Cicero had some unkind jokes to make about the oily character of the poets who resided around Corduba. We have many inscriptions of oil-merchants; the quantity that was exported, according to our authorities, is fully borne out by the finds that have been made at the Monte Testaccio, where heaps of broken jars and casks have revealed merchants and wares from almost every considerable town of Southern Spain, among those most frequently mentioned being Astigi, Hispalis, Malaca, and Corduba. There appears to have been a guild of "olearii" for the transport of oil from Baetica to Italy; one man declares himself to be "a merchant in Spanish oil from the province of Baetica," while another combines cargoes of Baetic oil with Gallic wine.

Another product was wine; the vine flourished exceedingly in various parts, but best of all in the district round Tarraco and in the Ebro valley, and also in Baetica, whence much was exported. That connoisseur the elder Pliny praises the Laletane wine for its body, and that of Tarraco

—"vitifera Tarraco" as it is called by a native poet—for its delicacy. A moderate vintage was produced by the Balearic Isles, and there was also a wine from Gades. Spanish wine is mentioned in Petronius, and we know from Varro that it was despatched in large jars from Baetica; these jars, too, have been found at Monte Testaccio.

Another article of export was flax, and the clothing and nets made from it. It grew extensively in the district round Tarraco, where it was woven into cloth and garments, and also into sails and nets; Pliny speaks of the extraordinary fineness of the sails of that coast; the excellence of the flax was attributed to the waters of a certain stream in the neighbourhood. From Saetabis near by came famous towels and cloths, and the men of Emporium further up the coast were renowned for working in flax. Even more famous was that of Zoelae in Gallaecia, which was used for making nets and exported extensively to Italy and over the world. In connection with this it is interesting to note that one historian tells us that the women of Spain used to have competitions in weaving and making cloth; at Tarraco, as we might expect, we find inscriptions of workers in linen. As well as this in the vicinity of Carthago Nova there was a plain called the "Campus Spartarius" from the quantities of esparto grass which covered its surface; the working of this gave employment to large numbers of men and women, and it was exported in bulk to Italy and the provinces.

The wheat of Spain, too, was highly esteemed; it was exported from Turdetania, and Baetic "triticum" was renowned. The Eastern coast of the peninsula was famed for fruit, and especially for figs. There was also abundance of vegetable dyes, and amongst the most used was the coccus, which was sent in quantities to Italy, and was also used as half-payment of their tribute by certain of the wilder tribes of Lusitania. A few plants that were not indigenous had been acclimated by enterprising men; thus the pistachio nut had been brought from Syria to Spain and successfully transplanted there; in the second century Galen tells us that the plums of Spain rivalled even those of Damascus.

In the more mountainous regions of the peninsula horses were reared and bred, and had been used by the savage tribes for warfare. So swift were the Lusitanian that they were credited with having the wind for their sire, and from among the Asturians came a famous breed of chariot horses. The valleys of the country abounded in herds of cattle and flocks of sheep, and in that ideal land Turdetania herds of every kind flourished greatly on the pastures of the Baetis and the Anas; in addition, there were no wild beasts to fear there. On the other hand, in the hills of the Sierra Morena there was abundance of game and the hunting was very good; Seneca the Elder gives us a delightful picture of the pleasures of life in Spain, with hunting during the day and then banqueting and genial conversation at night. The only thing approaching a pest was the rabbit, but it never became so annoying as it has in Australia or did in the Balearic Isles, where it plagued the people so much that they sent a special deputation to the Senate to beg for deliverance. History does not record the answer of that body.

In the valley of the Baetis and especially by Corduba there was raised a fine species of black-fleeced sheep, which was very valuable; the farmers must have devoted great attention to the bettering and crossing of their stock, for we are told that Columella's uncle sent across to Africa for rams. Down by Gades so rich was the milk of the cows that the cream had to be watered in order to make cheese. Spain was famed for the manufacture of woollen cloth, and we hear of togas of Baetic wool and of Spanish cloaks. The land provided plenty of vegetable dyes, among them the coccus, and dyeing was much practised, as we can gather not only from notices in our authors, but also from various inscriptions wherein the workmen employed upon the different technical processes are clearly named and distinguished. The hills and valleys of the North-Western country, with their forests, provided excellent raising ground for swine; we are told that the Cerretani and the Cantabri vied with each other keenly in the quality of their hams, which were exported from the country, and Varro speaks with approval of the sows of Lusitania. But these Northern regions though rich in minerals and in grazing lands did not foster the vine or olive, and the Hellenized Strabo observes that the wilder tribes of that district were wont to use butter instead of oil.

Every small town in the ancient world usually had its native pottery where lamps and cheap ware were manufactured, but Spain does not appear, like the neighbouring province of Gaul, to have given so much attention to the manufacture of vases or pottery, that is, of course, for export. We do, however, find traces of works in different parts of the country; in Baetica and elsewhere have been discovered vases and pots belonging to the "Figlinae Medianenses" and it appears likely that some ware at Rome marked with the name of Q. Fabius Rusticus emanated from that factory. Yet Saguntum produced ware of more than purely local fame; its pottery is praised by Pliny and its bottles and flasks by poets of the Empire.

But for more elaborate pottery Spain had to rely upon the products of foreign workmen, and Gaul with its workshops was near at hand to supply all deficiencies. Thus the vases of the famous craftsman, Mommo, have been found in Spain, and pots and utensils from the factories of the Ruteni have been discovered at Saguntum and vases of the same provenance unearthed during the recent excavations at Emporiae. Curiously enough, even lamps were imported into the Southern parts from the large factory of Iol Caesarea. But this is accounted for by the close connection which has already been shewn to exist between the two coasts.

We have now completed our survey of the resources and routes of the Spanish provinces. In its mineral and agricultural wealth it stood second to none of the provinces of the Empire; on the other hand, its manufactures and crafts were not so far advanced as in Gaul; in the latter province we are struck by the rapid increase of pottery works, glass-factories, textile industries and so on; but whereas the mines of Gaul were apparently failing or at any rate less productive than hitherto, those of Spain continued with undiminished output. The region of the North-West, owing to its metals, was one of great activity, while from the Southern valleys the oil, in its huge jars, was the main export, with other agricultural produce. In return for this produce Spain received from the East what she did not possess, jewels and precious stones and spices, while she sent out the tin and lead which India lacked. It is significant that we meet with an obviously Oriental pearl-merchant at Emerita, doubtless doing a flourishing trade, and so too we find a company of Syrians established at Malaca and busied in exchanging the spices and silks of the East for the Spanish metals. But it bears witness to another fact: all over the Empire during the first and second centuries the Hellenised Orientals were driving out the older established Italian traders, and they had occupied even Rome itself. In the South of Spain we meet with Africans from the neighbouring coast, and signs of close and frequent intercourse. But at the same time the Spaniards were not idle in carrying their own produce; we meet with many in inscriptions all over Italy, from merchants in oil, or salt, or cloth, or members of mining syndicates, and even in the other provinces, notably Gaul, near Nîmes and Bordeaux. They, too, had learnt to profit by the "Pax Romana."

CHAPTER TEN

ITALY AND THE NORTHERN FRONTIERS

"Vicina illa caelo Alpium iuga,
quibus Italiam natura vallavit."

MAMERTINUS

"Rarus ab Italia tantum mare
    navita transit :
litora rarus in haec portubus
    orba venit."

OVID at Tomi

CHAPTER TEN

ITALY AND THE NORTHERN FRONTIERS

BEFORE discussing the trade and routes of Gaul and of the adjacent province of Britain it is necessary to describe the means by which Italy maintained communication not only with the Western provinces and Germany but also with her Northern armies along the Danube and in Pannonia. The amount of traffic, however, that came from the North-East was comparatively small and these districts have not the same importance for trade as the other provinces, and for this reason we shall treat the subject with brevity.

Italy is encircled along her Northern boundaries by the frowning masses of the Alps, which bar all inter-communication except through certain passes. Now it was of importance to the Roman Empire that these passes should be in its hands, for only thus were its rulers secure of a way through to the armies on the Rhine and on the Danube; again communication between the camps on the two rivers was a necessity and this could only be assured by the command of the valleys beyond the Alpine barrier. We therefore encounter a number of roads leading in a northerly direction through the mountain passes, and the towns lying at the end of them all connected by an East and West route ensuring quick transit along the whole of the Northern frontier. Into the problems of frontier defence which here confronted the Romans and resulted in the massive "Limites" of Germany and Rhaetia it is not our task to enter, but merely to describe those routes which served trade and the sort of traffic that came down them.

To begin with the routes into Gaul: apart from the road along the sea-coast between Genua and Forum Julii the only possible pathways across the towering barrier of the Alps were formed by the valleys of such rivers as the

Druentia, the Isara, the Rhone, and their tributaries. Yet even so the dizzy heights attained by the passes, the narrow spaces where carts could not find room and traffic could only be conducted on baggage-animals, the storms of winter, and the robber tribes infesting the country round, made the journey dangerous at any season, and those merchants who ventured upon it did so only after payment of heavy tolls and often at the risk of their lives. In Caesar's time the pass that led from Augusta Praetoria to the territory of the Nantuates was exceedingly perilous and that traversing the Alpes Graiae little better.

It was left to Augustus to carry out the subjugation of the mountain tribes and he performed the work with his usual thoroughness. The passes before his time had been few and dangerous; he increased their number, made them safe, and constructed good road beds. The savage tribes were exterminated or tamed; new roads were undertaken and the obstacles of nature overcome; the whole country was pacified and garrisons placed at suitable spots. Upon the cliffs at Monaco stood a great trophy with the names of over forty tribes which had been made to feel the might of Rome and of Augustus. Cottius, who was left (under the title of "praefectus Augusti") in charge of his ancestral kingdom in the Alps, proved his gratitude to his suzerain by the repair of existing roads and the construction of new ones, thus stimulating trade and transport. To the North and North-Eastern mountains Augustus sent his stepsons, Tiberius and Drusus, who in a brilliant campaign utterly defeated the Rhaeti and Vindelici (with other tribes such as the Breuni and Genauni) near Lake Brigantium and stopped their raids, thus securing the passes over the Rhaetian Alps to the Rhine valley; at the same time the route along the Aenus to the Danube and the pass over the Carnic Alps and down the stream of the Dravus was assured. Eastwards, from Aquileia, a low and easy pass led by way of Ocra to Nauportus and the Save and Danube valleys. Throughout this region road-making went on busily, primarily for military reasons, but trade soon followed the flag.

To describe these roads a little more in detail; the coast road passed through the Ligurian land, traversing a thin ribbon of country lying between the sheer hills and the sea, along a harbourless coast; the inhabitants were a race of mountaineers, who could not grow vines or cereals in their land, but who hewed down the trees of their forests for ship-timber, which they brought to Genoa, together with cattle and horses, hides and honey, and a small amount of amber, in return for which they imported wine and oil. They made excellent troops and acted as wood-cutters or quarrymen, and sometimes hired themselves out for labour to Massiliots. Some even ventured to sea in their tiny boats and sailed as traders to Sardinia and even to Africa.

The second route led from Augusta Taurinorum up into the Regnum Cottii at Segovii, and thence to Brigantium: here it divided, the southernmost branch following the valley of the Druentia to Arelate and Nemausus, the northernmost going by way of Cularo, where there was a customs-station, to Vienna and so reaching Lugdunum. We have already recounted how this road was kept in repair by the king of the district, and doubtless it was much used by the guild of Cisalpine and Transalpine merchants which had its headquarters in Lugdunum. Soldiers too were employed during the early years of the Empire to police this route, and sometimes proved useful in quelling disturbances in neighbouring towns. The third route also forked: starting from Eporedia it mounted the valley of the Durias as far as Augusta Praetoria; here the Western branch climbed over the Graian Alps by a lengthy and slow route, but one open to waggon-traffic nevertheless, and down the valleys to Lemincum and Vienna; the other branch rose more steeply to surmount the Pennine Alps and could not be traversed by carts; it made its descent to Lake Lemanus and the land of the Nantuates. From that lake a continuation led over the Jura mountains into the territory of the Sequani and down to Vesontio; hence it passed through the country of the Lingones and forked at Andematunnum, either to the Rhine or to the coast, by roads that had been constructed by Agrippa. This route was important because it provided quick communication between Rome and the camps of Upper Germany, and all served mineral districts; a copper mine among the Centrones was the property of Sallustius, the friend and confidant of Augustus, while the country of the Salassi was rich in gold, for the washing of which the swift-flowing Durias was close at hand. Indeed, during republican times the natives who controlled the headwaters had sold their rights to Roman contractors through whose avarice quarrels often arose, which resulted in petty raids and retaliations.

We must now consider the roads which linked Italy with Rhaetia and Noricum and the lands that slope towards the Danube valley. There was firstly a route from Milan and skirting the lake of Como, which rose over the Rhaetic Alps and then descended into the Rhine valley; this it followed to the lake of Brigantium and then turning North-Eastwards reached Augusta Vindelicorum. But the latter town was also accessible by another route which started from Verona and went up the valley of the Athesis as far as Tridentum and Endida; here it turned aside to pierce the highlands of the Breuni, and descending crossed the Aenus near Veldidena, and so down into the lower lands of the Vindelici to its goal. This was a road which had originally been planned by Drusus, the stepson of Augustus; he did not live to complete the work, but his son, the emperor Claudius, was proud to finish it, and could boast that he had joined the Danube to the Po. These roads though constructed for military purposes yet carried much trade. For Rhaetia was exceptionally rich in timber, especially in maple and larch; there were curious fables about the latter tree, among others that it was incombustible, and so it was used in many public buildings at Rome; besides, the Rhaetian vines and the lampreys of Lake Brigantium were much in demand. The town of Augusta Vindelicorum, upon which these roads converged, was the most brilliant and flourishing of the whole district; here are found merchants of every kind, dealers in wool and clothes, sellers of purple, potters, cattle-dealers, and also makers of pickles and sauces. At Brigantium, too, we meet Roman merchants and business men, while in the towns of the district are to be found various others of differing nationality, among whom the Treviri are specially prominent.

Further towards the East there was also a route from Aquileia over the Carnic Alps to Virunum and Noreia and then over the Noric Alps to Gabromagus and the Danube near Lauriacum, but the way was difficult, the passes dangerous, and traffic preferred the easier and more frequented road over the Julian Alps. It is true that the former may have been used when urgency demanded, and it was doubtless by it that Maroboduus fled from his rebellious subjects to throw himself upon the mercy of Tiberius, but the latter was the easier and more natural highway for trade. Here the mountain-chain which encircles the North of Italy sinks to its lowest and provides a gentle ascent over the pass of Ocra. The road then led down to Nauportus, where we find soldiers employed in the construction of causeways and bridges over the marshy country early in the reign of Tiberius, and so to Emona, a notable junction. From this point the direct Eastern route followed the valley of the Savus to Segestica and Siscia; the rivers of the region were broad and navigable and conveyed much of the merchandise which came from Rome and was destined for the Danube and the East. But for those going Northward, the road forked at Emona and crossing a range of hills descended into the valley of the Dravus to the town of Celeia and on to Poetovio. There the level plains of Pannonia received it until the Danube was touched at Carnuntum; this place, which had been selected by Tiberius as the starting-point for his invasion of Maroboduus' realm, was subsequently fortified and became the seat of a garrison; it was also the natural centre for all commerce and traffic with Central Germany and the tribes beyond. Indeed, not far from Carnuntum, somewhat down the river, lay a town, by name Brigetio, where was discovered an inscription dedicated to "the genius of commerce and of our merchants" by some faithful slave of the customs officials there stationed. The country across the river, vaguely called Boiohaemum and the seat of the Marcomanni, was at the beginning of our era ruled by a man of remarkable ability and organising power, Maroboduus, who had gathered many distant tribes under his sway and built up an army and power which menaced Rome itself; among other measures he allowed the free right of trading to Romans, and many merchants had been lured by this inducement to take up their residence in his capital and carry on business in the surrounding country. Doubtless they sent back to Rome wild beasts for the games and hides of cattle, importing the wine and oil which the savages needed, or the gaudy wares and coloured beads in which they delighted, but besides this one very great motive must have been that by settling along the Danube bank they were enabled to come in contact with the amber trade. The route which conveyed this much-prized substance from the shores of the Baltic to the banks of the Danube and over the mountains to Aquileia and the land of the Veneti and the Padus valley was very old indeed, how old it would be hard to say; the mouth of the Padus had been for centuries connected with amber and the amber trade in Greek legend and fable; the reign of Augustus brought a clearer knowledge of the route, at any rate as far as the Danube, and the peace and prosperity of succeeding years produced many who were ready to pay for information. A Roman knight was despatched to collect amber and explore the trade-route. This ran from Carnuntum on the Danube up the valley of the March, through the Glatz Pass, into Upper Silesia and Posen: at Kalisz it touched the river Prosna, and after following it for some distance, till its junction with the Warthe, turned North-Eastwards by way of Lake Goplo to reach the Vistula and the Baltic coast. Here he visited the collecting places and trade factories ("commercia"), and finally returned in safety bringing quantities of amber back with him, which was lavished on the decoration of the amphitheatre by his patron. This knight must have brought back a great deal of information geographical and otherwise —such as Carnuntum being 600 miles from the Baltic— but, unfortunately, none of it has reached us; Tacitus may have used his account, but gives us merely a description of amber-gathering by the natives and none of those details of place and distance which would have been so instructive. Yet there existed a considerable traffic, for finds of Roman coins have been made in Northern Germany and near Posen. We would give much to know more of such men as Julianus or Maes Titianus, who financed expeditions for the purpose of trade, but at present they remain mere names to us. One of the most important products of the North was iron, which was found in plenty in Noricum where it was worked into swords and implements. Pliny speaks highly of the excellence of the workmanship, and we can well understand that the two routes converging on Aquileia were crowded with traders.

We have already mentioned the Eastern route; this separated from the other at Emona and followed the valley of the Savus down to Segestica. The river was navigable and carried a great deal of the merchandise and freight coming from Rome, and the road clung closely to it through Siscia and Sirmium until it finally reached the Danube at Singidunum and Viminacium. From Viminacium a road led South-East up the valley of the Morava to Naissus, where it forked, the left-hand branch leading direct to Serdica and Byzantium, the right-hand rising to cross the mountains of Dardania into the Axius valley, which it followed down to Thessalonica. Thus Rome was in speedy communication with Greece, with Thrace, and with Asia, and with the armies which guarded her against the hordes of barbarians across the Danube. Among these the Daci had been most formidable; about the time of Julius Caesar a king arose among them, by name Burebistas, who organised the tribes of Quadi and Iazyges dwelling round about, and threatened to descend upon Italy; but some petty quarrel sprang up, and the ruler who might have done so much was assassinated, opportunely enough for Rome, vexed as she was already by internecine strife. But over a century later the menace was renewed, and Trajan decided to reduce Dacia. As before, the route running through Segestica became the base from which to strike, and rivers such as the Danube, and its tributary the Marisus, were used for conveying supplies. Apart from military needs Trajan was powerfully influenced by the thought of the gold mines lying in the region to be annexed, which were profitably worked for many years. Gradually the road-system extended, until it included desolate Tomi, upon the Euxine coast, and it could be said that Trajan had linked up the Atlantic with the Black Sea. Upon this great East and West artery of traffic those merchants moved whose inscriptions and dedications are found in

the provinces of Dacia, Pannonia, and Moesia. It is not
our intention to treat of them at the same length as in the
other provinces, because these regions did not possess
anything like the same agricultural, mineral, or industrial
importance, but it may be worth while to call attention to
the fact that the great bulk of trade here appears to have
been carried on by the ubiquitous Syrians and by the
Treviri, who seem to have been their only serious rivals
and are found in large numbers over the Rhine territory,
in Gaul and Switzerland, and in Northern Italy. Thus we
find two Syrians, whose headquarters were at Salonae, and
who travelled between there and the Danube, another at
Celeia, and a man from Antioch residing as far North as
Carnuntum. In order to secure the successful working of
the mines and to guard against future insurrections in
Dacia, Trajan deported a large number of the original
inhabitants and filled the country with men of Dalmatian
and of Asiatic extraction, which measure alone must have
meant an added impetus to trade and communication.
Yet in spite of all this, in spite of the gold of Dacia and the
iron of Noricum, we may doubt whether these provinces
paid for the expenses of conquest; their interest to the
Empire was always primarily one of defence and the road-
system served military needs first.

CHAPTER ELEVEN
GAUL

"Culmina villarum pendentibus
edita ripis
et virides Baccho colles et amoena
fluenta
subterlabentis tacito rumore Mo-
sellae."

AUSONIUS

"'Αλλόβριγες δὲ μυριάσι πολλαῖς
πρότερον μὲν ἐστράτευον, νῦν δὲ
γεωργοῦσι τὰ πεδία καὶ τοὺς αὐλῶνας
τοὺς ἐν ταῖς Ἄλπεσι."

STRABO

"The Mashona have forgotten the
terrors of the Matabele raids.
They have come down from the
hilltops to cultivate the plains
and live unmolested."

Report on Rhodesia in
The Times, 1 Oct. 1923.

GAUL

THE creation of the first province beyond the Alps —that of Gallia Narbonensis—was due to the friendly relations of Rome with a foreign trading city. This city was the Phocaean colony of Massilia, planted not far from the mouth of the Rhone, at the end of an important trade-route leading from Northern Europe: founded about 600 B.C. it had prospered exceedingly and had sent out colonies in its turn to various spots on the coast around. Tradition said that the city had helped to pay the ransom exacted from Rome by the Gauls; in the first Punic war its fleet appears to have been of service to Rome, and it has been conjectured that its hostility towards the Carthaginian settlement in Spain was responsible for bringing Rome into the struggle against Hannibal. In the year 154 B.C. it appealed for help to hold back the raiding peoples of the Alps; the appeal was heard and their lost territory restored; again in 125 B.C. Roman legions were despatched to punish the marauding Salluvii and Vocontii, but this time a thin strip of land along the coast-line was reserved by the conquerors to give them direct land communication with the province of Spain; within this strip the victorious Domitius built his famous road. The establishment of a fort at Aquae Sextiae and the foundation of the colony of Narbo Martius finally secured the territory, and Roman merchants, money-lenders, and business men flocked in to this new field. The colony of Narbo grew rapidly; it had an exceptionally favourable site for commerce, while at the same time it acted as a "watch-tower and bulwark of the Roman people," keeping off the incursions of the Arverni and the mountaineers, and guarding the way to Spain. It was possibly owing to the growing commerce of the town that the Transalpine tribes were

forbidden by the Senate to plant vine or olive: wine and
oil were two great articles of import and so had to be safeguarded; merchants had discovered that the Gauls were
wine-loving people, and so (like modern traders with
"fire-water") they brought with them the cheap and fiery
wines of the South and gaudy pieces of pottery or painted
glass to give in exchange for the amber, the hides, or slaves
which the chieftains would offer; a cask of wine would often
purchase a slave. Thus Southern Gaul became crowded
with merchants and usurers; Cicero could boast that not
a single monetary transaction was carried out there without
an entry in some Roman account book; such men as
Fonteius or Umbrenus gained great wealth and power in
the province. The darker side of this is seen in the revolt
of the Allobroges, rendered desperate by debt and exactions.
But a few years later followed the amazing conquest of the
whole vast region by Caesar, which resulted in the creation
of some of the most loyal and most civilised of all the
Roman provinces. Wise measures were adopted to pacify
a high-spirited people and console them for their loss of
liberty; Roman citizenship was held out to them as a prize
to be attained by faithful service and the nobles were
taught to compete for such an honour. The tribes were
persuaded to leave their rugged hill-fortresses and come
down to occupy the new towns founded in the valleys
lying along lines of trade; every encouragement was
afforded to agriculture and industry. In spite of one or
two occasional outbreaks peace was imposed on Gaul, and
an era of surprising prosperity ensued. More still, the
barbarous practices of Druidism, the human sacrifices and
burnings, were forbidden; but while the old religion was
taken away from the people they were given a new cult
which should bind all cities and tribes together in a common
loyalty and unity. The solemn inauguration of the altar of
Rome and Augustus by Drusus marked an epoch in the

history of the provinces. Next after Augustus the emperor Claudius, by the interest he took in the land of his birth, as manifested in his construction of new roads and grants of citizenship, did most for bringing nearer the day when all Gauls were to be dressed as Romans.

To the Italians the country which Caesar had added to their Empire appeared as a region of great rivers flowing through wide and fertile plains, of mountains and hills concealing untold mineral riches, and of dark forests wherein the Druids practised their horrible rites. Its wealth in crops, especially in corn and cereals, was known to be large. The Southern province of Narbonensis was the more cultivated, and was so dotted with cities and villages that the elder Pliny could describe it as "more like Italy than a province." Though the Northern plains did not yield a return so readily, herds of cattle could find good grazing there, and swine wandered through the forests in search of food; the native Gallic coins shew how important these animals were; sheep, too, were to be found in abundance and the Gallic wool was considered exceptionally thick and good. It was the newest of all the provinces, a land of boundless possibilities.

We have already discussed means of communication with Rome by land; there remains the sea-route. The Southern coast of Gaul contained few harbours of any importance; the best were Narbo, Arelate, Massilia, and Forum Julii, where one of the imperial fleets was stationed. The mouth of the Rhone was confused by shifting sandbanks and approach to it endangered by the storms and mists that swept down upon it; to remedy this the Massiliots had built towers along the coast for the guidance of mariners. But the voyage can rarely have been a pleasant experience, though many merchants had to brave it; the Gulf of Lyons had, then as now, a sinister reputation, and we can sympathise with the unfortunate Claudius, who was caught there in a severe gale, and nearly drowned before he reached Massilia. We may well credit the report that after this experience he completed his journey by land.

The alternative was to proceed by the coast-road through Liguria and along the Riviera. This was the main highway for the West of Gaul and Spain and carried much traffic; Domitius built the road in about 120 B.C. and marked off the distances with milestones; from some belonging to the age of the emperor Tiberius we can see that it underwent repairs practically throughout its entire length during the years A.D. 31–32, probably owing to the stream of waggons and passengers which was ceaselessly pouring between such busy centres as Nicaea, Narbo, Arelate, Massilia, Tolosa, and the towns of Spain.

Most of the roads of Gaul were a creation of the Empire; all we can do here is to give a brief sketch of their development and some description of the completed system. Before the Roman conquest many native roads existed, though they were probably little better than tracks, and the conquerors often utilised and improved these. The rivers of the country played an important part in any scheme of communication; Strabo remarks upon the length and navigability of their courses, and the fact that many of them had their source in a common region or came close to one another during their journey to the sea made transport easy and portages short. The natural centre for all roadways was Lugdunum, lying as it did in the heart of the country like a citadel to command it, and the genius of Agrippa had seized upon the city as the point from which to drive his roads. These were five in all: firstly, one which went South following the course of the Rhone, past Vienna and Arausio to Arelate and Nemausus, where it connected with the Via Domitia; secondly, one through the territory of the Arverni and of the Lemovices almost due West to Aquitania and having as its special objective the port of

Burdigala; thirdly, one that used the valleys of the upper
Arar and of the Sequana, going North-West into the land
of the Ambiani and the Bellovaci, from which there was
a quick passage to Britain; fourthly, one driven North-
Eastwards to the Rhine, and the camps along it; fifthly,
one connected with the fourth, but giving more direct
communication with the capital, branching off at Vesontio,
and climbing the Jura mountains, to traverse the land of
the Nantuates and so over the Alpes Poeninae into Italy.
These great roads formed the nucleus of the future system
of Gaul; other emperors might make additions and open
up fresh parts of the country, but it was merely a development upon lines already laid down by Agrippa. Thus the
succeeding decades were spent in the attempts made to
conquer Germany and the planning of a system of forts
and camps along the Rhine, and during these years many
new roads were constructed in Northern Gaul. Drusus
in his campaigns not only made one over the Alps into
Rhaetia and the camps of the upper Rhine, but set garrisons along the course of that river in order to safeguard
Gaul from the inroads of the barbarians; fifty forts were
placed upon the river bank, a fleet was stationed at Bonna,
and that town joined to Gesoriacum on the Western coast
by a road which was carried over the marshy intervening
country along a series of embankments, causeways, and
bridges; the camps on the river, at Vetera, Moguntiacum,
and Vindonissa, must also have been connected by road.
Even Germany felt the might of the conqueror; Domitius
Ahenobarbus, who penetrated further into that country
than any other Roman general, built a famous "Long
Causeway" between the Rhine and the Amisia, which
opened that district to trade. We have, unfortunately, little
literary evidence for these works, and no milestones, but
the task went steadily forward, and we find Tiberius,
during his German campaigns, being welcomed at Bagacum,

which lay upon the road from Gesoriacum to the Rhine. Some years later, Germanicus, besides completing much of the work begun by his father, stationed a fleet at Fectio near the mouth of the Rhine, and this rapidly became a depôt for trade, especially to Britain.

But it was destined for another son of Drusus to do most for Gaul of any of the emperors; the despised Claudius loved the land of his birth and did everything he could to encourage industry and to forward civilisation there. On his way to the conquest of Britain he must have visited many towns for himself—to judge from the time he took, which is out of all proportion to the length of the journey. It is interesting to notice how many of the roads that he had built were in intimate connection with the commerce of the sea-ports of Gaul and especially with those which derived the greater part of their wealth from trade with the newly added province of Britain. Thus we observe a road being constructed through the land of the Lexovii from Autricum (Chartres) to Alauna and on to the modern Cherbourg, doubtless to receive the trade of the opposite Isle of Wight; in the very heart of Brittany, near Carhaix, there appears to have been a small network of roads, which not only served to link the harbours of the Veneti and the modern Brest with the valley of the Liger, but also were useful in developing the transport of iron, vast quantities of which were smelted in this region. An alternative route between the flourishing port of Burdigala and the federal capital at Lugdunum was provided by a road which ran up North to Mediolanum Santonum and repairs were effected upon the older way. From a junction at Augusto-nemetum (on the Lyons-Bordeaux road) a branch was driven Northwards to Avaricum which served the great ironworks of that city and the industry of working in silver that prevailed among the Bituriges. On the Rhine itself repairs were effected upon the road that led from

Moguntiacum down to Colonia Agrippina, which was dignified with this title during the reign of Claudius, and soon became the most important trading town in the whole valley.

Beside Claudius, the only other emperor who did a similar amount of work in road-construction and who took an equal interest in the resources of the province is Trajan. Something had been done to solve frontier problems by the Flavian emperors; Vespasian built a road leading direct from Argentorate into Rhaetia, and it was probably during his reign that the lands on the other side of the Rhine—the Agri Decumates—were occupied, and the great Limites of the Rhine and the Danube and the territory between constructed; Nerva had a road laid between Durocortorum and Divodurum (and presumably on to Augusta Treverorum), and repaired the road that Claudius had built fifty years ago between Moguntiacum and Colonia. But Trajan spent an immense amount of care and attention upon the question of intercommunication in Eastern Gaul; Argentorate was connected with the South by a road through the Jura to the land of the Nantuates, and the system of the Rhine roads received a thorough overhauling; from Noviomagus Batavorum they ran along the river to Moguntiacum, and from that town further South to connect with the Limes Transdanubianus and the armies of Pannonia. When we couple this with the work he expended upon the conquest of Dacia, and when we remember that the increasing military needs of the Empire made it essential to secure quick transit between the North of Britain or the mouth of the Rhine and the Black Sea or even the mountains of Armenia, we can appreciate the phrase of a biographer, that he had made one sure line of road stretching through barbarous peoples from Gaul right to the Black Sea. The result of all this toil can be observed, in the immense importance which the

Rhine valley later came to possess, both as a region of flourishing industrial towns, and also as a highway for the transport of the articles they produced.

Traffic by water was as common as by land. Before the days of the Empire British tin was brought by merchants from Ictis and conveyed across Gaul and down the Rhone in thirty days. Indeed, there were four main ways of communication with our island, all starting from the mouth of a river. The first led from Narbo, following the course of the Atax, which soon became too shallow for navigation, and waggons had to be used; but once the valley of the Garumna was touched it was an easy journey to Burdigala; a second route started up the Rhone valley, but turned aside into Arvernian territory in order to avoid the rapids of the river, and so reached the waters of the Loire; a third likewise went up the Rhone, but continued along the Arar, from which a short land-journey took it across to the stream of the Doubs, and so into the Seine and past Paris to the ports of Normandy; the fourth was merely a variation of the third, leaving the Seine to go by land to Portus Itius, in the district of the Morini, whence was the shortest passage to Britain. We find merchants engaged in this trade with Britain as early as Caesar's time, but he could get no information out of them as to the size or population of the island, since they knew no more than the coast-line; indeed, they actually gave the islanders news of his coming. Like the Veneti, who were ready strenuously to oppose Caesar, in order to prevent the British trade slipping from their control, these merchants seem to have been unwilling to impart to the general even the little knowledge they possessed. But though during the reign of Augustus Britain was not a part of the Empire, trade relations were kept up, and the native princes shewed themselves friendly; embassies visited the court of Augustus, and when soldiers of Germanicus' army were wrecked on the coast of Britain, they were sent back unharmed: Strabo gives us a list of articles imported into the island and mentions the slaves and hides which the natives sent in return.

Even into the Rhine valley some Roman merchants had penetrated before Caesar, and there was much shipping plying on the river, principally belonging to the Menapii, who had established trade-connections here. There was traffic from this point, too, to Britain, though not directly from the mouth of the river; vessels sailed down it, and then hugged the Gallic coast until they reached Itius, before putting across. The campaigns of Drusus and Tiberius had helped to open up this region, and much had been learnt from the voyage of exploration which the imperial fleet undertook; from the mouth of the Rhine this had sailed Northward up to the Danish peninsula, "further than any Roman had approached by land or sea," and the tribes of that district, the Cimbri and the Semnones, had sent to beg the friendship of the emperor. Indeed, a great deal was done for inland navigation and for coastal traffic by succeeding legates; Drusus constructed a canal leading from the Rhine into the North Sea by way of the Zuyder Zee, and also began the building of a large dyke or levee to restrain the waters of the river, which was only brought to completion under Nero. The Belgian and Frisian coast, with its shallow waters and its violent storms, was always unpleasant for navigation, and so we find Corbulo digging a canal twenty-three miles long between the Meuse and the Rhine, to avoid the sea-passage; the legionaries under his command were employed on the task. An even more ambitious project was that contemplated by a certain Vetus, one of the legates of Germany; his scheme was to connect the waters of the Mosella and of the Araris by a canal (its length need not have been more than sixty miles), which would then have provided a through waterway between the Mediterranean and the North Sea, by way of the Rhone, Araris, Mosella, and Rhine, thus effecting an immense saving of time and distance besides avoiding the dangers of the sea-route. Unfortunately the plan was never realised; petty jealousies were at work, and technical difficulties as to the employment of troops in another province and so on were easily raised. Yet it is a little surprising that under the Flavians or during the reign of Trajan such a scheme was not revived. For there was no lack of capable engineers—such as Frontinus, for example —and labour was to be had in abundance from the army. Perhaps the real cause is to be looked for in the fact that by the end of the first century Northern Gaul was no longer so important in the defensive scheme; the centre of interest had shifted to Pannonia and the lands lying Eastward.

Of the volume of traffic there can be no doubt; Horace speaks of merchants who have voyaged in the Atlantic, and we have already noticed the shipping that plied between Britain and the mouths of the Rhine and of the Gallic rivers. It was doubtless to aid this that Caligula erected a lighthouse near Boulogne, and that Claudius installed a fleet at the same spot. Still more convincing are the number of inscriptions in ports and towns recording merchants to foreign parts or mentioning the many guilds of sailors whose profession it was to navigate the various rivers of the country.

We may fitly start our survey by considering Gallia Narbonensis. It was the oldest Gallic province, and had for much longer been subjected to Roman penetration. It was a sunnier and more fertile region than the plains of the North, and had been far more cultivated. In its agricultural development, in its population, in the fullness of its resources, it was second to none of the provinces and more closely resembled part of Italy. The most interesting town, on account of its historical associations, though not now the most thriving, was Massilia. It owed its prosperity in no small degree to its well-chosen site at the end of the trade-route from North-Western Europe; when Marius dug the Rhone canal he gave the Massiliots the right of exacting dues from all vessels using it, and from this revenue they derived much wealth also; for the guidance of mariners along this tricky coast they had erected towers to act as landmarks at various points. Naturally a great part of their riches was derived from the sea, as was that of their colonies, such as Nicaea, Antipolis, and Rhoda. There were good coral-beds off the Stoechades, while oysters and tunnies were obtainable in abundance; the salting and pickling of fish was one of the great industries of Antipolis. The soil of their land was stony and rough and did not produce much corn, but was quite suitable for the cultivation of the vine and olive, and their oil and wine was exported. We do not know the quality of the oil, but their wine can hardly have been much in demand by those able to afford better, since we hear that it was thick and gross, while Martial complains of its smokiness, and Pliny says it was much adulterated for export! This, among other reasons, may possibly explain the existence of a flourishing medical school at the town, which trained many distin-guished physicians of the Empire, who could demand high fees, of which Pliny tells us. There appears to have been a fair amount of communication between students of this school and the famous one at Alexandria, and in some inscriptions we discover Massiliots in Egypt. But it was not only a busy mercantile town; commercial prosperity had been accompanied by the pursuit of culture, and schools of philosophy sprang up, which Romans attended instead of going to Athens; many chose it as a place of exile and even left their riches to it; here the fashionable Roman could find a spot which combined a Greek re-finement of culture with the simple living of a provincial town.

Although it had much to import and export the land was not well provided with harbours, and the coast was dangerous; an imperial fleet was stationed at Forum Julii, and such ports as Massilia, Arelate, and Narbo received most of the trade. Along the Southern bend of the coast fishing was the staple industry, and there were fisheries at Ruscino of which curious tales were told. The country to the West was rich in minerals; iron mines were opened on the bank of the Atax during the early years of the Empire, and gold was to be found among the Tectosages in some quantity. This gold had helped to build up the famous treasure of Tolosa, which Caepio so wantonly plundered, and had filled the land with hoards buried by the inhabitants in times of distress.

But the greater part of the traffic of the country arose from its agricultural produce, much of which was exported to Rome and Italy; it was the most fertile and the best cultivated part of all Gaul. The river valleys afforded good pasturage for flocks of sheep and goats, for cattle and pigs. Wool was much exported and Varro speaks with approval of the hams and sausages and pickled pork which were sent to Rome from this quarter; the cheeses of Nemausus and of Tolosa were considered especially good. After the establishment of the Empire, every encouragement was given to the mountain tribes to forsake warfare and take up agriculture, and Columella speaks of a sweet wine which was cultivated by the once warlike Allobroges. The town of Vienna had produced a new wine which had been unknown in Vergil's time, and Martial refers to "vine-bearing Vienna." In this export trade a great number of men were engaged and we find merchants in Gallic wines of various kinds stationed at Rome. In addition the clays of the Eastern region were very favourable for pottery; there were pottery-works among the Allobroges, and coloured ware was made at the workshop of Aricius in

Vasio, the capital. To carry all this traffic large guilds of sailors and mariners existed in every one of the more important towns, and the inscriptions still left to us testify to their number, variety, and importance. Every river, the Rhone, the Araris, the Dubis, the Druentia, and the Atax, had its separate guild; in every town of note the carpenters, the shipwrights, and the timber-merchants plied their trade, and business along the river-banks and in the dock-yards ran high; we have still left an inscription com-memorating a young shipwright whose grave was placed above the Rhone on the very spot where he used to stand at his work. Stamps of lead, too, that have been unearthed at Forum Julii shew the route by which the metal came from the islands of Britain across France and down the Rhone to Italy.

Among the towns of the region Vienna was prominent, standing at the end of the descent from the Alps, with its flourishing river trade and its vine-bearing soil. It was in continual feud with Lugdunum, and its public and private wealth were alike great, as we can judge from a silver statue erected to a benefactor. Arelate, with its good harbour, was another wealthy town; it had been raised to the rank of a colony by Caesar, and may even have been a customs-station. The ruins of a splendid amphitheatre and many inscriptions left by trade guilds and merchants witness its energy and prosperity. Further along the coast to the West lay Nemausus, which had been made a colony by Augustus. Though its commerce was not so large as that of Narbo, yet it must have been of considerable importance, since we find here the usual guilds of carpenters and shipwrights and sailors, of contractors and ship-captains and dealers in clothes and flax; furthermore it lay upon the main road to Spain, which was repaired under Tiberius, on which bridges of wood and stone were rapidly replacing the old fords and ferries; we possess inscriptions of Spaniards from Calagurris in the town. From such imposing remains as the amphitheatre or the aqueduct over the river Gard we can gather some idea of the wealth of the region.

But incontestably the most considerable town of the whole province, if not politically at any rate commercially, was Narbo, which lay a short distance up the river Atax. It was the greatest mart of all in the district and a writer of the Augustan age has noticed how favourably it was situated with regard to trade both from Spain and the West of Gaul. Many were the vessels that sailed between here and Ostia, with corn and wine and oil, and recently a mosaic has been discovered at the latter port, representing a ship discharging her cargo at the docks of Narbo, while there are inscriptions of Narbonese merchants and remains of their warehouses; jars at Monte Testaccio that once contained the products of the region bear painted on them the names of merchants and manufacturers of the town. Among a host of inscriptions discovered near by we find traders of various sorts; makers of flasks and pottery, halter-makers, dealers in wicker-work, carpenters, workers in stucco and plaster, sandal-makers, bakers, market-gardeners, butchers, sellers of flax, dealers in timber, and many others. In addition there was the traffic from the iron-mines higher up the river, the trade that came from the West by the Garonne, and merchants coming over the passes from Spain to swell the activity and bustle of this thriving town.

North of Narbonensis lay the country called the Three Gauls—Aquitania, Lugdunensis, and Belgica—protected by a thin margin of land along the Rhine known as Upper and Lower Germany. In contrast with the South it was a less sunny and sheltered land; olive and fig would not grow North of the Cevennes, and the vine gave only a poor return; but corn and millet grew in abundance, and the plains afforded grazing for cattle and flocks. "It is a country," says Mela, "exceptionally fruitful in corn and in food for animals, though it does not support plants that cannot stand the cold well." Corn was its main article of export to Rome, doubtless being conveyed by river, and it is worthy of remark that the guild of shipowners at Arelate chose as their patron an imperial procurator of the corn-supply for the province of Narbonensis.

Where the colder climate would not allow of the culti-vation of vine, olive, and fig, the Italian merchants had found that wine and oil were eagerly bought by the natives, and it was still imported in some quantity to these parts. As an intoxicating drink the Gauls brewed a kind of beer, which was called "zythos," but efforts had been made to acclimatise the vine with some success; beside the Vien-nese brand already mentioned, the Bituriges had started cultivating the plant with encouraging results. The trade in wine, whether for export or for import, was considerable; many of the amphorae found at Monte Testaccio bear names of Gallic tradesmen; one cask contains the alluring announcement "Here am I, five years old wine from Baeterra," and Pliny speaks of its export from the country. Again we find the presidency of the guild of the Arar sailors being held by a merchant in wine, and a Treviran merchant at Lyons occupied the same position. Oil would appear to have been exported mainly from Narbon-ensis, as we should gather from inscriptions of oil-merchants there and in Rome, but we come across one also at Lyons, and in Rome we find a financial magnate who traded in oil from Baetica (the best), and in wine from Lyons, and was at the same time president of the corporation of sailors upon the Arar.

For the rest we must remember that it was the continued policy of the Empire to persuade the inhabitants of Gaul to forego fighting with one another and turn to agriculture; in the North the same crops could be raised as in Italy. Corn and rye and millet and the usual common vegetables grew in abundance; figs would not flourish North of the Cevennes, but cherries had been imported from Lusitania and Italy and acclimated there, and Pliny speaks of Gallic peaches. Great success had attended the encouragement given to agriculture; the Gauls had taken it up eagerly, and every patch of ground was well worked, save where the extensive marshes or the thick forests made it an impossibility.

But though these three provinces had not the richness or the variety of the Southern crops, the plains of the North-West provided excellent grazing and pasturage for flocks of sheep and herds of cattle. On Gallic pastures, as Horace sang, the fleeces grew thick and rich; the best were produced by the sheep of the Belgae, and in this quarter of the country many flocks were owned by Romans. Swine wandered freely in the forests and found their food there; the export of hams, sausages, and pickled pork was large, and both the Sequani and the Belgae had a share in the trade; indeed it was said that the latter supplied woven cloaks and hams and pork to Rome and Italy in abundance, while Menapian hams were given as presents and are mentioned in the later Edict of Diocletian.

With such considerable flocks of sheep wool was plentiful and the weaving of it into garments was practised by nearly all the Gallic tribes; Pliny gives us a list which includes the Cadurci, Caleti, Ruteni, Bituriges, and the Morini; the Cadurci, especially, made bolsters and cushions, quilts and covers, which were exported to Rome, as well as weaving flax into linen garments. So, too, many tribes had varieties of their own, and different styles of cloaks and garments were made at Trèves and Arras, while we hear of a special kind of wrap woven by the Nervii. These manufactures gave rise to the employment of many men as sellers and peddlers and agents, and we find at Lyons a dealer in linen from the tribe of the Veliocasses, a cloak-maker, and a

clothes-cleaner; at Burdigala we meet with a Treviran
vendor of garments, and cloak-merchants at Vienna and
at Paris. Indeed, these hardy merchants went even farther
afield in search of profit; we find a dealer in cloaks and
hides at Milan, and there also dwelt there a cloak-merchant
of the Mediomatrices, while another Gallic trader in
clothes had actually travelled as far as Pola to set up his
business. The Treviri appear to have been especially successful as merchants and there is scarcely a country of the
Northern Empire into which they did not penetrate with
their wares.

There is no doubt that the whole country had been once
rich in minerals, and long before the Romans took control
of it veins of gold, of silver, and of iron were extensively
worked: Caesar tells us that the Aquitani were skilled in
the digging of pits and shafts owing to their experience in
mining, and also mentions great ironworks in existence at
Avaricum; the Romans imagined they had conquered a
country of immense mineral richness. They were destined
to meet with disappointment, as we shall see.

Gold was found only in the Western regions, among the
Tectosages, and in the land of the Tarbelli in Aquitania;
such tales as those of the largesse scattered by Luerius,
a king of the Arverni, shew how great had been the wealth
gathered and how extensive the working of the precious
metal, so that in imperial times it had been almost exhausted. On the other hand, silver appears to have been
more common; it was mined among the Gabales and among
the Ruteni; in the latter country it is interesting to find a
mine that was the property of Tiberius and worked by
imperial slaves under a bailiff of the emperor. At this
period there were still many mines left which had not come
under imperial control; in Spain the greater number were
owned by private persons or by syndicates during the early
years of the Empire, but according to all accounts Tiberius

took a decisive step towards making all such property part of the fiscus; yet even so progress was slow and it was probably only after the Flavian era that all were put under imperial procurators and that general regulations concerning them could be drawn up. The Bituriges were famous for their industry of inlaying and plating with silver, and doubtless there were veins of metal in their land, though most of them were poor and of small production, like the vein on the right bank of the Rhine which was opened and worked by a legion under the supervision of the legate; the work was severe and the experiment hardly worth the toil.

Copper was found in a few districts: the empress Livia had owned a mine (presumably in the Alps), but it was soon exhausted; there were mines at the modern Vaudrevange, and we can see traces of working at Lyons, but the output must have been disappointingly small. On the other hand, the land contained rich deposits of iron; it was mined and worked extensively among the Petrucorii and there were veins of iron along the banks of the Atax which were worked by a contractor. Even where it could not be obtained, the water or supply of fuel at various places was especially suitable for smelting and tempering it, and so we hear of ironworks at Anicium and of large iron furnaces at Avaricum, which employed much labour, as early as the time of Caesar. And all over the country traces are to be found of extensive manufacture; at Lyons we meet with iron-smiths and at Dijon with ironworks, while the Aedui were famous for their manufacture of armour and of breast-plates. Towards the close of our period all these mines and manufactures were brought under the supervision of the imperial officers, and there was a "procurator ferrariarum" who had his central bureau at Lyons. This activity was more widespread than literary references or inscriptions would incline us to believe; all over the Sambre valley vast remains of these ancient workings have been discovered in the form of iron, slag, and scoria, and the same is true of extensive districts in Brittany.

A certain amount of marble was quarried in Aquitania, and one inscription commemorates the opening of a quarry there, the owners claiming to be the first hewers and exporters of columns from the district; there was a "marmorarius" at Agennum, and we hear of the opening of workshops at Vaudrevaye. It must not be forgotten that the Empire, with its careful fostering of municipal life and ambition, gave a considerable impetus to trade in marble and to statuary; to have a statue erected in his honour by his native town was one of the greatest prizes a man could expect.

Yet in spite of all this we cannot help feeling that the mineral wealth of Gaul did not come up to the exaggerated anticipations of the Romans; the mines of silver and gold had been so well exploited by the natives that they were nearly exhausted by the time of the conquest. Iron was plentiful and was much worked, and marble was quarried for the statuaries to labour on, but the precious metals, gold and silver, were disappointing in their yield; Pliny has no word of praise for the gold or silver mines of Gaul, and he mentions some that were soon exhausted. The truth would appear to be that Spain far surpassed its neighbour in the production of gold and silver and tin, and the newly-conquered Britain yielded tin and lead in such quantities, and in return for so little labour, that any competition was impossible; between them these two provinces effectually swamped the production of Gaul.

On the other hand, in its manufactures Gaul occupied almost as high a place as Syria or Egypt. There had been a native pottery, but during the period of the Roman conquest and after, the so-called Arretine ware was imported largely into the country; it is found in various early imperial camps, and pottery of the Augustan age has been unearthed at Vetera, and also at Fectio, which was not only a station for the Rhine fleet, but an important depôt for the river and sea trade. The clays of Gaul were excellent for the production of earthenware; we have already noted the shops and factories of the Allobroges and their coloured ware, and as the natives shewed themselves quick at artistic design and imitation Gallic production soon began to compete with foreign importation. Its beginnings were unimportant; lamps made at Lugdunum and also pieces of decorated ware have been found at many of the Rhine camps, which date from the first quarter of the first century, but the industry flourished especially among the Arverni and the Ruteni, where great schools sprang up. The most famous of the Rutenian potters was Mommo; his factory was at La Graufesenque, and his wares quickly spread not only over all Gaul but to the adjacent provinces and even to Italy itself. Another centre was at Ledosus (Lezoux) where Dr Plique unearthed over a hundred furnaces and the names of nearly three thousand potters; a third was in the Rhine valley at the ancient Tabernae Rhenanae (now Rheinzabern). The two Southern manufacturies were producing imitation Arretine ware quite as early as the second half of the first century; production in the Rhine valley did not start till the beginnning of the second, and other centres then sprang up as at Trèves, Cologne, and Heiligenberg. But the wares of the South, especially Mommo's, were exported far and wide, and have been found in Britain, Spain, Africa, and Italy. The Atisii too exported pottery, and vessels from Lyons have been found in England, while ware from such centres as Cologne and Trèves (and also from Lezoux) has been found in Britain. But most interesting to notice is the fact that towards the close of the first century the Gallic ware was actually beginning to outsell the Arretine which it had started by imitating; in a case of pottery found at Pompeii, which had never been opened owing to the eruption, was found a large quantity imported from Gaul for use in Italy or beyond. And this is not a solitary instance.

Much the same was the result in the manufacture of glass. This industry had been carried on for centuries in Egypt, which exported over a very wide area, Egyptian glass being even found North of the Alps, while glass beads and vessels have been discovered among the treasures of Gallic chieftains. Before Caesar's time the industry had taken root in Syria, and the invention of the method of blowing glass had given an immense impetus to its manufacture. The ware of the famous Syrian artist, Artas, has been found in parts of France, and Sidonian decorated glass has been unearthed along the banks of the Rhine. But just as some of the Syrians found it more profitable to transfer their business to Italy, so others determined to travel even further West to meet the demand; the process of glass-making had spread to Gaul by the time of the early Empire and after the first century we discover that no more Syrian ware was imported. Instead, to meet the demand, large factories sprang up over the country, mostly in the Rhine valley and in Normandy, along the coast of the channel. (It is interesting to note that as early as the time of Strabo glass vessels were articles of import into Britain, and possibly the industry had been established among the Caleti early.) There were glass-factories at Lyons and we find one there sending for a brilliant young glass-maker from Carthage in order to supervise production and to inculcate proper methods. But the chief centre of production was in Normandy and it was here that worked the master-artist, Frontinus, specimens of whose delicate and brilliant art meet us all over Northern Gaul; he appears to have had agencies and branch factories in many parts. It was from this region that a great deal of the glass-ware found in Southern Britain came, or else apprentices of the

Gallic factories had settled in our island. As well, a certain amount was produced in the Rhine valley, especially near Cologne and at Tabernae, but these factories were later in date than the Norman; probably they were established by Syrian workmen, and their products were exported not only into Germany but even as far as the Cimbric peninsula.

Another industry, though a minor one, was the production of terra-cotta images; these were made among the Arverni, at Burdigala, and also in Brittany. This fact may be stressed because together with other evidence it indicates the course of the development of industry in Gaul. At first the South held the primacy, and later, when emperors reigned at Trèves, the centre of interest shifted to the North and North-East; but during the first century the regions of Brittany and Normandy appear to have burst into a vigorous industrial life; it is at any rate noteworthy that not only were the tribes of this district famous for their weaving, but there were the glassworks of Frontinus, the extensive production of iron, and all the trade of Britain. It is not without reason that Claudius paid special attention to the development of the road-system in those parts.

The agricultural riches of the land of Gaul, the degree of civilisation that was attained during the first and second centuries, and the consequent demand for articles of luxury and refinement gave an impetus to foreigners to settle in the country and to take advantages of the opportunities thus offered. A good many Italians took up their residence there, who dealt for the most part in corn, wine, and oil, while Syrians and Asiatic Greeks flocked in to offer the manufactures of the East. At such an important harbour as Burdigala we find a very cosmopolitan gathering; as might be expected, many Spaniards did business there, coming from Bilbilis and other towns of Northern

Spain; for the rest there are German merchants, Greeks
(one hailing from Nicomedia in Bithynia), and of course
Syrians. The federal capital at Lyons was, like Massilia,
a favourite resort for those who had been exiled, but as
well it was a thriving industrial centre; all the imperial
procurators had their bureaux here, and there were iron-
foundries, glass-factories, and pottery-works, while there
resided in the town many merchants for the sale of flax and
linen, and wool and clothing. Here we find a merchant
from Puteoli, and one from Rome, who owned ships sailing from the last-named port, Greeks, and again Syrians
(one of whom was an embroidery merchant), besides the
African glass-worker already mentioned.

Indeed, Syrians and Easterners formed a very large
portion of the foreign population of Gaul, as was only
natural: Gaul was ready to export natural produce and raw
material, corn and cereals, vegetables, fish and animals and
poultry, flax and wool and hides, and in return demanded
the more refined products of a civilisation which she had
begun to admire and assimilate. Hence the Easterners
came in with carpets and rugs from Asia, with gums and
spices from Arabia, rare fruits and fine silks from Syria
and beyond, and glass and paper and scents and cosmetics
from Alexandria and Egypt, or the finely-wrought articles
of precious metal which all the East produced. Thus it is
that we find among the Helvetii a goldsmith who hails from
Lydia, or a Grecian mosaic artist from Puteoli (for Campania, under the Empire, had at least as large a population
of Greeks and Orientals as it had of Italians), a merchant
from Berytus, another from Nicomedia, and fellow-countrymen of his. It would appear, however, that the Syrians did
not go in such numbers West, but frequented the Rhone
valley and that of the Upper Rhine, where the biggest
industrial centres lay. In the West and South-West, too,
local conditions made it natural that the bulk of the import

trade should be carried on by Spaniards from over the border, and that accounts for the number met with at Burdigala or in the various Narbonese towns.

In Gaul itself the traffic between the various centres was extraordinarily busy. Early in the imperial era lamps made at Lugdunum had found their way to the Rhine valley and to the trading centres ("canabae") which rapidly sprang up around the great camps; so, too, had the decorated ware we have already mentioned. It did not necessarily go by the land route; some from North Gaul was shipped at the Northern ports and up to the mouth of the Rhine, at Fectio, and so to its destination. Doubtless the sailors of the Northern rivers had their guilds, though they have not left so many traces; those of Paris, however, raised a magnificent monument during the reign of Tiberius, which shews in what a flourishing condition their finances were. In the South at Burdigala merchants from all parts congregated: traders from among the Treveri, the Bellovaci, the Parisii, the Sequani, and the Ruteni are all named on inscriptions, and it is noticeable that the majority of the traders belong to the Northern tribes; so, too, at Lugdunum we meet with merchants from the Treveri and the Triboci and a cloak-vendor from among the Carnutes; a Trevir is found in business at Agedincum and a Nervian at Cologne; it is obvious that commerce was largely in the control of these energetic Northerners. When we consider the lengthy journeys involved (as from the banks of the Rhine or Moselle to the Garonne), when we recall the export of cheeses from the region of the Menapii to Rome, or the traffic in wool from the same part, and remember Pliny's statement that geese reared by the Morini were driven all the way to Rome on foot, we can form some idea of the many cross-currents of trade, of the noise and crowds along the roads, and we may consider that the expression of Tacitus is not unjust, when he remarks that the roads between the Mediterranean and the Channel hummed with traffic.

Trade from out of Gaul was no less active; the Moselle and the Rhine with their long valleys drained the country of such tribes as the Treveri and the Mediomatrici and carried their goods down to the sea; traffic with Britain was frequent and considerable; we can still read the words with which a merchant in pottery records his thanks to a protecting goddess for having brought him and his wares safely across the sea. Vases from factories at Trèves were carried to London and to other towns, we find traces of merchants who traded with Britain at Cologne and Castel, while stone from quarries near the former town has been found in buildings in the South of our island. Far the greater part, however, of the trade in pottery was undertaken by the agents of the Arvernian factories at Ledosus; these ousted the Rutene manufacturers and for nearly fifty years enjoyed a monopoly, since the Eastern Gallic centres did not rise to prominence till after the first century. Still Rutene wares were exported to towns along the Eastern Spanish coast, such as Emporiae and Saguntum, and to others within easy distance. As regards longer journeys we have evidence (though from a very late author) for voyages to Egypt, and Narbonese pottery has been discovered in that land; as there was a famous medical school at Alexandria we may fairly surmise that the Massiliots, whose inscriptions we find in Egypt, had come there for the purpose of study; but it is not unlikely that men also journeyed there to learn technical processes and improvements in the art of glass-making.

We have now surveyed Gaul and can from this outline form some opinion of its place in the Roman world. Its reputation for wealth was considerable: King Agrippa (according to the account of Josephus), when his people were restive under a foreign rule, asked them if they thought themselves richer than the Gauls, "who possess springs of prosperity in their own country," and in another passage of his speech he referred to them as "flooding the whole world with their goods." There can be no doubt that the inhabitants were prosperous and rich: the tribe of the Arverni, during the reign of Nero, retained the most famous sculptor of the age, Zenodorus, at an enormous fee to make a statue of their native god for the capital. But it was not from any mineral resources of the country that these riches arose: rather it was the agriculture of Gaul and its industry, especially in the Northern regions, that were the important factors. In the North cloth had been woven and garments made from early times, but during the first century pottery factories also began to make an appearance, while the smelting and working of iron held a prominent place in Normandy and Brittany. The South relied more upon its agriculture and its export of wine and oil, though the Arvernian potteries were always important. The resources of the country were undoubtedly large; few could compete with it in natural wealth. In its prosperity and in its unshaken loyalty, together with Spain Gaul formed—as Tacitus well says— the strongest part of the Western domains of the Empire.

CHAPTER TWELVE
BRITAIN

" I would only add one remark, that nowhere
else does the sea make its power more felt :
the tide causes long stretches of the rivers
alternately to ebb and flow, nor does it
simply rise and sink upon the shore, but
it runs far inland, and winds about and
makes its way into the very heart of the
hills and mountain chains, as if the sea were
the lord of all."

TACITUS (trans. Townshend)

"O fortunata et nunc omnibus beatior terris
Britannia."

INCERTI PANEGYRICUS CONSTANTINO DICTUS

BRITAIN

ALTHOUGH the existence of Britain had long been known to the Phoenicians of Gades, who traded with the inhabitants, and although Greeks such as the explorer Pytheas had visited the island and noted both its fertility and its exceptionally moist climate, it is probable that few Romans even knew its name. It is almost certain that the tin which was brought from the mysterious Cassiterides came really from Cornwall, but those merchants who traded in it had every reason for keeping close such a valuable secret, and there is a tale of one Gaditane who deliberately ran his ship aground sooner than let a Roman merchant, who was following him, learn the way there. Yet a great deal of trade was carried on long before Caesar invaded our land: the Veneti had found it very profitable and so were prepared to offer a determined resistance to his advance: when conquered they refused to give any information which would have helped him in his invasion. Roman merchants, too, came hither, but since they knew no more than the coast-line, and even that not very accurately, their goodwill was useless. Yet like all distant lands Britain was supposed to contain fabulous riches: the disappointment of Cicero—and doubtless of other Romans—was great, when he learnt the facts about it. Caesar's campaigns threw a flood of light upon the situation, and give us the first careful account of our island. Gold and silver he found none, but he remarks that there is much lead in the land, though little iron; copper was imported from Gaul, and there was abundance of timber for building or for ships. But it may be doubted whether Caesar's object was really to conquer the island; he did not desire to annex a rich territory to the Empire, but rather to make a demonstration. He had met with much opposition

from Druidism in Gaul and had learnt that Britain was
the centre of training for the priests and their headquarters;
besides this the tribes that dwelt in the South of Britain
and the North of Gaul were closely related and were
continually sending help to each other. For these reasons
he determined to teach them a lesson, and his invasion
doubtless made a considerable impression.

But the impression was by no means lasting; after a few
years most Romans had more urgent matters to consider
than the loyalty of a little-known Northern island, and the
payment of tribute apparently ceased. Trade, however, did
not; we have a full account of how tin was brought from
a spot in Britain called Ictis (probably the Isle of Wight)
across the Channel to Gaul and so by river and down the
valley of the Rhone to Massilia; it was also taken to Narbo,
obviously by way of Burdigala. Gallic coins found at
Falmouth and in the South-Western counties attest the
antiquity of this trade, and later the fact that British coins
bear upon them inscriptions in Latin shews that considerable intercourse continued, and that the barbarians had
begun to understand the meaning of the Roman tongue.
It seemed as though Augustus in the earlier years of his
rule would follow the example of his father and annex the
land, and the contemporary poets have frequent references
to Britain as a country which needs to feel the conquering
arm of Rome; but some distraction nearly always occurred
to prevent this scheme, and in the end it was definitely
dropped, the reason alleged being that the island would
not repay the cost of subjugation and garrisoning. But the
various chieftains and petty kings were sufficiently wise to
send embassies and presents to Rome and Augustus, and
trouble was thus avoided. This policy was regarded as a
precedent by Tiberius and our island was left severely
alone, though it is noteworthy that some men of Germanicus who were wrecked on the East coast were promptly

sent back by the British chiefs. Caligula's vapourings and fantastic parades came to nothing, and it was reserved for Claudius to carry to completion what Caesar had begun. If we are to seek for an explanation, we need not find it in any vanity of the emperor: it is well to reflect that the pretext for the invasion was the exile of a British prince Beric, who fled to Claudius' court for revenge. It must have been he who pointed out to the emperor and his freedmen that Britain was worth the price of conquest, and told them of its hidden treasures of lead and tin; this news would be all the more welcome because by this time the capital had begun to realise that the mineral wealth of Gaul (in the more precious metals certainly) was nearing exhaustion. At any rate less than six years after the conquest the leaden veins of the Mendips were being worked and the ore exported, and after another decade the lead in Flintshire had been discovered.

From the time of the Claudian conquest the province went ahead rapidly, and in any mention of the civilisation of our island one cannot omit the honourable and useful part played by Agricola, who devoted no small part of his time to accustoming the natives to live in towns and adopt Roman habits, and in putting down the usual abuses of a new government. In nearly all places where excavation has been undertaken it has been found that the Flavian era always marked a great increase of activity, and for this we must hold Agricola responsible. It would perhaps be just to say that Britain only reached its full development in the late second and during the third centuries, when its production and export of wheat was of considerable importance, and skilled artisans were to be found in the island, while a constant traffic went on between the mouths of the Thames and of the Rhine: during the period we are studying Britain had not reached its full prosperity. But we have every right to regard Agricola as responsible for the start of Romano-British civilisation and for its success.

To the Romans Britain appeared as a lowland country watered by rivers running through moist plains, while the rest lay covered with marshes and forests: they noted also the fertility resulting from our damp climate. The longer rivers, such as the Severn, the Trent, and the Thames, together with their tributaries divide our country up so thoroughly that all parts are easily accessible and no spot is more than eighty miles from the sea-coast. There were undoubtedly many primitive trackways running through the island, and Stonehenge existed as a centre for trade and forwarding to Ictis long before our written knowledge begins, but it was the Romans who first made durable highways for commerce. Unfortunately, our knowledge for the first period of occupation is very scanty; remains are few, and we have to rely upon odd scraps of evidence for any reconstruction. No milestones of earlier date than Hadrian's reign have survived: for the rest we have to draw deductions from the foundation of colonies and the placing of camps and forts. There can be no doubt that the Eastern quarter of the island was soon developed; within twenty years after the Claudian conquest London was crowded with merchants, and famous for its commerce: the newly-founded colony of Camalodunum must have been connected by road with London and so through Kent with the Channel ports and Gaul. Again during the Claudian campaigns there was a great deal of fighting in the South and South-West in which Vespasian greatly distinguished himself; the fact that the lead of the Mendips was being worked by A.D. 49 and being exported as well points to road-communication with the Southern ports. A few years later one of the imperial legates secured the whole area between the Severn and the Trent, and to this period we can assign the foundation of Isca (in Monmouthshire), of Glevum, and possibly of Lindum as well. Thus the main lines of communication between London, Silchester, Bath, and Caerleon and between London and Lincoln had been laid before A.D. 70 (though the towns were little more than fortresses) and probably the route between London and Chester was already open since the lead-mines of the Decangi in Flintshire were being worked before the Flavian era. The expedition of Suetonius Paulinus to Mona, and the rapidity with which he was able to return and quell the revolt of Boudicca support this hypothesis strongly. The next few years were occupied with the consolidation of what had been won: Frontinus spent much of his time fighting the Silures of South Wales, and we read that he did good work in overcoming the difficulties of the country too, which suggests the construction of roads and causeways and the arrangements for a ferry across the Severn. One of the methods of ensuring peace was the establishment of forts and garrisons as advanced posts in semi-pacified country, and these can scarcely have been left without means of communication with the main camp; not only had the legate all the legions to draw upon for labour, but it appears that the natives also were compelled to give their services for the building of roads through swamp and forest. We have references too to the granaries which were placed at various points along the roads for the collection of the corn-tribute. Later, of course, the existence of the Hadrianic wall implies complete security of communication between the Northern counties and such centres as Deva, Eboracum, and Lindum, and from the Hadrianic period there survive three milestones. Their position is significant; they were found respectively at Conway, near Lancaster, and near Leicester. They go to prove that Hadrian took in hand the repair of the main road along the North Welsh coast (and it should be remembered that Conovium was the point of

departure for the Southern military road), that of the
Northern road towards Carlisle, and that of the North-
Eastern road through Leicester and Lincoln. Thus by the
end of our period England was covered by a network of
roads: London was then, as now, the centre from which
they radiated. The South-West was served by a road that
ran from London through Calleva and Old Sarum to
Dorchester and Exeter; from Calleva various branches led
to Winchester, to Gloucester, and to Bath, and so by ferry
across the Severn to Caerwent and South Wales. A second
road ran through St Albans and then turned West through
the Midlands and so to Wroxeter and Chester; the latter
was an important town and camp, and stood at the junction
of roads for North Wales and Carnarvon and for Lancaster
and Carlisle and the fortresses of the Lake district. A
third road served the Eastern counties, going by way of
Castor and Lincoln to York, whence a continuation led on
to Newcastle and the Great Wall. Besides these main roads
come other minor ones, such as that which led from London
to the Channel ports (Richborough, Dover, and Lympne),
or from London to Colchester, or the Fosse Way which
connected Exeter and Bath with Leicester and Lincoln,
and there were various military roads, which served to
link chains of forts, such as those of Wales or of the Lake
District. The only parts of the country which do not seem
to have been penetrated were Western Devon and Cornwall (though sea-communication probably existed with the
tin-mining districts) and a good portion of Central Wales.
But it may be remarked that the most populous and the
most civilised part of the Roman occupation could be
roughly bounded by a line drawn between Chester and
York: beyond this lay the forts and garrisons of the Lakes
and Northern districts and of the great walls; the roads
here were primarily for military purposes, whereas in the
South they served trade as well. All the important towns,

London, Camalodunum, Calleva, Venta Belgarum, Isca Damnoniorum, Aquae Sulis, Venta Silurum, Glevum, Uriconium, Deva, Ratae, Lindum, and Durobrivae, lay South of the line we have mentioned, the only exceptions of any moment being those of Luguvallum and Corstopitum, which were originally camps. A great part of Northern England was at this time covered with swamp or forest and was suitable neither for ploughing nor for pasturing; also there were no mines and no industry in this district which might have helped to build up towns.

The various means of communication with our island we have already enumerated in the section upon Gaul. Here it will suffice to say that they all had for their starting-point a river estuary, whether of the Garonne, the Loire, the Seine, or the Rhine, though in the latter instance the voyage was not made direct from the mouth but from Portus Itius. This was the harbour that had been used by Caesar for crossing over, and from here or from Gesoriacum the passage was quite short; at the latter port a fleet was stationed by Claudius to protect traffic upon the Channel; the same emperor paid a great deal of attention to the provision of roads and of transport facilities in the Western part of Gaul, as can be deduced from stones found on the routes to Cherbourg and Brest. The constant coming and going of soldiers and merchants must have kept the ports of Gesoriacum and Rutupiae very busy, and we are told by a second-century orator that "hundreds of private people cross over to Britain," some doubtless on visits of pleasure or to take the British waters, but most to buy the corn of the land, or the hides and skins, or the hunting-dogs, which were reputed excellent.

The moist climate of the island made crops plentiful, and the chief one was corn. In Caesar's time it was only sown in the South, but its culture must have been spreading rapidly, for half a century later it was being exported,

though we cannot say whether the export was great. The
soil was very fertile though the crops were rather late;
under Agricola the corn was exacted as part of the tribute,
and stored in granaries throughout the land. The Roman
rule aimed at extending the boundaries of the cultivated
land and persuading the tribesmen to take up agriculture
and farming; in other provinces we have watched the
experiment being tried, and in Britain too it was successful:
the production of grain grew larger and larger and in the
fourth century the emperor Julian was able to transport
great quantities of corn to the Rhine for the succour of a
famine-stricken land.

Among other articles of export Strabo mentions hides
and fleeces, cattle and flocks, slaves and hunting-dogs; the
latter were renowned for speed and fierceness, while the
geese of Britain were considered a great dainty. The olive
and vine and other Southern fruits would not grow in our
soil, but the cherry (originally an importation of Lucullus
from Pontus) and also the apple had both been brought to
the island and acclimated by the end of the first century,
and doubtless various other common fruits and species of
nuts were brought here by enterprising knights and merchants.

In regard to minerals, Strabo declares that gold, silver,
and iron were all exported, and the same list is given us
by Tacitus as being the "prize of victory." Curiously
enough, neither writer refers directly to the tin, which
had been for years before the Roman conquest a notable
article of export. Gold was obtained from the quartz rocks
near Lampeter, while silver-refineries are known to have
existed at Calleva, and ingots of silver have been found
near London and near Richborough, testifying to the
export of that metal. But though these precious metals
were rare and not found in sufficient quantities for the
Romans, lead was present in abundance; it was indeed the

most important article of export, being mined with the greatest ease, for, according to Pliny, one only had to scratch the soil to discover deposits; in fact, so large was the output, even immediately after the conquest, that a law was passed (doubtless upon the representations of mining companies in Spain) limiting the amount that could be brought out. As early as A.D. 49 the mines of the Mendips were being worked and pigs of lead inscribed with the imperial name have been found there; in other parts of the country veins were soon opened up, as at Wroxeter, and in Flintshire (whence it was taken South by way of Chester), as well as near Tamworth, and at the Metallum Lutudarense near Matlock. In later years there seems reason to believe that the metals of the North-West were exported from Chester, where there was a harbour, or from the Mersey (if that river had its present mouth). For not only was lead to be found in the district but copper also was mined extensively in North Wales. On the other hand, a mystery seems to overhang the problem of British tin; neither Strabo nor Tacitus mention it as an export, though we know from other authors that it was obtained from our island before; there was indeed a very small Roman settlement near Bodmin, dating from the late first century, which *may* be connected with the tinworks close by, but we can be certain that this mining was not pursued very actively until the late third or fourth century, and so far there has been but one piece of tin found in the West Country in contrast to the mist of legend and conjecture that has grown up about the commerce of it. On the other hand, iron was comparatively plentiful and was worked in several places; carpenters' tools, hammers, axes, saws, chisels, files, tools for farriers and shoemakers, shears, scythes, knives, padlocks and various other implements made from iron have been found all over the country, and we have remains that shew that iron was worked in Sussex and by the Forest of Dean. In that region within recent years excavations have been made on a site which must have been of some importance; near Ross, at the ancient site of Ariconium, there have been uncovered remains that indicate that a great industry was pursued there; iron was smelted and forged and worked into various implements and an industrial town had grown up round the ironworks; it has indeed been called a third-century Birmingham by the excavator. Further reports from this site will be awaited with much interest.

There were, however, several other articles of export from Britain which were prized by the Romans; as usual there had been exaggerated anticipations of the wealth which would result from the conquest; Seneca, in an early work, calls upon Claudius to open Britain to Roman trade: this was done, but the island was opened at the same time to the less welcome attentions of the Roman usurer, which were soon to cause trouble. There was a good export trade in wool and cloth; even in Strabo's time the sheep of Britain had been exported, and the country was peculiarly fitted for pasturage. We find reference to woollens being manufactured at Venta Belgarum, and in the Edict of Diocletian British cloth is mentioned together with the North Gallic products. Besides making woollens, the inhabitants naturally dyed them; although they had no shellfish, such as had made a great trade along the Phoenician or Mauretanian coast, they did possess vege-table and lichen dyes, which they used with skill. Traces of dyeing works have been found at various spots in the country and especially at Silchester. Other articles of export were baskets made from the willows and osiers of the marshland, and taken to Rome, where they were often given as small presents. From the point of view of the epicure, however, the most important thing exported was the famous British oyster, from the regions around

Rutupiae, which met with great praise; the pearls found
in them, however, had proved a disappointment since
they were of too dark a colour to command a really high
price.

Clay was also found in sufficient quantities for the making
of local pottery; but the industry in Arretine never developed as it had in Gaul. Presumably it never had a
chance, since the market was flooded with foreign wares
from the start. Even before the Claudian invasion the
products of Italian (and later of Rutene and Arvernian)
craftsmen had found their way to London and up to
Cambridge and along the Thames valley, while during the
whole of the Roman occupation the greater part of the
pottery used in the island came from the ovens of Ledosus,
while the North was supplied from the Eastern Gallic
centres; even in such a remote part as the village of Din
Lligwy, in Anglesey, fragments of Arretine ware have been
discovered among the ruins. But there were some native
manufacturies, such as those at Castor, near Peterborough,
which distributed its wares over a fairly wide area; it is
probable that the industry started here and spread to the
Continent, but the question does not admit at present of
a definite solution. There was also the stoneware of the
New Forest which was used a great deal in the South of
the island, and also the ware named after Upchurch in
Kent, where it was first discovered in any quantity; no
kilns have been found there, however, and it is probable
that the centre of manufacture was at Higham, near by.
But taken all in all such pottery as was produced mostly
served purely local uses, and the cultivated Roman Briton
preferred to buy for his table the more expensive imported
wares of Lezoux or of La Graufesenque.

We have mentioned the remarkable development of
London, and this is not a solitary instance; Camulodunum
had a large population of traders and business men;

among these were doubtless the agents of Seneca, who is reputed to have had immense sums of money out at usury in the different provinces; it was even hinted that the calling in of his loans occasioned indirectly the rising of Boudicca. But the rumour comes from a tainted source. There can be no doubt, however, of the great throng of merchants who made the voyage to Britain, especially from the lands of the Rhine valley, with the pottery and stone of the district. Inscriptions of such men are frequent at such places as Cologne and Castel, and at Walcheren we have a tablet erected by a pottery-merchant, wherein he thanks some strange goddess for having preserved his life and his wares on the voyage to Britain. Although goods from Trèves and Rheinzabern and Heiligenberg were taken to the South of the island and have been found at London, they encountered competition here from the Gallic agents, and the greater part of their trade must have been with Eboracum and Corstopitum and the North, probably by the Humber and Tyne valleys. But the competition of the wares from the South of Gaul was very keen. Even before the conquest Italian vases had found their way to Britain, and their import did not cease entirely until after the Flavian era. Then it was replaced by the productions of the South Gallic ovens, which spread all over the country. They have been found even as far North as the fort of Balmuildy on the Scottish wall, which was only occupied for a short time. Their importation reached a height during the age of the Antonines, and the quantity of pottery made at Lezoux and found in this country is far greater than that from any other centre.

Thus the number of merchants engaged in sailing to or from Britain must have been considerable: already in the Augustan age Horace tells of men who have sailed many times into the Atlantic: by the second century an orator can speak of the hundreds of private persons who cross over to Britain on various errands. But we should naturally assume that the greater part of these came from neighbouring lands, and this appears to be borne out by inscriptions. Thus we find (in London) traders from the North Gallic tribes, a Mediomatrix and a Sequane, and of course a Trevir. But other nationalities do occur: thus at Lindum a Greek was established, and even in the North we find the inevitable Syrian, this time a man named Barates from distant Palmyra. Doubtless he traded in the silks and spices and dried fruits of his native land, for among the finds on various sites have been the dried prune-kernels for which Damascus was famous. And in the end Britain paid well for what she had received: she became one of the most important provinces of the West. Later authors speak enthusiastically of the multitude of sheep pasturing on the island and the amount of wool which was exported; and artisans and carpenters could be found in plenty, and were often sent over to the Continent. More still our land gained renown as one from which the much-needed corn was despatched; a late historian speaks of the supply which was usually brought across from Britain, and British corn enabled Julian to check a German famine.

Thus trading activity penetrated the whole island, and went even further; certain very adventurous merchants crossed the sea and landed upon the shores of Ireland, bringing back news of the country and information about the shore-line and the harbours. Indeed, some attempt was apparently made to subjugate it. But Agricola must have been a man of unusually sanguine temperament if he thought that one Roman legion and some few auxiliary troops would be sufficient for the conquest and garrisoning of that island. Juvenal declares that Roman arms had been carried beyond the shores of Juverna. Tacitus' statement that the shores of the land were known by merchants is borne out by coin-finds there—the greater part of them have been unearthed, as we might expect, in the North of Ireland, where the sea-passage to Scotland is short and easy; most of the coins belong to the age of Trajan and Hadrian, and to later epochs; the earliest so far discovered is Neronian. Systematic excavation is almost certain to bring more information. Till then we must wait.

We have dealt with Britain somewhat more briefly than with the other provinces, because it only reached its full development at a later date than we are considering, and also because more information upon the subject is readily available; roads and routes have been discussed in more than one excellent monograph and in numerous local antiquarian publications. Yet much remains to be done. A man can walk but few miles from his own home without striking some track that was originally laid under Roman supervision, some camp built by the Roman soldiers, or some town wherein Roman civilisation flourished. No task can be more pleasant than to follow the road where it leads, whether it be down from the Welsh hills to the Severn ferry, or straight as a die across the level spaces of Lincolnshire, or up the sides of some Cumbrian fell. Many are still in use; the main lines of communication are but little changed; though much has perished the roads remain, a direct legacy from Roman occupation.

CONCLUSION

"Sed et mundus pacem habet per
Romanos, et nos sine timore in
viis ambulamus et navigamus
quocunque voluerimus."

IRENAEUS

" καὶ οὔτε Πύλαι Κιλικίαι φόβον παρ-
έχουσιν οὔτε στεναὶ καὶ ψαμμώδεις
δι᾿ Ἀράβων ἐπ᾿ Αἴγυπτον πάροδοι,
οὐκ ὄρη δύσβατα, οὐ ποταμῶν ἄπειρα
μεγέθη...ἀλλ᾿ εἰς ἀσφάλειαν ἐξαρκεῖ
Ῥωμαῖον εἶναι μᾶλλον δὲ ἕνα τῶν
ὑφ᾿ ὑμῖν."

ARISTIDES

We have no fear now either of
the Cilician Pass or of the narrow
tracks through the Arabian sands
into Egypt, we are not dismayed
by the height of mountains or
the breadth of rivers....To be a
Roman citizen, nay, even to be
one of your subjects, is a sufficient
guarantee of personal safety.

WE have now completed our survey of the provinces of the Roman Empire, and have seen what were the nature and the extent of its resources; we have examined briefly the means of communication available during the first two centuries of its existence; we have watched the merchants and traders of various nationalities in their travels between the different countries, exchanging their goods and wares, and have passed even beyond the bounds of the Empire to observe by what routes the silks and spices of China or India reached Roman purchasers, or how the amber and hides of the Baltic coast were brought to the centre of Italy. There can be no doubt that great opportunities lay open to business men during this period, and that much activity prevailed. Philo declares that "at the present day in our search for wealth we ransack every corner of the earth, and dig our mines in plain and mountainside to discover gold and silver, copper and iron, or precious stones," while Seneca bewails the fact that "desire of trafficking drags a man headlong over every land and sea in the hope of making gain." It was a time of large developments in commerce, like the early nineteenth century.

Comparisons are often instituted between ancient and modern commerce, not always with justice to the former. The first difference that occurs to anyone is of course the vastly increased speed with which articles of commerce can be conveyed between country and country. Yet to concentrate attention upon such a point is wrong. It is true that we may congratulate ourselves that where an ancient sailing-vessel with a favourable wind might keep up a steady average of five knots, a modern tramp can maintain twelve to fifteen, but the difference is only one of degree, not of kind. The real alteration has been brought about by the use of electricity; it is not in the transport of goods but in the transmission of news that a change has occurred. The early nineteenth century was little better off than the Roman world as regards the time taken by letters and news, which had always to be brought by a courier or letter-carrier of some sort; but now we have eliminated the personal element (that is the carrying of documents) and the advent of wireless telegraphy has introduced a change in the habits and minds of men, which we can only dimly realise at present. In the olden days a general—say Corbulo in Armenia—had very full powers delegated to him, despatches travelled slowly, and the emperor could make up his mind at leisure as to what reinforcements to send: the wealthy business magnate of Rome or of Alexandria would send out his fleet of ships or his caravan, handing over all responsibility to the captain or leader, and then would wait in hope for news; he could afford to take long views and think out his decisions. But now a merchant in Liverpool can learn from his agents within a quarter of an hour of an advantageous parcel of cotton waiting at Galveston, and has to make up his mind in as short a time whether he will risk buying or not; in the sphere of international politics the utterances of statesmen, whether enthusiastic or gloomy, pacific or threatening, are learned almost as soon as they have been made, and minds are apt to be governed by the passion or excitement of the moment; there is no time for a statesman to think slowly and come to a cool decision. In comparison with this momentous change, which means that men have to be flurried and worried to adjust their minds to a celerity of decision at which our grandfathers would have gasped, all those other differences which are so often paraded—the substitution of free for slave labour, mechanical improvements, the factory-system, and so on— appear rather small, for the Romans possessed the germ of all of them.

Yet the perils of land and sea could never be entirely overcome. On land there was always the risk of robbery or of confinement in "ergastula": Largus relates how the steward of a certain Calvisius, after escaping from shipwreck, reached shore only to be imprisoned in this way. Under good emperors the evil was suppressed, but it was liable to break out again in disturbed times. Both Augustus and Tiberius dealt with it severely, and the slave-dungeons were carefully inspected to discover cases of wrongful imprisonment; Hadrian finally abolished them. After the wars of the triumvirs bands of footpads infested lonely places—such as the Pomptine marshes—but they were gradually stamped out and peaceful intercourse made possible.

On sea, sailing in winter was considered perilous: ships were usually beached during the stormy season and only the most urgent business would take them abroad. We read in Josephus that the approach of winter made voyaging risky, and that the fear of a winter voyage induced Mucianus to march the Vespasianist troops round through Cappadocia and Phrygia instead of taking them by sea to Greece; it is typical of the wild and passionate nature of the elder Agrippina that in her vehement grief she would not let even winter storms deter her from putting to sea: St Paul on his voyage to Rome was compelled by adverse weather to winter in Melita. Spring is often hailed by the poets as the season when the boats are brought down again to the water.

Again lack of steam-power prevented ancient vessels from making headway against strong contrary winds; the blowing of the Etesian winds, which lasted about six weeks, practically cut off Rome from all news of Alexandria during that time, as Caesar and Vespasian both found; the only way to reach the capital was to creep slowly along the Asiatic coast and take advantage of every local wind. The region of the Hellespont was very bad for contrary winds and strong currents; thus we find Herod, who was hastening after Agrippa, being held up for some days at Cos, by strong head winds. The Mediterranean has a sinister, and deserved, renown for its sudden storms; these swept down upon the unhappy Claudius in the Gulf of Lyons, when he was on his way to subdue Britain, and nearly drowned him off the Stoechades, while death actually befell the Vitellian general Valens, when he was endeavouring to make his escape by this way to Gaul. These were all, however, disadvantages inherent in the use of wind-power and before the advent of steam our own forefathers were scarcely better off.

Piracy was another evil against which Augustus had to contend, just as even in the early nineteenth century the pirates of Algiers gave trouble. In the record of his life-work he could write: "mare pacavi a praedonibus." If there had been no other motives the instinct of self-preservation must have urged the emperors to take an interest in ships and harbours, for it was upon the ships of the corn-fleet that they relied in order to keep the populace of Rome contented. Thus Augustus took particular pains to keep the irrigation channels of Egypt in good order, using even military labour, and a law was passed during his reign which laid severe penalties upon anyone who did anything to hinder the corn-supply, or entered into any combination with the object of raising its price, or hindered or delayed the sailing of a corn-ship. His successor, Tiberius, offered bounties to corn-merchants, and a speech of his shews that he was fully alive to the dependence of Italy for its food upon the winds and waves. To mitigate the danger of the Sicilian straits for these ships Caligula is said to have contemplated the construction of harbours of refuge, but the scheme was never completed. During the reign of Claudius at one time there was only fifteen days' supply left in the city, and the emperor promised definite rewards to all who would sail during the winter, guaranteeing them against loss or damage by storm, and held out various privileges to all who would build ships. Later, Nero, among other enactments, declared that owners of corn-ships should not be liable to have them included in the assessment of their total property. Both Claudius and Nero paid attention to the improvement of the port facilities at Ostia, which were not too good, for in the latter's reign we hear of ships being sunk by a violent storm even in the harbour itself. But a very great advance was made, as in other departments, by the businesslike Trajan. Measures were taken to ensure regular sailing, the corn was carefully stored in properly constructed granaries, and so large was the surplus that once on the occasion of a famine in Egypt the grain-ships were able to return at once to Alexandria to succour the population.

Quite apart from measures in connection with the corn trade we have enough definite evidence to enable us to state boldly that the emperors took a real interest in trade and did all they could to encourage it. Thus Claudius undertook the widening and improvement of the port at Ostia and the building of a lighthouse, and it was the same emperor who stationed a fleet at Gesoriacum (where his predecessor had already set a lofty beacon for the guidance of mariners) in order to protect channel trade. One of the earliest exploits of Nero was to dig a new harbour for his native town of Antium, which enjoyed a busy trade, and he also projected the making of a canal from Ostia to the city itself, in order to improve navigation between the capital and its port. The policy of retrenchment inaugurated by Vespasian would not permit much expenditure upon public works, and it was reserved for Trajan to give a splendid opening to a new era by the construction of great harbours for Italy; we hear of activity on his part at

no less than three places: thus he greatly enlarged the
Claudian port at Ostia and provided it with vast moles and
a breakwater to protect ships against the violence which
they had so often experienced there, and he constructed
an entirely new port at Centumcellae; we possess a letter
of Pliny's describing the building of it, from which we can
see that it was carried out on a generous scale. Finally he
provided a harbour on the East coast at Ancona, and thus
made the approach to Italy safer, as the inscription on the
local arch informs us. All these works of his go together
with his laying of roads and purification of the coinage,
and the result was an immense impetus given to commerce.
And there were other schemes, even grander, which unfortunately it was given to none of the emperors to realise;
both Caligula and Nero had thought of cutting through
the isthmus of Corinth, anticipating the modern canal, and
it comes as a surprise to us to find that the later emperors
did not take it in hand. Probably the reason is to be found
in the comparative smallness of the vessels of those days,
which could be easily brought across the isthmus on rollers;
even if not, the unloading of its cargo and the portage to
the other side would not entail the same relative trouble
and expense as nowadays.

The work of the Romans upon roads was no whit less
important. It is possible that too great stress is laid upon
the fact of their making roads, and not enough credit given
to the previous inhabitants; recent research has shewn
fairly conclusively that the natives of Britain and Gaul had
a good system of inter-communication, well aligned and
laid out, but that does not make the achievement of the
Romans any the less remarkable. Instead of mere paths
or cart-tracks on soft and spongy ground, liable to floods
and landslides, they provided a broad paved stone track,
direct and well aligned, and properly drained, fit for the
movement of large bodies of troops and men, and able to

withstand the wear and tear of constant traffic; in some places (as in Syria) where the black basalt of the region might have proved too hard, a softer road-bed was specially laid. Augustus saw the need for the construction of new roads and for the repair of the old ones; Rome was to lie at the centre of a great system of ways stretching out to the farthest outposts of the Empire, and placing her in speedy communication with them. He himself set about the repair of the important Via Flaminia, which led out from the city Northwards, and allotted the other roads to various high nobles. He also instituted an imperial post or news-system, whereby messages of importance were brought by specially selected couriers or drivers; the roads were divided into convenient lengths, and provided with resting-houses and stables. The cost of maintenance appears to have fallen upon the country through which the roads ran, and the tax was very unpopular, even Italy being called upon to contribute to it; Claudius attempted without success to alter the system, for later we find Nerva remitting the tax, and making it one of the imperial charges. The amount of traffic that passed along these roads is shewn by the frequency with which they had to be repaired; sometimes the restoration is mentioned upon the milestone, but more often the stone has been entirely recarved, and so the date of construction is left doubtful. In the reign of Tiberius an ex-praetor protested against the bad condition of the Italian roads, and he was entrusted with their repair. The same emperor was so keenly interested in their upkeep, that he endeavoured to secure for that purpose some money that had been left to the people of Trebia for a theatre, but was defeated; his nephew Claudius even employed gladi-ators upon road-making. Wherever there was a region to be developed, and where trade would follow, there we find the emperors providing communication; Tiberius provided a special road to the gold-mines in Spain which he had confiscated, and both he and succeeding emperors constructed a regular network of roads to serve the rich mineral district of Asturia and Gallaecia. Similarly, the North-Western district of Gaul, which was full of iron ore and also provided easy access to Britain, was given roads by Claudius and much was done to open up the country: we may compare the new road that was laid down by Hadrian in Egypt, communicating with the Red Sea, and providing a more level and safe route than the old one. The frontier road constructed by his predecessor, Trajan, in Arabia Petraea received all the traffic that flowed to Damascus and the towns of the North from Aila and the ports of the Red Sea. The whole road-system of Asia Minor was thoroughly reorganised by the autocratic emperor Domitian; even where roads had been constructed primarily for military purposes traffic soon came to use them.

The policy of the Flavian and succeeding dynasties was to perfect the system of communication between the Rhine, Danube, and the Euphrates; it was along the Northern and Eastern frontiers that the real dangers lay, and it was here that quick transport of troops became absolutely essential. Hence the activity of these emperors in Germany, Pannonia, and Moesia, and in Bithynia, Pontus, and the border marches of Armenia; hence too in later years the gradual emergence of Constantinople as the inevitable capital for an Empire which wished to be able to move its armies upon interior lines to strike at the savage hordes of North-Eastern Europe or against the Parthians and Persians. Trajan stands out as one of the great organising figures of the Empire, a second founder equal to Augustus: there was scarcely a province which did not benefit from his activity. We know of his great bridge over the Danube and the roads that he constructed to serve his Dacian campaigns, but many useful works were executed in Italy itself, such as the draining of the Pomptine marshes and the making of a way through them. In fact a thorough revision of the roads of the Empire was carried out: those that were worn and out of repair, with bad surface, climbing steep passes and liable to flood by rivers, were replaced by solid roadways with stone paving and proper drainage; rivers were spanned by bridges, causeways were thrown over marshy or insecure ground, shorter ways were found, gradients lessened, valleys filled and hills cut through. In connection with all this building stands his construction of harbours, his care of the corn-supply and his purification of the coinage: these measures and their importance for trade cannot be overestimated.

Pliny has laid it down as a principle that Roman generals on their campaigns gave especial thought to trade, and though this sentiment may not be true of the early republic we cannot doubt its applicability to the Empire. We may instance Nero, who sent instructions for the erection of shops and shelters along the military road through Thrace, and who in the first years of his reign had made proposals for something like the establishment of free trade throughout the whole Empire, proposals which were met by heavy advice from his astonished counsellors. The founder of the Empire himself, Augustus, had certainly cherished schemes for the subjugation of Arabia and the control of the precious freights that came from that country; hence the expedition of Aelius Gallus, which only miscarried through native treachery; hence later the intention that his grandson, Gaius, should inaugurate his career by some striking conquest; a Roman fleet operated in the Red Sea, a handbook was drawn up by the learned Juba, and the explorer Dionysius of Charax (if this is not a slip for Isidore) was specially despatched to the Orient by the emperor. So, too, with the Southern regions; the gold and reputed riches of Aethiopia tempted the Roman rulers, and Petronius was sent on an expedition against the country. Seventy years later the project was renewed by Nero, and in order to carry out a preliminary survey a small party was sent up the Nile, and returned with a map and some curious information. Again, during the first century of the Empire we observe a gradual reaching out towards the region of the Tauric Chersonese and an attempt to gain possession of the once rich corn lands. The Euxine was to become a Roman lake; after Nero's abolition of client-princes in the region of Pontus and Lesser Armenia there came the expedition of Plautius Silvanus, the governor of Moesia, to the help of the Bosporan kingdom against peoples unknown to Rome: it is significant that the same governor first sent a great quantity of grain from his province. Later the Bosporan kingdom was annexed and garrisons placed in various parts, while a fleet of forty ships enforced peace upon a once dangerous sea. But Nero intended to carry his conquests even further East; an invasion of the Caucasus was meditated by him, and achieved by Vespasian a few years later; a small force was established at Harmozica to control the trade-route up the Cyrus valley, and in the reign of Hadrian garrisons were established at various points to protect traders. A way was thus found to circumvent the Parthian control of the Eastern trade. The Periplus of Arrian is an informal document, but in it he refers to a governmental paper which had been despatched to Hadrian, and many such reports were received from the various legates, and filed in the imperial offices. We can be sure that the work of such men as Juba, or Dionysius, or Isidore, the papers of such governors as Suetonius Paulinus (on his African expedition), or Agricola, or Plautius Silvanus, or Arrian were carefully preserved. And doubtless the labours of such savants as Strabo, or Marinus of Tyre, or Ptolemy, if not encouraged in their inception were rewarded upon accomplishment by grateful rulers: Agrippa in drawing up his map made use of the best scientific brains of the day, such as could be found at Alexandria and at the other great centres of learning. Vitruvius mentions large maps of the world in Rome, and we have still preserved the inscription of a legionary who had been sent on survey work in Egypt. Much of the most valuable labour of the geographers must have consisted in collecting and codifying the information sent home by imperial legates: in the lost work of Marinus there was an account of a march made by Septimius Flaccus across the desert to Aethiopia, and of an expedition in which the Roman commander, Julius Maternus, accompanied the king of the Garamantes over the Sahara to some mysterious country. It may be true to say that the Romans conquered the world without maps; to assert that they ruled it without them is absurd and contrary to all known facts.

We have already seen how swiftly merchants and traders had spread over the provinces. But it was not only the mercantile classes that profited by the peace and security given by the Empire; the very agents of it, the soldiers themselves, found time to indulge in advantageous selling of wares to ignorant natives; great markets were often held outside the frontier camps, and gradually there grew up settlements there, called "canabae," where all could buy and sell; these settlements were the germ out of which developed important towns. When a legionary left the service, a well-meaning government presented him with a tract of land in some country, and expected him to till it; but the veteran soon found it much more profitable to forsake the monotony of farming and return to the province wherein he had served and was known, to the travel and excitement of a merchant's life. Apart from such soldiers and from the smaller provincial or Italian traders there were the men of money who joined together in companies for the exploitation of a district or the working of a mine, as at Sisapo and elsewhere, and knights who had large financial interests in the various provinces often resided there for some time, even neglecting their duties in the capital. These business men had penetrated everywhere; in India they had erected at one of the busiest ports, Muziris, a temple to the divinity which they chiefly revered, the Fortune of Rome and Augustus; the pages of the Periplus and of Ptolemy are sufficient evidence for the number of voyagers to that country and for the information which they brought back. In the opposite half of the world, by the second century of our era, they had pressed on into Ireland and brought back news of its harbours and coast; in the Atlantic the fishers from Gades and the Southern Spanish towns went far down the Western coast of Africa, as did the dealers in Gaetulian purple; others turned North and circumnavigated the coast of Spain to take in cargoes at Brigantium from the mineral district of the North-West, to anchor at the busy port of Burdigala, or to thread their way in and out of the rivers and islands along the shores of Brittany and Normandy, and ultimately to reach Britain: an orator of the second century declares that hundreds of people—apart from the military forces—cross over to Britain, and that the sea is covered with ships. In North-Eastern and Central Europe Italians were often met, especially at the court of the Suebic king, Maroboduus, whither tempting terms had attracted them; pottery and vases from Gallic manufactures have been discovered as far North as the province of Posen, and there was the venture of the unnamed Roman knight to reach the Baltic and the depôts of the amber trade. Romans were to be found in the Tauric Chersonese, and also upon the Black Sea especially at such ports as Phasis and the others which were near to the mouth of the river and which received the traffic coming up from the Caspian. Pliny, too, speaks of men who have made the journey down the Euphrates to ports such as Charax and Vologesias and brought back information, and the itinerary of Isidore is an example of a type of hand-book which must have been common.

Something of the stigma attaching to trade was slowly disappearing. One of the main features of the Empire, as has been noticed, is the gradual breakdown and decay of the old noble families and their replacement by a new aristocracy dependent upon and devoted to the Emperor. But we may note also the rise of a new class, almost corresponding to our professional class of to-day; we can observe it in the honours paid to physicians and to teachers, in the position held by a man like Galen or Dioscorides, Seneca or Quintilian. It was no longer so shameful to engage in business. Domitius Afer, who made a fortune and reputation under Tiberius, was the owner of some brickyards; his heirs profited probably by the great fire at Rome and the subsequent building activity, and greatly enlarged their business; ultimately it came into the hands of Marcus Aurelius, and helped much to enrich the imperial estate. Again, from the Histories of Tacitus, we learn of a woman called Calvia Crispinilla, who appears to have been a favourite at Nero's court; she is described as rich and influential. How she gained her influence it is not our task to enquire, but we need not doubt that much of her wealth was due to the very successful trade, which she carried on through her freedmen agents in the exportation of oil and wine and other liquids to the North: large amphorae bearing her trade-mark (so to speak) have been found in various places along the route to the Danube, as at Tergeste and near Poetovio. The time was one when men were prepared to embark on large enterprises in order to gain a profit. Indeed, when the emperor himself set

an example we cannot be surprised if his subjects were
inclined to follow. In Egypt, as we have already seen, he
was at the head of a vast business concern: no seed could
be sown, no crops reaped, no corn bought or sold, without
the imperial permission exercised through his agents; the
manufacture of beer, and bricks, and cosmetics, and of
other articles was an imperial monopoly. A client-prince
followed his example, and Juba of Mauretania, besides
indulging in liberal studies, increased his revenues by
working purple-factories off the coast of Gaetulia. Then
again there is the mysterious Annius Plocamus (who was
surely a Greco-Egyptian), of whom little is known beyond the fact that he had bought up the collection of
the Red Sea taxes; it was his freedman who was caught
and blown by a monsoon to Ceylon, a detail which
shews that in collecting the dues he must have voyaged
at least as far as Aden; possibly the reduction of Arabia
Eudaemon (mentioned in the Periplus) had already taken
place.

If we endeavour to estimate the relative importance of
the provinces to Rome, a very obvious line of distinction
soon forces itself upon us. It is, roughly speaking, that the
East was the region of industry and manufacture, and the
West the great storehouse of raw material. It is true that
a certain amount of raw material was brought from the
East, but the mines there were exhausted and worked out:
the red lead of Ephesus was reputed to be the best in the
world, but much the greater part of Rome's supply came
from Spain. Some of the Oriental fruits too had been
transplanted to the West with some success; Galen declares
that the Damascene plums were rivalled by the Spanish.
The West was the richest region for mineral deposits; in
wealth of gold and silver, of copper and lead, of tin and
iron, and of other metals it excelled. On the other hand,
the East was unrivalled for its manufactures; cloaks and

blankets and garments, rugs and tapestries and carpets, were all made there, together with pottery of the finest kind, and glass vessels, both cheap and expensive; scents, perfumes, and cosmetics, jewellery and ornaments, rare and fragrant spices and gums, all came from the marts of Damascus or Antioch or Alexandria. Yet during the first two centuries of the Empire a gradual movement of industry took place Westward; skilled Greeks, Syrians or Egyptians, determined to ply their trade nearer to the centre of demand; in the Western provinces, in Gaul and Spain and Africa, wealth had been acquired by the owners of cornland or by the possessors of mines, and this wealth the provincials were ready to surrender in return for artistic and fashionable products. It was the familiar tale of the new rich desiring " culture " and polish: Greek and Syrian doctors, literary men, artists, sculptors, and musicians were only too ready to supply their wants, and Eastern glassware, pottery, mosaic-work, jewellery, and other articles of luxury and refinement were welcomed. If a man reads through the inscriptions of physicians and artists, or the monuments of the dealers in jewellery and scents and precious stones, he will be surprised to find how large a majority of them bear Greek or Asian names. In Gaul numerous Syrians are encountered; one enterprising Palmyrene had travelled as far as Britain to do business; there is the Syrian colony at Malaca, and a copy of an inscription dealing with the shipowners of Arelate has been found on Lebanon. Many craftsmen were attracted to the Western centres of manufacture: the quicksilver-melters of Ephesus migrated to Rome, Alexandrians flocked Westwards, and musicians from Egypt are found upon the banks of the Rhine. Some hardy Alexandrians even journeyed to Rome to earn a living as gladiators.

Thus over lands that had been pacified and secured by

Roman arms and upon seas that had been freed from piracy by Roman ships we see a stream of traffic flowing; merchants and traders of every nationality were passing and repassing. Within the Empire itself long voyages and journeys were made; without, men penetrated to far-distant lands, and the Roman name became known far and wide. The agents of the Roman business man had reached Ireland and touched the margin of the Baltic Sea, knew the Scythians of the Tauric Chersonese, and had met the Chinese traders beyond the lonely Stone Tower of Tash-kurgan, had bought and sold in the marts of India, and bartered goods with the Aethiopians. The purity and good standard of the Roman coinage, the prowess of the Roman armies, the fair-dealing of the Roman merchants every-where commanded respect. Much the same was the record of the British trader in Eastern lands. We are reminded how a Persian sage, during the war, discussing the situation with a British officer, gave his verdict upon the modern European nations: "Should the Germans be beaten," he said, "we should be without Science, and perhaps that would be no great loss; should the French be conquered, we should have to forego Art and Letters, and that would be grievous; but if the British should be defeated, we should be left without Justice, and Justice we cannot afford to lose."

This unceasing intercourse, this far-reaching interchange of goods and products, was a result of the beneficent policy of the emperors, and is one of the surest proofs of the utility of the government exercised by them and of the health of the Empire. Augustus realised that the right ordering of an empire is of far more importance and difficulty than the winning of it, and both he and his successors laboured hard for the welfare of their subjects, a fact which was not always appreciated by the writers of the day. What the result was we have endeavoured to portray in the preceding pages. For two whole centuries a large portion—by far the most civilised—of the ancient world enjoyed more peace and prosperity than it has known ever since. This is no mean achievement for any government, and we can echo the words of the elder Pliny: "the might of the Roman Empire has given unity to the world; all must agree that human life has benefited, both in the general intercourse made possible, and in the common enjoyment of the blessings of peace."

LIST OF ABBREVIATIONS

Ac. des Ins. et B.-L. = Académie des Inscriptions et Belles-Lettres.
Acts = The Acts of the Apostles.
ad Att. = Cicero, Epistulae ad Atticum.
ad Fam. = Cicero, Epistulae ad Familiares.
A.E., Ann. Épig. = *L'Année Épigraphique.*
Aelian, De Nat. Anim. = Aelian, De Natura Animalium.
Agric. = Tacitus, Agricola.
A.J.A. = *American Journal of Archaeology.*
Amm. Marc., Ammian. = Ammianus Marcellinus.
Ann., Annals = Tacitus, Annales.
App. Bell. Civ. = Appian, Bellum Civile.
App. Bell. Ill. = Appian, Bellum Illyricum.
Archaeol. = *Archaeologia.*
Arch. Cambrensis = Archaeologia Cambrensis.
Archiv = *Archiv für Papyrusforschung.*
Aristides, Orat. Aeg. = Aristides, Oratio Aegyptia (Dindorf).
Arrian, Anabasis = Arrian, Anabasis Alexandri.
Arrian, Perip. = Arrian, Periplus Maris Euxini.
Aug. = Suetonius, Vita Augusti.
Aur. Vict. = Aurelius Victor.

B.A. = Caesar, Bellum Africanum.
B.C. = Caesar, Bellum Civile.
Bell. Hisp. = (Caesar), Bellum Hispaniense.
B.G.U. = *Berliner Griechische Urkunde.*
Boletin = *Boletin de la real Academia de la Historia* (Madrid).
Bonn. Jahrb. = *Bonner Jahrbücher.*
Brambach = Brambach, Corpus Inscriptionum Transrhenanarum.
Bull. Archéol. = *Bulletin Archéologique du comité des travaux* (Paris).
Bullet. Comunale = *Bulletino Comunale* (Rome).

Cag.-Laf., C.-L. = Cagnat-Lafaye, Inscriptiones Graecae ad Res Romanas pertinentes.
Calig. = Suetonius, Vita Caligulae.
Catull. = Catullus.
C.I.G. = Corpus Inscriptionum Graecarum.
C.I.L. = Corpus Inscriptionum Latinarum.
Class. Quart. = *The Classical Quarterly.*
Claud. = Suetonius, Vita Claudi.
Clement, Paedag. = Clement of Alexandria, Paedagogus.
Cod. Theod. = Codex Theodosianus.
Colum. = Columella, De Re Rustica.
Cosmas = Cosmas Indicopleustes, Topographia Christiana.
C.-R. de l'Acad. des I. = *Comptes-Rendus de l'Académie des Inscriptions et Belles-Lettres.*

Déchelette, Manuel = Déchelette, Manuel d'archéologie préhistorique, celtique, et gallo-romaine.
Déchelette, Vases = Déchelette, Les Vases céramiques ornés de la Gaule Romaine.
Dessau = Dessau, Inscriptiones Latinae Selectae.
Dio = Dio Cassius.
Diod. = Diodorus Siculus.
Dio Prus. *or* Chrys. = Dio Chrysostom of Prusa.
Diosc. = Dioscorides (Wellmann).

Ed. Dioc., Edict. Diocl. = Edictum Diocletianum.
E.E., Eph. Ep. = Ephemeris Epigraphica.
Epist. = Pliny, Epistulae.
Epist. ad S.P.Q. Ath. = Julian, Epistula ad Senatum Populumque Atheniensium.
Eumen. Paneg. Const. Augusto = Eumenius, Panegyricus Constantino Augusto.
Euseb. Hist. Eccl. = Eusebius, Historia Ecclesiastica.
Euseb. Mart. Palaest. = Eusebius, Martyres Palaestini.
Eutrop. = Eutropius.
Expos. Tot. Mund. = Expositio Totius Mundi.
Ezek. = Ezekiel.

Flor. = Florus.
Fölzer, Die Bilderschüsseln... = Fölzer, Die Bilderschüsseln der Ostgallischen Sigillatamanufakturen (Römische Keramik in Trier, vol. I). Bonn, 1913.

Gal. = Galen.
Geog. Graec. Min. = Geographi Graeci Minores.
Geog. Rev. = The Geographical Review (New York).
Germ. = Tacitus, Germania.
Gk Pap. in B.M. = Greek Papyri in the British Museum.
Griech. Ostr. = Wilcken, Griechische Ostraka aus Ägypten und Nubien.

Hist. = Tacitus, Historiae.
Hist. Aug. = Historia Augusta.
Hor. = Horace (Odes, unless otherwise stated).

I.G. = Inscriptiones Graecae.
Isid. = Isidore of Charax, The Parthian Stations (in Geog. Graec. Min.).

J., Jos. = Josephus, Antiquitates Judaicae.
J., Jos., B.J., Bell. Jud. = Josephus, Bellum Judaicum.
J., Jos., Vita = Josephus, Vita.
Jahresh. des öst. arch. Inst. = Jahreshefte des österreichischer archäologischen Instituts.
J.A.O.S. = Journal of the American Oriental Society.
J.R.A.S. = Journal of the Royal Asiatic Society.
J.R.S. = Journal of Roman Studies.

Jullian = Jullian, Histoire de la Gaule.
Juv. = Juvenal.

Liv. Ep. = Livy, Epitome.
Logan, Malabar = W. Logan, Malabar (2 vols.), 1887.
Lucan = Lucan, The Pharsalia.
Lucil. = Lucilius, the fragments.

M.A., Mon. Anc. = Monumentum Ancyranum.
Mart. = Martial.
Mela = Pomponius Mela, Chorographia.
Mélanges Univ. Beyrouth, Mél. Beyrouth = Mélanges de l'Université
    de Beyrouth (Syria).
Mon. Antich. = Monumenti Antichi (Rome).
Monuments et Mémoires = Monuments et Mémoires: publiés par
    l'Acad. des Inscr. et B.-L.
Morin-Jean = Morin-Jean, La Verrerie en Gaule, 1913.

Nero. = Suetonius, Vita Neronis.
N.H. = Pliny, Historia Naturalis.
Nic. Damasc. = Nicolaus Damascenus, fragments in Fragmenta His-
    toricorum Graecorum (Didot).
Norden = Norden, Die Germanische Urgeschichte, Leipzig, 1922.
Notitia = Notitia Dignitatum.
Notiz. = Notizie degli Scavi (Rome).

Odes = Horace, Odes.
O.G.I.S. = Dittenberger, Orientis Graeci Inscriptiones Selectae (2 vols.).
Orelli, D.I.L. = Orelli, Dilectus Inscriptionum Latinarum.
Oswald and Pryce, T.S. = Oswald and Pryce, Terra Sigillata, 1922.
Ox. Pap. = Grenfell-Hunt, Oxyrhynchus Papyri.

Pais = E. Pais, Supplementa Italica ad vol. v. C.I.L.
Paneg. Messal. = Panegyricus Messallae.
Pap. Fay. = Fay'um Towns and their Papyri, 1900.
Pap. Tebt. = The Tebtunis Papyri, 1902–1907.
Paus. = Pausanias, Graeciae Descriptio.
P., Perip. = Periplus Maris Erythraei (Geog. Graec. Min.).
Petronius = Petronius, Satyricon and Fragmenta.
Philo, Leg. = Philo, Legatio ad Gaium. (Cohn-Reiter.)
Plut. = Plutarch.
Polyb. = Polybius.
Posidonius = Posidonius, Fragmenta (Hist. Graec. Fragm. Didot).
Proc., Procop. Anec. = Procopius, Anecdota.
Proc., Procop. Hist. Arc. = Procopius, Historia Arcana.
Prop. = Propertius.
Ptol. = Ptolemy, Geography.
P.-W. = Pauly-Wissowa, Real-Encyclopädie.

Rev. Arch., Rev. Archéol. = *Revue Archéologique* (Paris).
Rec. d'Arch. Orient. = *Recueil d'Archéologie Orientale.*
Rev. d'Assyr. = *Revue d'Assyriologie.*
Rev. Ép., Rev. Épig. = *Revue Épigraphique.*
R.É.A., Rev. Ét. Anc. = *Revue des Études Anciennes.*
Rev. Law of Ptol. = Grenfell-Mahaffy, Revenue Law of Ptolemy Phila-
   delphus.

S. = Strabo, Geographica.
Sagot = Sagot, La Bretagne Romaine.
Schoff = W. Schoff, The Periplus of the Erythraean Sea.
Sen. ad Polyb. = Seneca, ad Polybium.
Sid. Apoll. = Sidonius Apollinaris, Epistulae.
Sil. It., Sil. Ital. = Silius Italicus.
Silvae = Statius, Silvae.
S. Silviae Aq. Pereg. = Sanctae Silviae Aquinatis Peregrinatio.
St Chrys. ad Stag. = St Chrysostom, ad Stagiritos.
Stat. Silv. = Statius, Silvae.
Stein = Sir M. A. Stein, Ruins of Desert Cathay.
Suet. = Suetonius (Lives of the Caesars).
Sulpic. Dial. = Sulpicius Severus, Dialogi.

Tac. Agric. = Tacitus, Agricola.
Tac. Germ. = Tacitus, Germania.
Tac. Hist. = Tacitus, Historiae.
Thucyd. = Thucydides.
Tib. = Suetonius, Vita Tiberii.
Tot. Orb. Descr. = Totius Orbis Descriptio.
T.S. = Oswald and Pryce, Terra Sigillata.

Varro, R.R. = Varro, De Re Rustica.
Vell., Vell. Pat. = Velleius Paterculus.
Vesp. = Suetonius, Vita Vespasiani.
Vict. de vir. ill. = Aurelius Victor, De viris illustribus.
Vict. Hist. Northants = Victoria History of Northamptonshire.
Vita Apoll. = Philostratus, Vita Apollonii Tyanensis.
Vitr., Vitruv. = Vitruvius, De Architectura.

Waddington = Lebas-Waddington, Inscriptions grecques et latines....
Walters = Walters, Catalogue of Roman Pottery in the British Museum.
Willers = Willers, Neue Untersuchungen über die Römische Bronze-
   industrie von Capua und von Niedergermanien. Hanover,
   1907.
W.-M. = Wilcken-Mitteis, Grundzüge und Chrestomathie der Papyrus-
   kunde. 1912.

Zosimus = Zosimus, Historiae.

$\mathcal{N}OTES$

CHAPTER ONE: ITALY AND THE ESTABLISHMENT OF THE EMPIRE

For this view of the 'ius fetiale' and for an account of the un-aggressive character of early Roman policy see the opening pages of Tenney Frank's book, 'Roman Imperialism.' Agricultural peoples are always shrewd bargainers and tenacious of rights or of money.

Page **3**. 'Even the grain dole...,' for we may be sure that Gaius intended to organise the corn supply properly and thus lower the cost of transportation: hence his building of granaries, etc.

On Italians in Delos and elsewhere, consult Hatzfeld's brilliant work 'Les Trafiquants Italiens dans l'Orient Hellénique.'

p. **4**. Pliny's dictum (N.H. xxvi. 19) is, 'Romani duces semper in bellis commerciorum habuere curam': cp. the campaign of Vinicius to avenge murdered merchants and business-men, in Dio LIII. 26. 4.

Italy. General remarks on Italy, harbours, climate, crops, etc. in S. 286. Padus valley, S. 212. 4, 5; vineyards, S. 214; its eminence in Italy, S. 218. Timber in Etruria, S. 222. 5. Sabine produce, S. 228. 3. Wines of Campania, S. 234, cp. Varro, R.R. I. 2. 6, 'Quid vinum Falerno?...' (cp. S. 238). Land round Brundisium, S. 282. 6. Wool of Apulia and of Tarentum, Colum. VII. 2 (cp. S. 284, Apulia is πάμφορος καὶ πολυφόρος). 'Grata Calabriae armenta,' Hor. Odes I. xxxi. 5, cp. Mart. XIV. 155. Praise of Italy, Verg. Georg. II. 134 ff.

p. **5**. Mines of Italy, N.H. xxxvII. 202. Limitation of mining, N.H. xxxIII. 78. Copper of Bergomates, N.H. xxxIV. 2; worked at Comum and Sulmo, ibid. 144. Iron of Elba, S. 223 (end), N.H. xxxIV. 142, and Diod. v. 13.

p. **6**. Wool and stuffs from Patavium, S. 213. 7 and 218; Mart. XIV. 143. Cheeses, N.H. XI. 240. Huge wine-casks, S. 218. Cups at Pollentia, N.H. xxxV. 160. Aquileia, S. 214. 8. Marble from Luna, S. 222; stone of Tibur and Gabii, S. 238. 11. Glass-factories on Volturnus, N.H. xxxVI. 194. East-bound cargoes always smaller, S. 793. For glass-blowing see chapter II. Egypt.

p. **8**. First export of olive oil, N.H. XV. 3.

It does not do to criticise Octavian's early years too closely; he was young and unfriended and had to fight for his life with the same weapons as his opponents, but his clemency was a real thing, not 'exhausted cruelty.'

p. **9**. The sailors of Alexandria hail Augustus as 'Saviour,' Suet. Aug. 98. 2. For Philo's panegyric see 'Legatio,' c. 21, 'τί δέ; ὁ τὴν ἀνθρωπίνην...' etc. Inscription at Philae, O.G.I.S. 657. Altar to 'Fortuna Redux,' C.I.L. x. 8375; cp. M.A. 11, and Horace, Odes IV. 5. 15 (note the emphasis on 'Fides').

p. **10**. References to imperial property will be found in the chapters on the provinces. Measures against brigands, Suet. Aug. 32; roads relaid, ibid. 30 and cp. Dio LIII. 22 ('τὰς ὁδοὺς...δυσπορεύτους ὑπ' ἀμελείας ὁρῶν...') and M.A. 20 ('Consul sept. viam Flaminiam ab urbe Ariminum feci'). Pirates put down, M.A. 25 (add passages of Philo and Horace quoted).

p. **11**. Augustus' declaration is in M.A. 32, 'Plurimaeque aliae gentes expertae sunt p. R. fidem me principe, quibus antea cum populo Romano nullum extiterat legationum et amicitiae commercium.'

p. **12**. For Gaius Caesar's expedition to Arabia cp. the following passages: N.H. XII. 56, N.H. II. 168 (where a fleet in Red Sea is implied), and see also chapter IV. on South-Eastern Routes.

CHAPTER TWO: EGYPT

A good introduction to the whole subject of Egypt will be found in Wilcken-Mitteis, 'Chrestomathie der Papyrus-kunde,' I.; Rostow-zew, 'Geschichte des Rom. Colonates,' and also his article in *Archiv Pap. Forsch.* III. 201.

p. **16**. Herodotus' phrase in II. 5, 'δῶρον τοῦ ποταμοῦ,' refers to Delta only, but is equally true of whole land.

The Ptolemies and trade, Berenice road, S. 815. 45, and Phila-delphus' expeditions, S. 789. 5.

Caesar's early attempts to gain Egypt, Cic. de leg. agr. I. 6, 22; II. 23, 65.

Augustus and Egypt, Ann. II. 59, Dio LI. 17. Desired to seem legal heir, did not overthrow Cleopatra's statues, brought up some of her children, Dio LI. 15, 7; declares it part of the empire, Mon. Ancyr. 27, and cp. C.I.L. VI. 701, 'Aegypto in pot. P.R. redacta.'

p. **17**. Difficulty of access, 'δυσείσβολος,' S. 803. Aethiopian raids, S. 820, 821. Three legions and nine cohorts, S. 797. 12; one with-drawn under Tiberius, Ann. IV. 5, and one by Trajan, *B.G.U.* 140. Soldiers used on irrigation works, Aug. 18, Dio LI. 18. 'Drunken debauch,' παροινουμένη, S. 797. 12. Increase in crops, S. 788. Few ships dared 'ὑπερκύπτειν' beyond Ad-n, but now large fleets go, S. 798. 13. Cleansing of canals, under Nero, C.I.G. III. 4699; Trajan's new cut, Ptol. IV. 5. Rich dues (τέλη διπλάσια), S. 798. 13. For monopolies, Cicero, Pro Rab. Post. 14. 40 and S. 798. 13.

p. **18**. For river-transport see Egyptian bas-reliefs and frescoes showing floating of obelisks, etc. down Nile. ἀναπλοῦς or ἀναπλεῖν used in S. 803. 22, 806. 29, 807; in Ox. Pap. XIV. 1666; also in Pap. Tebt. III. 33, 5; transport of waterwheel, Ox. Pap. X. 1292. For full references see pp. 19, 20: paved roads in Alexandria, S. 793. 8.

pp. **19, 20**. Smallness of Nile mouths, S. 801. 18. Various ports, S. 799 ff. Inter-connecting canals, S. 803. 22 and 788. 4 (ὅλην γενέσθαι

πλωτήν). Revellers from Alexandria on canal, S. 801. 17. Nile-Red
Sea channel, S. 804. 25, 26; the Τραίανος ποταμός at Clysma, Ptol.
IV. 5. Channels to various towns: to Arsinoe, S. 809. 35; to Tanis,
S. 813. 41; to Coptos, S. 815. Restoration of canal between Bubastis
and Arsinoe by Trajan, Ptol. IV. 5.

pp. **21, 22.** Rough water in Gulf of Suez, S. 815. 45. Shoals and
winds at Berenice, S. 770. Road from Coptos to Myos Hormos and
stations, S. 815. 45. The Mons Claudianus, imperial freedmen, Cag.-
Laf. I. 1255, 1256. Land roads converging on Arsinoe, N.H. VI. 167 ff.
Road from Syria to Pelusium, through desert, S. 759. 30, 760. 33 (cp.
Joseph. Bell. Jud. IV. 659 ff. for Titus' march). Road to Ammon,
S. 799; to the Abydos-oasis, S. 813. 42. Cyrene road and restoration,
Ann. Epig. 1919, no. 90. Hadrian's new Red Sea road (C.-L. I. 1142)
through level country, guards provided.

Waggon-journey past Syene, S. 818. 50; a Trajanic milestone,
C.I.L. III. 14148[2].

p. **23.** Augustus and 'cura annonae,' Mon. Anc. 5, Dio LIV. 1; cp.
Vell. Pat. II. 94 (Tiberius). Offers to corn-merchants and shippers,
Ann. II. 87; Claud. 18, 19; Ann. XIII. 51. The Etesians—stoppage of
westward sailing, Caes. Bell. Civ. III. 107; Tac. Hist. II. 98. Night-
sailing, N.H. II. 127 (Etesians drop at night). Passengers on corn-
ships, Jos. Vita 15 (about 600).

Passage times: 9 days from Rome, 7 from Straits (Pliny, N.H.
XIX. 3), 7 days from Utica (Sulpic. Dial. I. 6. 1), from Crete (S. 475. 5),
from Rhodes (Appian, B.C. II. 13. 89). Galba's death known in 27 days
(C.I.G. 4957), whereas news of Pertinax's accession (on 1st January)
took 65 (B.G.U. 646), while his death on 28th March had not reached
the Fay'um 52 days later (B.G.U. 46). Nero's death known at Elephantine in 57 days (Griech. Ostr. 799).

Voyage to Massilia, Sulpic. Dial. I. 1. 3; to Coptos, N.H. VI. 102.
Alexandria-Bethlehem in 16 days, Sulpic. Dial. I. 8. 1.

p. **24.** Copper, iron, gold, round Meroe, S. 821. 2. Gold in Ethiopia,
N.H. VI. 189. Gold and silver from Nabat, S. 784. 26. Basalt, N.H.
XXXVI. 58; red granite of Syene, N.H. XXXVI. 63. Porphyry, N.H. XXXVI.
57; serpentine, Lucan IX. 714; various marbles, N.H. XXXVI. 55. Syene
marble, Statius, Silvae IV. 2. 27. Inscriptions of imp. freedmen, see on
pp. 21, 22. Egyptian granite in Belgian villas, Cumont, 'Comment la
Belgique...,' p. 46. Island of Σμαράγδινον, Epiphanius, de Gemmis
(see *Class. Quart.* 1909, p. 218). Export of stone to Rome, Statius,
Silvae II. 2. 86. Memphis quarries, S. 809. Precious stones, S. 815. 45
(emeralds), N.H. XXXVII. 121 (amethysts). Nitrum found, N.H. XXXI.
109 ff. (adulterated on export), S. 803. 23. For guilds of σκυτεῖς, etc.,
see Griech. Ostr. I. 331 ff.

pp. **25, 26.** Fertility: 'frugum fertilissima,' N.H. XXI. 86. S. 819. 53
remarks on τὸ αὔταρκες of the country. 'Triticum ponderosum,' N.H.
XVIII. 62, 63; flax, N.H. XIX. 7; βύβλος and bean, S. 799. 15; olives, vine,

and corn at Arsinoe, S. 809. 35; εὐοινία near Alex., S. 799; 'vinum Sebennyticum,' N.H. XIV. 74; Pelusiac wine, Pap. Oxy. XIV. 1692; 'Mareotica vina,' Silvae III. 2, 23. Delta palm poor but Theban good, S. 818. 51; 'palmae quadrimae ferunt,' N.H. XIII. 38. Mali punici, cerasus, and ficus in N.H. XIII. 113, XV. 102, XIII. 56, and a long list of orchard fruits in Pap. Oxy. XIV. 1631. Oil from raphani, cyprus, and sesame, N.H. XIX. 79, and XIII. 12; oil in Fay'um, S. 809. Register of sheep and goats, Ox. Pap. XII. 1458; wool, X. 1293 (N.H. VIII. 191); cheese, XIV. 1673. 'Porrus laudatissimus,' N.H. XIX. 110. 'Niliaca lens,' Mart. XIII. 9.

For information on industries, monopolies, etc., see Wilcken-Mitteis I. pp. 258 ff. and articles by Rostowzew: refs. to sesame-, olive- and κίκι-oil are found broadcast in the Revenue Law of Ptolemy. Prohibition of import of oil for sale, Rev. Law, 52. Restriction of papyrus growth, S. 800.

p. **27.** Alexandria, μέγιστον ἐμπόριον τῆς οἰκουμένης, S. 798. 13, cp. Vitr. II. 4. Augustus thought of rival foundation, Dio LI. 18. 1. Two seaward harbours and Pharos, S. 792; inland harbour, S. 793. Exports far outnumber imports, S. 793. Population μιγάδων ἀνδρῶν, S. 807. 32.

Westerners in Egypt, *Rev. Ét. Anc.* 1920, p. 50. Indians, Dio Prus. XXXII. 40. Jews in Alexandria, under own ethnarch, Jos. Ant. XIV. 117, XIX. 281 ff. (for their riches, cp. Jos. XVIII. 159 and *B.G.U.* 1079.). Anti-Jewish riots and embassies, Philo, contra Flaccum, Legatio; Jos. Bell. Jud. II. 457 ff.; cp. Ox. Pap. X. 1242. Romans make for good order, S. 798. 13, 'ἐπηνώρθωσαν τὰ πολλά.' Alexandrian mob, Prop. III. xi. 33, 'noxia Alexandria.' Alexandrian marble, Senec. Ep. 115. Egypt was a 'loquax et in contumelias praefectorum ingeniosa provincia,' Sen. Dial. XII. 19. 6.

pp. **28, 29.** For imports generally see the excellent list drawn up by Louis C. West in *J.R.S.* IV. For Eastern imports see chapter on Eastern trade.

Glassware to Rome, Mart. XIV. 115. Perfumes, 'Pharii liquores,' Stat. Silv. II. 1. 161. Glass factory in Campania, N.H. XXXVI. 194; and by Porta Capena (ibid.); and new processes discovered there, S. 758. 25. Imitations of foreign glass-ware, Athen. XI. 784 c. Glassmakers of Alexandria, S. 758 and Clement, Paedag. II. 3. Apprentice to weaver, Pap. Oxy. II. 275, XIV. 1647, *et passim.* Export of cloth to Africa and India, Perip. 6, 8, 9, and 49, 56, etc. ἐργαστήρια of Alexandria, S. 800. So-called Hadrianic letter in Vopiscus, Vita Saturnini, 8. Coolness of Alexandria in summer, S. 793. Revellers, S. 801. The Bucolic War, Dio Cass. LXXI. 4. Massacre of Alexandrians, Dio Cass. LXXVII. 22. Decline in trade mirrored by lack of Roman coins of period in India, *J.R.A.S.* 1903, p. 591.

pp. **30, 31.** Corn-transport, W.-M., Chrestomathie, nos. 440–46, Rostowzew in *Archiv* III. p. 201, and article 'Frumentum' in Pauly-

Wissowa. Amount of corn-supply, Aurel. Vict. Epit. 1 'ducenties centena milia,' cp. Jos. Bell. Jud. II. 386. Arrival of corn-convoy, Senec.
Epp. 77. 1, 2. Harbours of refuge, Jos. Ant. XIX. 205 ff. Supply runs
short, Ann. XII. 43. Inducements to ship-builders, tax remitted, Ann.
XIII. 51, cp. Claud. 19. Harbour at Ostia, Claud. 19; Trajan enlarges
it, Juv. XII. 75, and coins. Herod applies for corn, Jos. XV. 307.
Germanicus opens granaries, Ann. II. 59. Trajan sent back corn,
Pliny, Panegyric, 31 (rumour that Rome depended on Egypt was
refuted). Commodus and African corn-fleet, Hist. Aug. Commodus,
17. Corn-granaries, 'fraus advehentium,' Senec. ad Paulin. 19. Much
later, Athanasius was accused of detaining corn-fleet from Alexandria
to Constantinople, Athanas. I. p. 729 (Gibbon).

p. 32. On trades and professions see interesting summary in Pârvan,
pp. 101 ff. Linen- and stone-workers on lower Nile, S. 813. 41. Most
to be found in Pârvan, l.c., but wool-dealer in Ox. Pap. XIV. 1669;
ταπητέμπορος in X. 1253; transport of jars and waterwheel, X. 1292; and
an ἀργυροκόπος in XV. 1653. Money difficulties, 'keep away from
Jews,' B.G.U. 1079. Business advice, Pap. Fay. 111.

p. 33. Italians at Alexandria, Dittenberger, O.G.I.S. I. 133 and 135.
Aethiopian products, S. 821, 822. Ivory from Aethiopia viâ Syene,
Juv. XI. 124. Little use of Red Sea, though some Aethiopian trade
comes by it, S. 791 and 815. 45. Nero sends tribune up Nile, N.H.
VI. 181. Cp. Senec. Nat. Quaest. VI. 8. 3 (helped by Aethiop. king).
An Egyptian at Palmyra, J.A.O.S. 1904, p. 320. Egyptians at Greek
games, Paus. V. 21. 12; in Italy, Mart. Spectac. 3. Roman merchants
going far South in Egypt, Vitr. IX. 5. 4.

For Nero's Eastern policy I collect the following: intended visit
to Alexandria, attempt to dig Corinth canal, projected expedition to
Caspian Gates (Nero. 19), Aethiopian expedition (see above), and
see note at end of chapter IV.

CHAPTER THREE: SYRIA

p. 36. Rivalry of legates and native rulers, cp. Pilate and Herod
(Luke xxiii. 12). Herod sends first news of a treaty, Jos. XVIII. 104, 105.
Marsus disperses a gathering of princes, J. XIX. 338–42. Herod's
buildings, Jos. XV., especially 331 ff. and 409 ff.; at Chios, XVI. 18.
Philip, the model Jewish king, going his rounds as judge, J. XVIII. 106–
108. Burden of taxes, cp. Ann. II.42. 7 'Judaea Syria... fessae oneribus.'

p. 37. Annexation of Cappadocia and Commagene, Ann. II. 56. 3;
later by Vespasian, Suet. Vesp. 8. 4. Tiberius orders an attack on
Aretas, J. XVIII. 115, 120.

p. 38. For route to and from Egypt cp. Jos. Bell. Jud. IV.659 ff. Herod
gave Augustus food and water for desert-journey here, Jos. XV. 200.
Desert-road of Gaza to Jerusalem, Acts viii. 26. The Petra-route,

250 NOTES

S. 781. 24 and N.H. VI. 144. On North Syrian roads and bridges see Butler in Princeton Expedition records, Cumont in 'Études Syriennes,' also *J.A.O.S.* XXVIII. 155. Roads near Tiberias, Jos. Vita 241, 276. Practically all milestones are Trajanic or later. A relief map of Syria is excellent for throwing light on natural routes.

p. **40**. Abila inscription, Cag.-Laf. III. 1086. Road at Antioch, St Chrys. ad Stag. II. 6. Road swept away by flood, C.I.L. III. 189.

Robbers and turbulence, Herod puts them down, J. XVI. 282, cp. the edict of Agrippa, C.-L. III. 1223; a native soldier on guard in Trachonitis, O.G.I.S. 415; guard of soldiers for journey, J. XVIII. 112; perils of Jerusalem to Jericho, Luke x. 30; cp. Bands of Barabbas, Luke xxiii. 19; of Theudas and Judas, Acts v. 36–37; 'the Egyptian and his 4000,' Acts xxi. 38. Arab raids and tolls, S. 756, 'τοὺς ἐμπόρους... λεηλατοῦσιν οἱ βάρβαροι,' cp. N.H. XII. 64.

Trajanic milestones, re-laying of roads, later repairs, etc., see C.I.L. III. nos. 14149–19 ff. and 117, 199, 203, 208, 6715, 6722. The soft road-surface preserved, H.C. Butler, Appendix on 'Trajan's Road' in Div. III of Princeton Expedition. Care of roads, filling up holes, municipal guards, St Chrys. ad Stag. II. 6.

For Roman εὐνομία see S. 756 and St Chrys. *ibid.* 'νῦν μὲν γὰρ καὶ σταθμοῖς διείληπται (ἡ ὁδός) συνεχέσι καὶ πόλεσι καὶ ἀγροῖς, καὶ ὁδοιπόροις δὲ βαδίζων ἄν τις ἐντύχοι πολλοῖς.'

pp. **41, 42**. Antioch-Seleucia, S. 751. River-traffic, S. 755. 16. Voyages on Lake Tiberias, Jos. Vita 96, and cp. the Gospels, *passim.* New port at Caesarea built by Herod, Jos. XV. c. 8. Improvements at Seleucia under Vespasian, *Rev. Archéol.* 1898, p. 42. ναῦται and ἄποροι in riots, Jos. Vita 66.

p. **42**. Ports and coasting traffic: Seleucia, Acts xiii. 4, Ann. II. 69. 4 and 79. 2; Laodicea, Ann. II. 79. 2; Tyre, Ptolemais, Caesarea, Acts xxi. Coasting, Acts xxi. 6–7. Agrippa wanders by Ptolemais–Anthedon–Alexandria to Rome, Jos. XVIII. 155–8; returns viâ Alex., Philo, In Flacc. 5. Up the coast and round Cyprus, Acts xiii. 4 ff. and xxvii. 4.

Greece–Syria: Herod's voyage, Jos. XVI. 62; Germanicus and Piso, Ann. II. 55; St Paul viâ Ephesus–Cos–Rhodes–Cyprus to Tyre, Acts xxi. 1–3.

Trajan sets fleet in Red Sea, Eutrop. VIII. 3. 2 (hardly to ravage India!).

p. **43**. Time and Speed: Petra–Jericho, S. 779. 21; Edessa–Jerusalem, S. Silviae Aq. Peregr. 47; Antioch–Babylon in 70 days, St Chrys. (l.c.); Antioch–Beroea, Procop. de Bello Persico, II. 7.•2; Alexandria–Jerusalem, see Egypt.

About 18 miles per day is Ramsay's estimate, which the late Prof. H. C. Butler confirmed in conversation with me. St Paul went up to Jerusalem by horse; 'ἐπισκευάζεσθαι,' Acts xxi. 15, is a word used of equipping horses (Souter).

NOTES

251

For republican era cp. ad Fam. XII. 12, or ad Att. XIV. 9. To usual passages on difficulty of winter sailing add Jos. XVI. 15. Herod's voyage, J. XVI. 62. Pliny quotes exceptionally fast times in N.H. XIX. 1. ff.

pp. 44, 45. Iron mines at Germanicia, Cumont, Études Syriennes, pp. 151–71. Χαλκοῦ μέταλλα and official mentioned in Euseb. Mart. Palaest. XIII. 1 and Hist. Eccles. VIII. 13. 5. Marble at Sidon, Stat. Silv. 1. 5. 39. Soldiers at quarries of Enesh, Cumont, op. cit., pp. 151–71. Syrian architecture, see works of De Vogüé and H. C. Butler. Forests of Lebanon part of Hadrianic domain, Mélanges Univ. Beyrouth, 1910, p. 210. Cedars for fleets, N.H. XVI. 203. Irrigation channels, S. 755. 'λάκκος καὶ ἀγωγός' at Safa, C.-L. III. 1338. Transplantation, N.H. XV. 83 (Syrian figs to Alba).

p. 46. Antioch, described by Strabo, 750. 5, Libanius, and others. One-day sail to Seleucia, S. 751. Improvement channel, cp. Pausanias VIII. 29. 3 and *Rev. Archéol.* 1898, I. p. 42.

Apamea, S. 752. 10.

Laodicea. Its wines (πολύοινος) exported to Alexandria, S. 752; to Africa and India, Perip. 6. 49. Its linen and cloths, Totius Orbis Descriptio 31. Edict. Dioclet. in 19. 20 and 19. 51 mentions βίρρος Λαδίκηνος and φαίνουλα (paenula) Λαδικήνη.

Merchants of Aradus, C.I.G. 2626, I.G. XII. 3. 104, Cag.-Laf. III. 1019.

p. 47. Damascus, S. 756. Well-watered and fertile, N.H. V. 74. Early trading, cp. Ezek. xxvii. Chalybonian wine, Posidonius, fr. 58. Its fruits, Edict. Diocl. 6. 86. 'D. monaea sicca,' cp. Diosc. I. 121. Athen. II. p. 49 D speaks of κοκκυμῆλα. Galen VI. 613 (also in De Attenuante Victu, 51) says next after Spanish. 'Pruna et myxae,' N.H. XIII. 51. 'Damascena' in Italy, XV. 43. 'Pruna et cottana,' Juv. III. 83; given as presents in Italy, Mart. XIII. 29. 'τύλη μετὰ προσκεφαλαίου Δ' mentioned in Ed. Diocl. 28. Import of Syrian oil to Egypt, Rev. Law of Ptol. 52. A boundary dispute with Sidon, large territory, Jos. XVIII. 153. Alabastritis at Damascus, N.H. XXXVI. 61.

p. 48. Palmyra. Antony's expedition, App. Bell. Civ. v. 9. 'Urbs nobilis situ, divitiis soli et agris amoenis,' N.H. v. 88. Alterations to Ba'al temple, S. B. Murray in *A.J.A.* XIX. p. 268. Reference to Germanicus' and Corbulo's rescripts in Cag.-Laf. III. 1056, where the imperial freedmen Barbarus, Statilius, and Cilix are mentioned. Use of modius and denarius in same tariff-list. ''Αρχέμποροι' and 'συνοδιάρχης' of merchants in C.-L. III. 1045, 1050. ' Συντέλεια χρυσοχόων καὶ ἀργυροκόπων,' ibid. 1031. All articles mentioned to be found in tariff-list: also dried goods (ξυρόφορτον). Account of river-route in Isidore of Charax, Geog. Graec. Min. I. 244 ff.

p. 50. 'Suavitas' of Berytus wine, N.H. XV. 66. Silk, Procop. Hist. Arc. 25. Berytus and Roman detachments, S. 756. A navicularius (probably) of the town, Mélang. Beyrouth, 1910, p. 225. Weaving here and in Galilee. Scythopolis, Laodicea, Tyre, Byblus, Berytus, send out 'linteamina' through world: all rich in corn, wine, and oil, Tot. Orb. Descript. 31. 'Οθόναι from land of Hebrews, Clement. Paedag. II. 10; cp. Paus. V. 5. 2. Scythopolis later a λινυφεῖον, Cod. Theod. X. 20. 8. Tyre: its silk (Procop. l.c.); a city 'ebulliens negotiis,' Tot. Orb. Desc. 24. Anti-silk edict of Tiberius, Ann. II. 33 and Dio LVII. 15. 1. Silk sold in Rome, Mart. XI. 8. 5, 27. 11. Tyrian wine, N.H. XIV. 74.

p. **51**. 'Pretiosaque murice Sidon,' Lucan III. 217. Its purple-making in Tot. Orb. Descrip. 31; cp. S. 757 'ἡ Τυρία καλλίστη πορφύρα': so many dye-works it makes city difficult to pass through! Bitumen near Sidon, N.H. XXXV. 178. It also had a school of philosophy! S. 757. 'Sidon, artifex vitri,' N.H. V. 76. Legendary origin of glass, N.H. XXXVI. 191. Glass-blowing in Sidon about the time of Caesar, *Rev. Arch.* 1908, p. 211 ff. Finds of glass in Syria and Palestine shew immense increase in early imperial period, A. Kisa, Das Glas in Alt., p. 97. Works of Aristo, Artas and others found in Rome, C.I.L. XV. Pars vi. no. 6958; and also in Gaul, C.I.L. XIII. 3. Vases with Sidonian reliefs on the banks of the Rhine, *Bonn. Jahrb.* 1888, p. 86. Factory at Porta Capena, N.H. XXXVI. 194. Tale of unbreakable glass, Dio LVII. 21, N.H. XXXVI. 195, Petronius 51, all point to some technical improvement.

pp. **52, 53**. Fertility of Judea: best date-palms at Jericho, N.H. XIII. 44. Genesara, surrounded by pleasant towns, Julias, Taricheia, etc., N.H. V. 70. Tiberias and its cold waters, ibid. 71. Fishing, at Taricheia (see above) and cp. the Gospels *passim*. Salome bequeathed Jamneia and district of Archelais-Phaselis (where the most fruitful φοίνικες are) to Livia, Jos. XVIII. 31. Tuberes, zizipha, N.H. XV. 47 (first sown in camp). Bitumen from Dead Sea into Egypt, S. 764. 45. Export of wine from Gaza and Ascalon, Exposit. tot. Mund. 29. Onions of Ascalon! S. 759. 29. The 'New Bostra of Trajan,' O.G.I.S. 626.

Roman residents at Petra, S. 779. 21. Caravans like an army, S. 781, 'μὴ διαφέρειν μηδὲν στρατοπέδου.' The 'new' Trajanic road: 'viam novam a finibus Syriae usque ad mare Rubrum aperuit et stravit' (see notes on p. 40 for refs.). See the monumental Brunnow-Domaszewski 'Arabia,' and cp. H. C. Butler's appendix on Trajanic road already noticed. The 'caravan-master' constructs a gateway at Petra, *J.A.O.S.* XXVIII. 350. Description of Nabataea in S. 779. 21 and 784.

pp. **54, 55**. Men of Aradus in Rhodes and Nisyros, see notes on p. 46. Tyrians at Delos, C.I.G. 2271. Men of Berytus there, O.G.I.S. 591. A 'conventus civium Romanorum' at Antioch, Caes. Bell. Civ. III. 182; in Syria, Ann. II. 82; in Jerusalem, Jos. XIV. 83; cp. also 'οἱ ἐπιδημοῦντες Ῥωμαῖοι' in Acts ii. 11; in Petra, S. 779. 21. 'In Tiberim Syrius defluxit Orontes,' Juv. III. 62. A Sidonian met at Aegium by Paus. (VII. 23. 7).

pp. **54–56**. Spread of Syrians. In Alexandria, Dio Chrys. XXXII. 672, C.I.L. III. 6617. In Italy: at Luna (C.I.L. XI. 1360), at Ravenna (Apoll. Sid. I. 8), and in Verona (C.I.G. 9875); from Berytus (C.I.L. X. 1634), from Heliopolis (ibid. 1579, and cp. 1576 a dedication to Jupiter Damascenus), from Caesarea (ibid. 1985), from Ascalon (ibid. 1746). Further abroad: at Sirmium (ibid. III. 2006), at Celeia (ibid. 11701), and in Dacia (ibid. 1431, 7761); in Sicily (Cag.-Laf. I. 486, 493). From Tiberias, *Jahres. des öst. arch. Inst.* VI. 1903. In Gaul: from Germanicia (C.I.L. XIII. 1945), in Lugdunum (C.-L. I. 25). Man of Berytus at Palmyra, *Rev. d'Assyr.* II. p. 26, no. 5. A Greco-Nabataean at Miletus, Mél. Beyrouth, VII. p. 305. A Sidonian in Alexandria, *Rec. d'Arch. Orient.* 1907, p. 60. Syrians in Spain: at Malaca, C.-L. I. Letter of Tyrians at Puteoli, C.-L. I. 421. Jews in Damascus, Jos. Vita 27. Disgusted exclamation of some Roman: 'οἱ Σύροι κακὸν γένος,' C.-L. III. 1384.

CHAPTER FOUR: THE SEA-ROUTE
TO INDIA AND CEYLON

p. **58**. South-eastern trade. Of the three routes mentioned the first is to be found in Strabo p. 509; the second in Isidore of Charax, Σταθμοὶ Παρθικοί, and in Ptolemy; the third mainly in the Periplus Maris Erythraei, here discussed.

Ptolemaic colonies: Droysen, Hellenismus III. 332 ff. (at Socotra, Cosmas Indicopleustes, III. 169 B). The Red Sea Canal, Diodorus I. 33, N.H. VI. 165, S. 38. Road from Coptos, S. 815, N.H. VI. 101. Açoka's missionaries, V. Smith, Açoka, p. 131 (Edict 13). Canarese language in a farce, Oxy. Pap. III. 413, and an article by Hultzsch in *J.R.A.S.* 1904, pp. 399 ff. Indian dedication to Pan, Lepsius, Denkmäler VI. 166.

pp. **60, 61**. Soldiers used to repair silted canals, Aug. 18. Expeditions against Arabs (S. 780–2, Aelius Gallus), and Aethiopians (S. 820–1, Petronius). Trade at Myos Hormos, S. 118 and 798; he speaks of the ἐπιμέλεια bestowed on trade and the στόλοι μεγάλοι now sailing. Hippalus in Perip. 57; is alluded to in N.H. VI. 100–1. His date therefore falls roughly between 20 and 60 A.D.

Voyage from Ocelis to Muziris 40 days, down Red Sea 30, N.H. VI. 104. Made about July, Perip. 56.

Sack of Eudaimon by a certain Καῖσαρ, obviously after Hippalus' discovery, Perip. 26. Pliny's lament, N.H. XII. 84, 'milies centena milia sestertium.' Roman coins in India, article in *J.R.A.S.* 1903, p. 591. Residents in India, Ptolemy, Proleg. I. 17.

pp. **61, 62**. Coptos-Berenice, 12 days on canal, water and stations, N.H. VI. 102. Gallus' expedition to Arabia, N.H. VI. 160, 161 (reports of wealth and gold), S. 780–2. Dio LIII. 29 says it was against Arabia Eudaimon! Gaius' expedition, N.H. XII. 56. A fleet there: implied in N.H. II. 168. Was it this fleet that later destroyed Eudaimon? Philostorgius calls the town a ''Ρωμαϊκὸν ἐμπόριον.' The trade of Gerrha to Petra: πεζέμποροι, S. 766. 3.

Indian embassies 'saepe missae sunt,' Mon. Ancyr. 31. Cp. Suet. Aug. 21 and Eutropius VII. 10 and S. 719. 73. The letter he gives is not spurious; its meaning is clear: obviously it was Roman merchants who asked (in the name of their emperor) for a δίοδος to the mine district.

Tiberius sent Vitellius against Aretas, Jos. A.J. XVIII. 115, 120. Trajan subdues Nabat, Dio LXVIII. 14. 5. Trajan cleans out Red Sea canal and cuts new one (Ptol. IV. 5); puts a fleet in Red Sea (Eutrop. VIII. 3); receives Indian embassy (Dio LXVIII. 14. 15). Hadrian's road, Cag.-Laf. I. 1142. Voyagers to India, Paus. III. 12. 4. An Egyptian in India, Kenyon, Gk Pap. in B.M. II. pp. 48–49. Indians in Egypt, Dio Chrys. XXXII. 40; cp. XXXV. 23. 'Templum Augusti' at Muziris shewn in Tabula Peutingerana. Parrots and other τέρατα brought from India, Paus. II. 28. 1.

pp. **63, 64.** On rough water and shoals at Berenice and Arsinoe, see S. 770, 'ὑφάλοις χοίρασι.' Leuce Come and small vessels, Perip. 19. Huge caravans from Leuce Come in S. 781, ' μὴ διαφέρειν στρατοπέδου.' Roman merchants at Petra, S. 779. 21.

Leuce Come and centurion, Perip. 19. Tax of 25 per cent. on imports. Was it in order to drive trade to cheaper Egyptian ports?

As doubt is expressed on the matter I adduce following proofs of Nabataean clientship: S. 779. 21, 'νῦν δὲ κἀκεῖνοι (Nabataeans) Ρωμαίοις εἰσιν ὑπήκοοι.' Sullaeus, minister of Obodas, condemned to death by Augustus (J. XVI. 352). Augustus also arbitrates between vassal-kings, Herod and Aretas (J. XVI. 335 ff.); is angry with Aretas for assuming crown without leave, though eventually he confirms him (J. XVI. 353–4). Aretas sends a contingent of troops (J. XVII. 287; cp. S. 780. 23). Sends gifts and gold crowns to Augustus (J. XVI. 296), and same to Germanicus at Cyrrhus (Ann. II. 57. 5), an act of homage. Tiberius sends Vitellius against Aretas for his attack on Herod (J. XVIII. 115, 120). Malchus brings his contingent to Titus for Jewish war (B.J. III. 68).

It seems not impossible that Fabatus, the Καίσαρος διοικητής of B.J. I. 574 ff., may have resided also at Petra. Annius Plocamus and Red Sea dues, N.H. VI. 84.

pp. **64, 65.** Coast of Arabia dangerous, Perip. 20. Armed guards, N.H. VI. 101. Adulis, Perip. 4–6, N.H. VI. 173 (it lay two days from Ptolemais Theron). The king was 'miserly.' Some trade by Nile valley, S. 791, 815 (Red Sea little used). Exports and imports, Perip. 6. Adulis ivory best, c. 17. Towns in Perip. 8–14. Quantity of cinnamon from Mundus (c. 10), slaves of better sort from Opone (c. 13). Indian imports (c. 14).

Rhapta and 'unexplored ocean' (c. 16). But note that Ptolemy (I. 9. 1) knows of towns farther South and of voyagers thereto. Under

Arab domination, and Arab products sent there (c. 17). Ptolemy knows of Auxuma as the king's residence, '$\dot{\epsilon}\nu$ $\hat{\eta}$ $\beta\alpha\sigma\dot{\iota}\lambda\epsilon\iota\omega\nu$' (IV. 8. 25), and also speaks of 'the lakes from which the Nile flows' (I. 9. 1); it is worth remarking that a coin of Antoninus Pius has been found as far South as Zimbabwe, but one coin does not make a commerce.

p. 66. Dangerous shore and pirates, Perip. 20.

Town of Muza (P. 21); tool-trade to Africa (P. 17); gifts and embassies to Rome (P. 23); exports Gebanite-Minaean $\sigma\tau\alpha\kappa\tau\dot{\eta}$ (P. 24). Port for spices and incense, N.H. VI. 104. Legates from Arabia, N.H. XII. 57.

Sabaei famous for incense, N.H. VI. 154. Cassia from Arabia, called $\delta\alpha\phi\nu\hat{\iota}\tau\iota\varsigma$ by Alexandrian merchants, Diosc. I. 13. $Z\iota\gamma\gamma\dot{\iota}\beta\epsilon\rho\iota$ from Arabia brought in jars to Italy, Diosc. II. 160.

Ocelis, Perip. 25. Best port for sailors to India, N.H. VI. 104. The shrunken town of Eudaimon, Perip. 26. The emendations of $K\alpha\hat{\iota}\sigma\alpha\rho$, which is perfectly rational and explicable, to 'Ελίσαρ or even Χαρι-βαήλ (!) are put out of court by their preposterousness. Dioscorida, Perip. 30; its native garrison, P. 31. First colonised with Greeks by Philadelphus, Cosmas III. 169 B.

p. 67. Strabo mentions $\pi\epsilon\zeta\dot{\epsilon}\mu\pi\sigma\rho\sigma\iota$ of Gerrha and speaks of sea-voyage from that town, 766. 3 and 778. 19. For Chinese silk-trade see chapter VI.

Market-towns of Persian Gulf and Indian imports (Perip. 35, 36); pearls (P. 36); frankincense from Cana (P. 36).

Route from Gerrha (or Charax) up Euphrates (S. 766. 3), and cp. inscriptions of Palmyrene $\sigma\upsilon\nu\sigma\delta\iota\dot{\alpha}\rho\chi\alpha\iota$ from Charax: a portion of the route also given in Isidore. Treachery and low state of inhabitants, Perip. 34.

p. 68. Barygaza: great tides (Perip. 44); pilots in king's service tow vessels in. Exports from town (P. 48 and 49). Imports in P. 49 (cp. N.H. XXXIV. 163), lead and tin being imported, which India does not possess. Bright girdles are still used among the Bhīls (Schoff). Gold and silver coin, P. 49: cp. the story of the Tamil king's appreciation of Roman standard in N.H. VI. 85.

pp. 68, 69. Muziris, Perip. 54. 'Indiae emporium' (N.H. VI. 104), but our captain is not as afraid of the pirates as Pliny is. Greek and Arab vessels, P. 54. Exports and imports, P. 56. High price of pepper and its adulteration, N.H. XII. 28. Dioscorides (II. 159) mentions $\pi\dot{\epsilon}\pi\epsilon\rho\iota$ from India. Cp. Alaric and his tribute of pepper in Gibbon, c. XXXI. On coins see article in *J.R.A.S.* 1903, p. 591.

Finds in Nilghiri tombs, V. Smith, 'The Early History of India.' Tamil poems quoted from Pillai, 'The Tamils 1800 years ago,' c. III. Cp. also Mookerji, 'History of Indian Shipping,' pp. 135–6. Notice of merchants and sailors, S. 685. 3, 4, N.H. VI. 139, 146, Ptolemy, Proleg. I. 17 and Paus. II. 28. 1. Story of Justinian coin in Cosmas XI. 448 D.

256 NOTES

p. **71**. Pearl-fisheries, P. 59. Camara and other market-towns, P. 60. The country of This, P. 64. Notices upon Chinese intercourse in Hou-han-shu, ch. 88, quoted from Hirth, 'China and the Roman Orient.' The Legend of St Thomas will be found in Wright, 'Apocryphal Acts of the Apostles,' II. pp. 146–7.

Since this chapter was written there has appeared a pamphlet by Dr Werner Schur entitled 'Die Orientpolitik des Kaisers Nero' (Leipzig, 1923), but I do not think it alters any of my conclusions. It is hard to believe in the large and consistent policy there attributed to Nero and his advisers, and I am convinced that the reduction of Arabia Eudaemon had taken place before Nero's reign, and hope to prove as much later.

CHAPTER FIVE: ASIA MINOR

p. **76**. For any study of the condition of Asia Minor under the Empire Sir William Ramsay's books are indispensable, especially his 'Historical Geography of Asia Minor' and 'Cities and Bishoprics of Phrygia,' and also his recent articles on Galatia in *J.R.S.* Hogarth's 'The Nearer East' is also useful.

p. **77**. On the Italian 'negotiatores,' see Hatzfeld, 'Les Trafiquants Italiens dans l'Orient Hellénique,' who puts the first century B.C. as the period of their greatest expansion.

For the importance of Delos at this period cp. S. 486 and 668. 2 and Pliny, N.H. XXXIV. 9.

For 'mercantilism' see T. Frank's 'Roman Imperialism,' c. XIV. p. 277.

Moneylending to native princes, Appian, Bell. Mith. 11 (Nicomedes), Cicero, ad Att. VI. 1. 3 (Pompey's loans).

Conspiracy: Archelaus charged with it, Ann. II. 42; and cp. the curious echo in Philostratus, Vit. Apollonii I. 12. Cp. Marsus' treatment of Agrippa in Jos. Antiq. XIX. 326 and the suspicious gathering of kings in XIX. 338.

pp. **78, 79**. Fertility of Halys valley: ἀρετὴ τῆς χώρας, S. 572. Lycaonia's bare chill plains, S. 568.

Wealth of Asia: 'pingues Asiae campi collesque...,' Horace, Ep. I. 3, 5, and see special references further. For the ἐρημία of Asia see S. 605. 50 (Satnioeis), 606. 51 (Kisthene), 612. 63 (Chrysa), 614, 619, 621, etc.

The 'Royal Road' is described in Herodotus V. 52 (distances), and the Sinope-Tarsus route in Herodotus II. 34. Cp. also the march of Cyrus, and the journey of Alcibiades to Persia in Xenophon, Anabasis I. and Plutarch, Alc. 39, where he died 'ἐν κώμῃ τινι τῆς Φρυγίας.'

pp. **80, 81**. Aquillius' remaking of road, C.I.L. I. n. 557.

Efforts at putting down piracy: by Antonius in 103 B.C. (Livy, Ep.

68), by Sulla as praetor in Cilicia (Victor, de Vir. Ill. 75), and by Isauricus (Florus I. 41).

Pompey and the Caspian, S. 492 and N.H. VI. 52. Pompey's foundations (Nicopolis, Diospolis, Megalopolis, Neapolis, and Pompeiopolis) on trunk-road from Armenia: Comana was a great ἐμπόριον, S. 559. 36. For Cicero's route see ad Atticum v. (*passim*), and article by Hunter in *J.R.S.* III. p. 73.

Amyntas entrusted with pacification, Appian, Bell. Civ. v. 75.

Augustus' colonies in Pisidia, Mon. Ancyr. 28. Milestones of Augustus, C.I.L. III. 6974, 14185, 14401. Bridges by Selge and in Eurymedon country, S. 571.

Provincial troubles, Lycian outbreaks (Suet. Claud. 25. 3), Homonadensian war (Tac. Ann. III. 48), suspected kings (Jos. XIX. 338).

Vespasian's annexation of Cilicia Trachea, Commagene, and Cappadocia, Suet. Vesp. 8. Milestones of Vespasian, C.I.L. III. 306, and cp. n. 6052.

Complete restoration and organisation of roads under Domitian, C.I.L. III. 312, 318, and 14184. 48.

Mm. of Nerva (Tavium–Amasea), C.I.L. III. 14184. 44. Titus' road (Derbe–Lystra), C.I.L. III. 12218. Mm. of Hadrian, C.I.L. III. 13625 (near Elaeusa), 14402 (Iconium), and 14184. 58, 60, 61.

pp. **82, 83.** Ephesus and its busy harbour, S. 641. 24, 'ἐμπόριον οὖσα μέγιστον τῶν κατὰ τὴν Ἀσίαν.'

Laodicea, S. 578.

Apamea: second largest town, S. 577. 15. Greeks and Italians there. 'Nothing in the city idle: five ways converge,' Dio Chrys. XXXV. 14 ff.

Iconium, S. 568.

Wealth of Sardis and its good land, S. 626, 627.

Synnadic marble: exported to Rome, S. 577, cp. Hor. Odes III. 1. 41.

Pessinus, S. 567. 3.

Ancyra and Tavium, S. 567. 2.

Pliny's request for Juliopolis, Epist. IX. 77.

Description of Sinope, S. 545. 11 ff.

Comana, centre for trade from Armenia, S. 559. 36.

Sinope–Tarsus route: an 'isthmus,' S. 664.

References to roads in Strabo, 625. 4 (Pergamum–Thyateira–Sardis), 632. 2 (Ephesus–Smyrna), 648. 42 (Magnesia–Tralles), 649. 44 (Tralles–Nysa), 569. 5 (Sagalassus–Apamea). Road between Mazaca and Tyana, Vitr. VIII. 3, 9.

pp. **84, 85.** Usually it was the approach of winter that made land travel necessary: cp. Mucian's march through Cappadocia and Phrygia, Jos. Bell. Jud. IV. 632. Again it appears to have been exceptional to go by land back from Sinope instead of by sea, Jos. Ant. XVI. 23.

Sinope, its harbour and timber, S. 546.

Pharnacia, tunny-fishing and timber, S. 549. 19.

Amastris, S. 544. 10. Boxwood there and on Cytorus, S. 545; cp. Catull. IV. 13.

Sangarius navigable through Bithynia, S. 543. 7.

Smyrna, S 646.

For products, see further sections: into Apamea came the wares and wines of Italy, S. 577. 15.

Voyaging: Byzantium–Sestos–Abydos–Caria, S. 584 (currents of Sestos, S. 591. 22). περιπλοῦς longer than land-journey from Ephesus to Smyrna, S. 632. 2. πλοῦς and παρὰ γῆν, S. 636. Εὐθυπλοία and ἐγκολπίζειν contrasted, S. 643. 29. For Etesians, etc., see notes on Egypt. Ship from Adramyttion, Acts xxvii. 2. Alexandrian ship at Myra, Acts xxvii. 6. Herod sails viâ Rhodes to Byzantium and Sinope, Jos. XVI. 16 ff. Pompey's flight, Lucan VIII. 245–60, 456–65. Antipater: from Tarentum to Celenderis, then to Judaea, Jos. XVII. 85. Piso, from Cos coasts by Lycia to Celenderis, Ann. II. 75, 80; note that Domitius is ordered to proceed 'lato mari' to Syria. A rising of the Clitae harms 'navicularii,' Ann. XII. 55; cp. merchant in Bithynian wares, Hor. Ep. I. 6. 32.

p. 86. Cicero's mail, ad Att. V. 19. 1 (46 days); usually much longer, cp. 21. 4. Death of Gaius Caesar known at Pisae, Orelli, D.I.L. 643. Picked men used on postal service, Suet. Aug. 49. 3. Ephesus–Tralles in one day, 'pulverulenta via,' ad Att. V. 14. 1. Sagalassus–Apamea, one day, S. 569. 5. Mazaca to Cilician Gates, six days, S. 539. 9. Phasis to Sinope, three full days, S. 498. There seems no reason to doubt this: 100 miles per diem was quite possible for an ancient ship. Meineke asterisks it.

Winds off Troad, Pliny, Ep. IX. 17 A.

Coasting-vessels: 'orariae naves,' Pliny, l.c. Note that he went 'partim navibus, partim vehiculis' (15).

Merchant of Hierapolis: Φλάβιος Ζεῦξις, obviously a Greek, Hatzfeld, p. 191.

pp. 87, 88. Mines and Minerals. Some workings exhausted, S. 680. 28 ('ἐκλελειμμένα ἅπαντα') and 591, 23. The μεταλλευταί of Archelaus, S. 540. Mines at Tamassos, with wood near by, S. 684. 5. Silver also found, S. 684. 5. Lead and white-lead, N.H. XXXIV. 170–5. Workshops on island of Rhodes, N.H. XI. 119 ('aerariae fornaces'), also in XXXIV. 103, 107, 121 and XXXVI. 137. Copper down Red Sea coast to India, Periplus 24, 28, 49 etc. Cp. Pliny's remark in N.H. XXXIV. 163 on India's lack. Caesar's gift to Herod, Jos. XVI. 129. Precious stones in Cyprus, N.H. XXXVII. 58, 66, 67. Exhausted workings at Astyra, S. 680. 28 and 591. Gold near Caballa in Armenia, S. 529. 9. Gold and silver among Suani in Colchis, N.H. XXXIII. 52. Nero's projected expedition, Dio LXIII. 8.

p. 89. Copper near Cisthene, S. 607. Iron in Cappadocia, N.H. XXXIV. 142; above Pharnacia, S. 549. 19; at Andeira (and process of making ὀρείχαλκος), S. 610. Beaten iron-work of Cibyra, S. 631. 17.

Molybdena at Zephyrium, N.H. xxxiv. 173. At Pompeiopolis, σανδα-
ράκη (realgar), S. 562. On conditions, cp. with Diodorus v. 38
(Spain and Laurion). The best realgar found in mine near the river
Hypanis, Vitr. vii. 7. 5.

p. **90.** Quarries on Mt Argaeus, S. 538. 8. Marble of Synnada,
S. 577. 14 (now worked better, 'διὰ τὴν πολυτέλειαν τῶν 'Ρωμαίων').
'Phrygius lapis,' Hor. Odes iii. 1. 41. 'Phrygia Synnas,' Mart. ix.
75. 7. Marble in Ariusia, S. 645, 35. Proconnesus, S. 588. Fragments
of this marble found in Gallic villas, Cumont, 'Belgique,' p. 46.
Carians may have invented marble-cutting, N.H. xxxvi. 47. μεταλλευταί of Archelaus, S. 540. Σινωπικὴ μίλτος in Cappadocia, S. 540.
'Sinopis...optuma...in Cappadocia,' N.H. xxxv. 31. Pontic μίλτος,
ibid. 36; cp. Vitr. vii. 7. 2. Specularis lapis, N.H. xxxvi. 160. For
the φεγγίτης stone, see ibid. 163 and Suet. Domit. 14. The best
'minium' found near Ephesus, N.H. xxxiii. 114. (The Colchian was
adulterated.) But note that nearly all was brought to Rome from
Sisapo, ibid. 118; cp. Vitr. vii. 9. 4. Whetstones from Cilicia, N.H.
xxxvi. 164. For precious stones see N.H. xxxvii. 79 (beryls in Pontus),
and xxxvii. 92 and 96.

p. **91.** Sinope and the hilly seashore of Bithynia have abundance
of ship-timber, S. 546. 12. 'Silvarum abundantia,' Vitr. ii. 1. 4.
Good fir, N.H. xvi. 197. Pontic maple, N.H. xii. 56. Larches of
Bithynia, N.H. xvi. 197. Maple and mountain-nut for tables, S.
546. 12, 'ἐξ ὧν τὰς τραπέζας τέμνουσιν.' The 'phaselus,' Catull.
iv. 1. Lycian cedar, N.H. xii. 132. Olives in Sinopitis, S. 546. 12,
'ἅπασα δὲ καὶ ἐλαιόφυτός ἐστιν.' Boxwood from Cytorus, S. 545;
cp. Catull. iv. 13. Pityan pines, S. 588. 15; wood-cutting on Ida,
S. 606. 51. Large woods on Olympus, S. 574. 8; beech there, S. 572. 3.
Catacecaumene treeless, S. 628. 11. Cappadocia lacks timber, save
on Argaeus, S. 538. 7. Timber on Mycale, S. 636. 12. The olive in
Melitene, S. 535. 2; round Phanaroea, S. 556. 30; in Pisidia, S. 570;
by Selge, S. 570. 3; in plain of Synnada, S. 577. 14. Inscriptions of
'olearii,' see Hatzfeld, op. cit., pp. 213 ff.

pp. **91, 92.** Wine-district of South-West: towns given in S. 637. 15.
The wine of Ariusia in S. 645. 35, and cp. for its medicinal use Galen,
De Vinis, and De Victu Attenuante 94. Pliny's remarks in N.H.
xiv. 73 ff. Wine of Priapus, S. 587. 12; of Lampsacus, S. 589. 19;
of Ambleda, S. 570. 2; of Catacecaumene, S. 628. 11; cp. N.H.
xiv. 75; of Cos, Cato, de Re Rustica 112. Melitene: the Monarite
wine rivals the Greek, S. 535. 2. Phanaroea, S. 556. 30.

p. **92.** Sinope and its trade, S. 546. 12. Themiscyra and its fruit,
S. 548. Lucullus and his transplantings in N.H. xv. 102. Flocks of
sheep, S. 546. 13. Pontic ducks in N.H. xxv. 6, and bees in xi. 59.
The wax, N.H. xv. 65. It was καθαρός, Diosc. ii. 83. Tribute paid
in wax by Sanni, N.H. xxi. 77. Cappadocian carpets, Ed. Diocl.
xvi. 5. Gums and plants of Pontus, N.H. xii. 47, 49, and 72.

p. **93**. Deer and boar in Cilicia, N.H. VIII. 115, XI. 280.

The saffron of Corycus, N.H. XXI, 31; S. 670. 5. The best, according to Diosc. I. 26. Cereals: 'zea, oryza, tiphe,' N.H. XVIII. 81. Cilician 'passum' good, N.H. XIV. 81; beans, XVIII. 122; figs, XVI. 113; palms, XIII. 48; lettuce, XIX. 128. Styrax, N.H. XII. 125 (Pisidia, Side, Cilicia); S. 570. 3. The 'coccus' for dyeing, N.H. XVI. 32. Rose-perfume of Phaselis, Athen. XV. 688 E. Fertile Selge, S. 570. 3

The 'cilicium,' a garment of goats-hair, Varro, R.R. II. 11, 12. For socks and leggings of this stuff, cp. Mart. XIV. 141. Imported to Rome in Augustus' time; cp. Aug. 75.

p. **94**. Shellfish of Linon, S. 588. 15. The oysters of Ephesus, N.H. XXXII. 62.

Wealth of Caicus plain, S. 624. 2, and cp. 626 (the plains around Sardis) and ἀρετὴ χώρας, 627. 8. Milesian and Laodicean wool, N.H. VIII. 190 and XXIX. 33. Milesian purple, Ed. Diocl. XVI. 90. Laodicean cloak, XVI. 12. Use of radicula for refining wool, N.H. XIX. 48. Hierapolis water splendid for dyeing, S. 630.

Lydia of Thyateira, Acts xvi. 14.

'Tubera nobilissima' from Mytilene and Lampsacus, N.H. XIX. 37. Resinous trees, N.H. XXIV. 32. Kings of Asia planted incense tree, N.H. XII. 57. Aloes, N.H. XXVII. 14. Apples, XV. 39. Jars of figs, XV. 82.

pp. **95, 96**. 'πολὺ πλῆθος 'Ιουδαίων' in Asia, Jos. XVI. 27. Aquila of Pontus, travelling, Acts xviii. 2. Demetrius of Ephesus, Acts xix. 24. For immigration of Greeks cp. Juvenal's complaints in Sat. III. 69–70 (mostly Asiatics). A Nicomedian at Moguntiacum, C.I.L. XIII. 4337, and Bithynians, 6851, 625 (at Burdigala), a Lydian aurifex, 5154, a Carian, 8343, a Cappadocian, 6496. And cp. the Asiatic freedmen of the emperors, or physicians like Xenophon of Cos! Even as far as Britain, C.I.L. VII. 190 (at Lindum).

CHAPTER SIX: THE OVERLAND ROUTE
TO CHINA AND INDIA

The Roman policy with regard to the sea-route has already been discussed but notice the centurion stationed at Leuce Come to collect dues (Perip. 19) and the Red Sea tax-collectors (N.H. VI. 84).

p. **99**. Zeugma, 'transitu Euphratis nobile' (N.H. v. 86) and north of river route. Or up the river and across desert to Palmyra; cp. inscr. of ἀρχέμποροι and συνοδιάρχαι from Persian Gulf, in O.G.I.S. 632 and in chapter on Syria. Men of Gerrha grew rich on spice traffic, S. 778. 19; came overland probably whole way (S. 766). Petra also a great centre, S. 779. 21. Merchants accused of adulterating the ξυλοβάλσαμον brought from there, Diosc. I. 19. 3. Nero's extravagance on spices, N.H. XII. 83. Silk much sought after, Mart. XI. 8. 5.

Increase of knowledge, S. 508. 4. Isidore's work in Geog. Graec. Min. Might he not have belonged to Charax Mediae and hence his interest in the route?

p. **100**. Camp at Cyrrhus first, Ann. II. 57. Incorporation of Commagene and Cappadocia, Ann. II. 56 and finally, Suet. Vesp. 8. Zeugma, start of journey, Isid. 1. Caravans and customs-duties there, Vita Apoll. 1. 20; a camp there under Claudius, Ann. XII. 12. Cp. N.H. v. 86.

River-route: across to Anthemusias, down Bilechas valley, then by Phaliga–Circesium (where route from Palmyra joined), to Seleucia and Ctesiphon, Isid. l.c.

pp. **101, 102**. Exactions of riverside tribes, S. 748; therefore detour through land of Scenitae at three days' distance from river. Older route through better country: Carrhae–Resaina–Nisibis to Nineveh and down Tigris, cp. Arrian, Anabasis III. 7. (See *Geog. Rev.* September 1919, pp. 153–79.) Or even farther North, by Edessa and Tigranocerta to Nisibis. Cp. Trajan's march in A.D. 115, Dio LXVIII. 19. Antioch–Babylon in 70 days, St Chrys. ad Stag. II. 6. Sura–Ctesiphon in 10 days, N.H. v. 89.

Seleucia, 'civitas potens,' Ann. VI. 42. 'Πόλιν ἀξιολογωτάτην,' inhabited by Macedonians, Greeks, Syrians, and Jews, Jos. XVIII. 372, 373. Ctesiphon, the capital, near by, S. 743. 16; cp. Jos. XVIII. 377 (Jews there). Depôt of Vologesias, O.G.I.S. 632; cp. N.H. VI. 122. Down river to Phorath, under king of Charax, N.H. VI. 145 and cp. O.G.I.S. 632, 'οἱ συναναβάντες...ἔμποροι ἀπὸ Φοράθου καὶ Ὀλογασιάδος.' Charax, 12 miles away; originally at river's mouth, N.H. VI. 139. Market-town of Apologus chief depôt, see Perip. 35. Trade with India, P. 36.

pp. **102, 103**. Up through Zagros mountains (Isid. 3), to Bagistana and Ecbatana (Isid. 6), through Pass of Caspian Gates (Isid. 7), to Apamea and through Hyrcania on to Hecatompylos (Isid. 8 and Ptol. I. xii). Then to Margiana Antiochia (Merv), Isid. 14. Isidore's route ends at Kandahar (Alexandropolis), Isid. 19.

Maes' route went on to Bactra (Balkh), across the mountains of the Comedi and through land of Sacae to the Stone Tower (Tashkurgan), standing at convergence of routes from Oxus, Indus, and Yarkand.

pp. **104, 105**. Constant struggle for Armenia. Caucasus rich in timber, S. 497. 15. Crops of Phasis valley, timber too and flax, wax, pitch; linen works famed, S. 498. 17 ff. River-gold, S. 499. 19. The fertile valleys of Armenia, S. 528. 4. Gold near Caballa, S. 529. 9, also σάνδιξ.

Pompey used pass of Cyrus (Harmozica) for entry into Iberia, S. 501. Learnt of Indian trade viâ Oxus and Caspian, N.H. VI. 52. Canidius beats the Iberi and makes them 'socii,' Dio XLIX. 24. Tiberius sets up Tigranes as king of Armenia, Suet. Tib. 9. Kings of Albani

262 NOTES

and Hiberi seek friendship, Mon. Anc. 31. Hiberi and Albani 'protected' by Rome, Ann. IV. 5; they send help to Rome and Corbulo, Ann. XIV. 23. Garrison at Gorneae in A.D. 52, Ann. XII. 45. Nero annexes Pontus and Armenia; thought of sending expedition to Caspian Gates! Nero. 19. 2; Dio LXIII. 8; cp. Tac. Hist. I. 6. Legions added to Cappadocia by Vespasian, Vesp. 8. 4. Domitian's roads, C.I.L. III. 312 (Samosata–Melitene–Satala–Trapezus). A garrison at Harmozica in Iberia, C.-L. III. 133. Trajan's route viâ Satala, Dio LXVIII. 19.

p. **106**. Ancient trade-route viâ Caspian: Patrocles' account, S. 509. 3. Besides Indian trade region was rich in timber, S. 497. 15; crops from Phasis valley, S. 498; pheasants from Phasis, N.H. XIX. 52. Phasis two days from Amisos, S. 498.

Route viâ Phasis, navigable to Fort Sarapana, then a good waggon track to Cyrus valley in four days, S. 498. 17; Pliny says five days, N.H. VI. 52. Cyrus and other rivers navigable to Caspian, S. 500, or down Alazonius valley and stone-paved road in Albania, S. 500. 5. Another way viâ Satala–Elegia–Araxes valley: provisions from Trapezus to Armenia, Ann. XIII. 39; cp. Dio LXVIII. 18, 19.

By Hadrian's time a garrison at Hyssou Limen, Arrian, Perip. 3; five cohorts at Apsarus; 400 picked men to garrison Phasis, well placed 'πρὸς ἀσφάλειαν τῶν ταύτῃ πλεόντων,' P. 9. 3. Safety for veterans and merchants ('ἄλλων ἐμπορικῶν'), P. 9. 5. Dioscurias has a garrison, P. 10. 3. List of kings set up by Trajan and Hadrian, P. 11. 2, 3. Garrison at Harmozica, near Dariel Pass too, C.-L. III. 133.

pp. **108, 109**. Raw silk, silk yarn, and cloth brought by Chinese; some sent South to Barygaza, Perip. 64. Silent exchange of merchandise, Ammian. XXIII. 68. Ganges–Palibothra route known to Ptolemy, I. 17. 4.

Extracts from Hou-han-shu in Hirth's 'China and the Roman Orient.' Report of ambassador Kan Ying in A.D. 97. Postal stations (6); gold and precious stones (22); and gums and spices (25); honest dealers (29); wish for intercourse (32); sea-voyage round Arabia (37). Roads marked into stages and security for travellers (38, 39). Embassy from Marcus Aurelius viâ Annam resulted in direct intercourse (33).

pp. **109, 110**. Silk came in about Augustan period, cp. Vergil, Georgics II. 121; Lucan, Phars. X. 141. Edict against its being worn by men, Ann. II. 33, and cp. Dio LVII. 15. Among most precious productions, N.H. XXXVII. 204. Silk in houses of very wealthy, Mart. XI. 8. 5; sold in Tuscus vicus, ibid. 27. 12. Tyre and Berytus famous for its production, Procop. Hist. Arc. 25. Silkmaker at Berytus, Waddington 1854; Heliodorus of Antioch at Naples, C.I.G. 5834; Epaphroditus at Gabii, his rich gifts, C.I.L. XIV. 2793, cp. 2812; another merchant at Tibur, C.I.L. XIV. 3712; a woman at Rome (Greek), C.I.L. VI. 9892.

North Indian gold coins same weight as aurei of A.D. 95, *J.R.A.S.*
1903. Word 'denarius' long used in India, Logan, Malabar I. 269.
Roman attitudes, faces, and saddlery in Miran frescoes, Stein, 'Desert
Cathay,' I. pp. 470, 480, 483, 487. Bale of ancient silk found at Lop
Nor, ibid. I. p. 381.

Additional Note. I have not been able to see Hermann, 'Die
Verkehrswege zwischen China, Indien, und Rom um 100 nach Chr.
Geb.,' published at Leipzig in 1922, but from a review in the *Geographical Journal* I do not think any modification of the account here
given is necessary.

CHAPTER SEVEN: GREECE

p. **114**. Accounts of first Illyrian war in Polybius II. 8 onwards,
and in Dio Cass. fr. 49 and App. Illyrica 7 and 8. Appian gives the
version of help to Issa. Dio says Ardiaei made raids on ships coming
from Brundisium. Polybius says '$\sigma v v \epsilon \chi \hat{\omega} s \ \dot{\eta} \delta \acute{\iota} \kappa o v v \ \tau o \dot{v} s \ \pi \lambda o \iota \zeta o \mu \acute{\epsilon} v o v s$
$\dot{a} \pi'$ '$I \tau a \lambda \acute{\iota} a s$.' The Ardiaei were common enemies of all Greeks,
Polyb. II. 12. 6. Rome wanted security of commerce.

Lucullus in Moesia and Thrace, App. Ill. 30. Augustus' conquests
in Illyria, ibid. 16. Tiberius and Moesia, ibid. 30. One of his best
generals, Poppaeus Sabinus, was in charge, Tac. Ann. I. 80.

Customs immunity at Ambracia, Livy XXXVIII. 44. But this was
claimed for all Rome's allies as well.

p. **115**. The Via Egnatia. Its route described in S. 322; it was
'$\beta \epsilon \beta \eta \mu a \tau \iota \sigma \mu \acute{\epsilon} v \eta \ \kappa a \tau \grave{a} \ \mu \acute{\iota} \lambda \iota o v \ \kappa a \grave{\iota} \ \kappa a \tau \epsilon \sigma \tau \eta \lambda \omega \mu \acute{\epsilon} v \eta$.' Cicero's journey
into exile, ad Att. III. 7. 3. The earliest milestone in Achaea is of
Arcadius and Honorius. Vespasian's road in Cyprus, C.I.L. III. 6732.
In Crete, Ditt. Syll.² 929. Legate of Claudius restores roads, Cag.-Laf.
I. 980. Hadrian's benefactions, Paus. I. 36. 3. Milestones at Hypata,
C.I.L. III. Supp. 7359, 7362. Corinth–Athens road, along sheer cliffs,
S. 380, 391. 4; and improvements made by Hadrian, Paus. I. 44. 6.

p. **116**. The 'Ladder' pass on road from Argos, Paus. VIII. 6. 4.
Narrow Titane road, Paus. II. 11. 3. Argos–Tegea, Paus. VIII. 54. 5;
cp. S. 376. 17. Roads from Corinth: S. 377. 19 (to Argos), S. 380 (to
Athens), Paus. II. 5. 5 (to Sicyon). Sicyon–Phlius, Paus. II. 11. 3.
Argos–Cleonae, Paus. II. 15. 2. Roads from Mantinea to rest of
Arcadia, Paus. VIII. 10. Dyme–Elis, S. 340. Elis–Olympia, S. 341
sub fin.

$\Pi a \rho \acute{a} \pi \lambda o v s$ of Messenian Gulf, S. 348. 23. Malea, '$\tau \rho a \chi \grave{v} s \ \dot{o} \ \pi a \rho \acute{a} -$
$\pi \lambda o v s$,' but plenty of harbours, S. 368. Pamisus navigable, Paus.
IV. 34. Aegium–Cirrha ferry, S. 389. 5. Cyllene, a good port, Paus.
VI. 26. 4. Corinth newly restored, S. 379; cp. 381. 23, '$\dot{a} v \epsilon \lambda \acute{\eta} \phi \theta \eta$
$\pi \acute{a} \lambda \iota v \ \dot{v} \pi \grave{o} \ K a \acute{\iota} \sigma a \rho o s \ \delta \iota \grave{a} \ \tau \grave{\eta} v \ \epsilon \dot{v} \phi v \acute{\iota} a v$.' Plans for cutting isthmus,
Suet. Caes. 44, Nero. 19.

pp. **117, 118.** Aetolia devastated by wars, S. 427. 11 and 460. 23.
Chaeronea–Phocis pass, Paus. x. 35. 8. Thebes–Chalcis road, S. 404.
11. Thebes–Anthedon, S. 408. 22. Route of Via Egnatia described
in S. 322 ff.

Byzantium, 'confluente undique in eam commeantium turba,' as
Trajan says, Trajan-Pliny 78; its fisheries, N.H. ix. 51.

St Paul lands at Neapolis, Acts xvi. 11.

p. **119.** Hebrus navigable to Cypsela, S. fr. 48; Ludias to Pella,
S. fr. 20. South-east wind necessary for voyagers putting into Athens
from Sunium, Dio Chrys. i. vi. 3. Boeotian harbours, S. 400. 2.
Big harbour near Aulis, S. 403. 8; 'capaci nobilis portu,' N.H. iv. 26.
Chalcis, first city of Euboea, S. 448. 11. Pyrasos, S. 435. 14.

Road up Axios valley, a natural route, S. 389. 5; taken from a
military expedition. Nero provided 'tabernas et praetoria per vias
militares,' C.I.L. iii. 6123. Hadrian's Black Sea road 'per ora Ponti
Euxini,' C.I.L. iii. 7613, 7615.

pp. **120, 121.** Messenia and Pamisus valley, well-tilled, Paus. iv.
34; cp. S. 366. 6. Elis and its fine flax, Paus. v. 5. 2 and cp. vi. 26.
'Tubera,' N.H. xix. 37. Triphylia, S. 344. 15. Horses and asses of
Arcadia, S. 388. Sicyon, large quantity of olive-oil, Paus. x. 32. 19;
cp. Diosc. i. 35. Phelloë and its vines, Paus. vii. 26. 10. ''Η Λακωνικὴ
λειπανδρεῖ,' S. 362. 11. The rich Eurycles of Sparta, in Jos. Antiq.
xvi. 301 ff., 'τῶν Δακεδαιμονίων ἡγεμῶν,' S. 363, and owned Cythera:
see *Klio*, xvii, pp. 44 ff. Martial speaks of large estates in Patrae,
Mart. v. 35. Landowner in Euboea; see further in chapter.

For ruin and desolation cp. S. 388. 2, 'ἢ οὐκέτ' εἰσὶν ἢ μόλις
αὐτῶν ἴχνη φαίνεται,' and Paus. iii. 19. 6 (Amyclae), viii. 25. 3
(Thelpusa), iii. 22. 3 (ruins of Helos), iv. 33. 6. 7 (Andania and
Dorium).

pp. **121, 122.** Attic honey, S. 399. 23. The finest in the world,
Diosc. ii. 82; cp. N.H. xi. 32, Scribonius Largus 16. Boeotia culti-
vated διὰ τὴν εὐκαρπίαν, S. 406. 16. Epaminondas reopens Copaic
tunnels, C.I.G. 1625. Dates of Aulis, Paus. ix. 19. 8. Flower-per-
fumes of Chaeronea, Paus. ix. 41. 7. Hellebore of Oeta, S. 418. 3;
and of Anticyra, Paus. x. 36. 7. Coccus of Ambrosus, Paus. x. 36.
Fertility of Crisa, S. 418. 3. Oil of Tithorea, Paus. x. 32. 19; cp.
Plut. Sulla 15. Deserted cities of Boeotia, S. 403. Only acropolis of
Thebes inhabited, Paus. ix. 7. 6; cp. Dio C. vii. 121. Scolus and
Ascra ruined, Paus. ix. 4. 4 and 29. 2.

pp. **122, 123.** The flocks of Euboea, S. 449. 14 (corn, N.H. xviii.
70). Rest of description taken from Dio Chrys. vii. (Euboicus). Two-
thirds of territory deserted 'δι' ἀμέλειάν τε καὶ ὀλιγανθρωπίαν' (34).
A former landowner: his possessions confiscated. By Nero? (11).
Another large landowner speaks in 34 ff. Anything to get land back
to cultivation.

Thessaly and its fertility, S. 430. 2. Floods of Peneus, ibid. Rich

plain of Larisa, S. 440; still a town, S. 430. 3. Thessalian horses,
S. 388; cp. Dio C. XV. 30. Fruitful country round Datum, S. fr. 33.
'Materies laudatissima' of Macedonia, N.H. XVI. 197.

pp. **123, 124**. Quarries of Croceae: stone hard to work, but veined
and beautiful, Paus. II. 3. 5 and III. 21. 4. Taygetus stone, S. 367. 7,
recently opened, and large. 'Lacedaemonium viride,' N.H. XXXVI. 55.
'Taygeti virent metalla,' Mart. VI. 42. 11. Whetstones, N.H. XXXVI.
164. Also old quarries in Taenarus, S. 367. 7.

Attica: quarry at Amphiale, S. 395. 13. Marble of Hymettus and
Pentelicus, S. 399. 23; cp. N.H. XXXVI. 7. 114; cp. Paus. I. 19. 6.
Stone used by Herodes.

Scyros and its variegated marble, S. 437; cp. N.H. XXXVI. 130.
Parian white marble, N.H. XXXVI. 14, and numerous references in
Pausanias. Carystus and marble, N.H. IV. 64 and S. 446. 6. Stone
of Thasos, Paus. I. 18. 6; cp. N.H. XXXVI. 44. 6. Laurion exhausted,
Paus. I. 1; S. 399. 23, 'νυνὶ δ' ἐκλείπει.' Copper and iron of
Lelantine plain exhausted, S. 447. 9.

Mines of Macedonia: gold mines at Datum, S. fr. 33 (bk VII); cp.
fr. 36. Gold mines at Crenides, near Philippi, and gold and silver in
Mount Pangaeus, S. fr. 34. Copper-green in Macedonia (chrysocolla),
Vitr. VII. 9. 6.

p. **125**. Purple-fishing off Laconia, Hor. II. 18. 7. Spartan purple
best in Europe, N.H. IX. 127. Purple dye-works at Amyclae, Mart.
VIII. 28. 9 and IX. 72. 1. 'Spartana chlamys,' Juv. VIII. 101. Women
weave Elean flax at Patrae, Paus. VII. 21. 14 and cp. N.H. XIX. 20.
Statuary-making at Athens, Philost., Vita Apoll. V. 20 (export).
Unguents of Chaeronea and Tithorea, Paus. IX. 41. 7 and X. 32. 19.
Pottery at Aulis, Paus. IX. 19. 8. Purple-fishing at Bulis, Paus. X. 37. 3.

p. **126**. Vanished cities, cp. S. 322, 388. 2, 403, 455. 13 etc., and
Paus. III. 19. 6, III. 22. 3, IV. 33. 6, VII. 23. 4, etc., besides previous
references.

p. **127**. Corinth, Hor. I. 7. 2; 'μεγάλη καὶ πλουσία,' S. 381. 23.
Dio Chrys. XXXVII. 8 and ff. 'You did not treat me,' he says, 'ὡς ἕνα
τῶν πολλῶν καὶ κατ᾽ ἐνιαυτὸν καταιρόντων εἰς Κεγχρέας ἔμπορον
ἢ θεωρὸν ἢ πρεσβευτήν.' Later he says, 'καίτοι πόλιν οἰκεῖτε τῶν
οὐσῶν τε καὶ γεγενημένων ἐπαφροδιτοτάτην.'

Hadrian's gifts: Corinthian aqueduct, Paus. VIII. 22. 3; Scironian
road, Paus. I. 44. 10. Hadrian made Greek people thrive, Paus. I. 36. 3.
Dedication by Greeks to Hadrian, 'σωτῆρι, ῥυσαμένῳ καὶ θρέψαντι τὴν
ἑαυτοῦ Ἑλλάδα,' in Ditt. Syll. 835 A.

p. **128**. For Greeks flocking to Rome see Juv. III. 69 ff. Pallas and
Narcissus, Suet. Claud. 28. Xenophon of Cos, Tac. Ann. XII. 61
and cp. Ditt. 804. Peaceful state of Greece, Plut. Praec. ger. reip.
32 (824 C), and cp. Epictetus III. 13. 9, who says 'ἀλλ᾽ ἔξεστιν πάσῃ
ὥρᾳ ὁδεύειν, πλεῖν ἀπ᾽ ἀνατολῶν ἐπὶ δυσμάς.'

CHAPTER EIGHT: AFRICA

p. **132.** 'African soil wholly given to Ceres,' N.H. xv. 8. Coast well inhabited, especially near Carthage, S. 825. Rivers and large forests in West, S. 826. 4. The nomads' desire for land and pasture, cp. Ann. III. 73. Mago and Carthaginian farming, Varro, R.R. I. I. 10; Cicero, de Oratore I. lviii. 249; N.H. XVIII. 22; Colum. III. I. March of Agathocles through garden country, Diod. xx. 8. 3–4.

p. **133.** It is true that some portions of the 'Lex Thoria' dealt with the African land, but the Senate merely rid itself of an encumbrance, and attempted no development.

Gracchus' African schemes, Liv. Ep. LX; Plut. C. Gracch. 10; Vell. I. 15. Caesarean colony at Carthage, S. 833 (sub fin.).

Cp. the vast amounts of fines Caesar exacted from African cities in corn and oil; at Leptis 'xxx centenis milibus pond. olei in annos singulos multat' (Bell. Afric. 97).

pp. **133, 134.** Augustus' colonies: see his own statement in Mon. Ancyr. 28, and Pliny, N.H. v. 2, 5 ff.

Juba: first received Numidia (Dio LI. 15), then later Mauretania (Dio LIII. 26). Cp. accounts of him in Vell. II. 116 and Dio LV. 28: Athenaeus calls him πολυμαθέστατος. See collected fragments in Müller, and cp. De la Blanchère, 'De rege Juba.'

The Mauretanian colonies under Baetica, N.H. v. 2, 'regum dicioni exempta.'

For the right to raise levies and lead them in case of raids or emergencies, see the very interesting inscription recently unearthed at Volubilis and discussed in *Journal des Savants*, 1917, p. 36, where M. Valerius Severus was 'praefectus auxiliariorum' against the forces of the rebel freedman Aedemon.

Expedition of Cossus against rebels in A.D. 6, Orosius VI. 21; Florus IV. 12. 40. Tacfarinas' revolt in Ann. II. 52, III. 20, etc. Aedemon's rising, N.H. v. 11.

pp. **134, 135.** Roads: Carthage–Utica, and bridge over Bagradas, Polyb. I. 75. 4, 5, 10; cuttings through hills and presumably up valley to quarries at Simitthu. Theveste, a prosperous city, ἑκατόμπυλος, Polyb. I. 73; 'χώρᾳ καταρρύτῳ καὶ καρποφόρῳ,' Diod. IV. 18. The Eastern road, Perip. Scylacis 110, p. 89; S. 835. 18. Cp. also Curio's two-day march from Clupea to Bagradas, Bell. Civ. II. 24.

Fertility of Byzacium, called Ἐμπόρια, Polyb. III. 23. 2.

Colony at Simitthu, Eph. Ep. v. 1114.

For revolts of Gaetuli, Musulamii, and others see Dio LV. 28; Florus IV. 12. 40, and Orosius VI. 21. 24.

p. **136.** Rising of Tacfarinas, Ann. II. 52 (see on p. 134).

Tacape-Theveste road built about A.D. 15, C.I.L. VIII. 10018, 10023; and also a bridge over Wadi Bêdja built, ibid. 14386. Extension of

- Carthage to Straits, Pseudo-Scylax III. p. 89. Ebusus-Africa,

NOTES 267

limits of province under Vibius Marsus, C.I.L. VIII. 22786; cp. *Mémoires prés...à l'Acad. des Insc. et B.-L.* XII. p. 341. Theveste–Hippo Regius by Vespasian in A.D. 75, C.I.L. VIII. 10119. Carthage–Hippo Regius, by Vespasian, ibid. 10116, and a new bridge built by legion under Trajan, ibid. 10117.

Trajanic roads. Theveste–Thamugadi–Lambaesis, built in about A.D. 100, C.I.L. VIII. 10186, 10210. Cp. an Antonine road in the heart of the Mons Aurasius, C.I.L. VIII. 10230. Milestone of Trajan near Simitthu, C.I.L. VIII. 14560. This road repaired soon after by Hadrian, C.I.L. VIII. 10048, 10080, and a milestone also near Simitthu, 14564.

Sitifis–Djemila, C.I.L. VIII. 10355, and the 'Via Nova Rusicadensis,' 10296, both Hadrianic.

p. **137**. Hadrian repairs transcontinental highway: inscr. on portion from Cyrene to Apollonia, *Ann. Epig.* 1919, no. 90. For municipal and other roads cp. C.I.L. VIII. 10296, 22397. See the Antonine Itinerary for the gap between Portus Magnus and Tingis. For fortified estates see C.I.L. VIII. 8209 and 21531.

pp. **138, 139**. Navigable rivers, N.H. V. 18. The traffic along western side of Africa: 'magna pars meridiani sinus ambitu Mauretaniae navigatur hodie,' N.H. II. 168.

Search for purple of Gaetuli, N.H. V. 12, 'omnes scopuli Gaetuli (exquiruntur) muricibus purpuris.'

Neapolis–Selinus passage, Thucyd. VII. 50. Lilybaeum–Hadrumetum, Caes. Bell. Afr. 2 (in four days). Sicily–Clupea, Bell. Civ. II. 23. Carthage to Straits, Pseudo-Scylax III. p. 89. Ebusus–Africa, Diod. V. 16 (who gives times to other points). Africa–Carales in three days, Bell. Afric. 98. Marius from Utica to Rome τεταρταῖος, Plut. Marius VIII. 5, and the figs of Cato in N.H. XV. 74. Pliny mentions a two-day voyage (!) from Africa to Rome, N.H. XIX. 4.

Utica became capital on ruin of Carthage, S. 832. 13.

p. **140**. Mauretania: the country, in spite of desert portions, good; lakes, rivers, and large forests of good trees, S. 826. 4. Small light horses, S. 828. Sheep wandering over plains, Georgics III. 338 ff. Fertile growth, huge vines; lions, elephants, gazelles, big game, S. 826. 4; cp. Hor. Odes I. 22. 15. Pitch and bitumen and copperworks near Siga and along coast, S. 830. 11. Copper-mines near Cartenna, Gsell, Atlas; cp. Polyb. XII. 1. 3. Precious stones, S. 830. 11. Ebony and citrus wood, N.H. V. 12. Export of tables to Rome in S. 826. 4. Murex found on rocky coasts of Gaetuli, N.H. V. 12. Juba's dyeworks of purple on islands off Moorish coast, N.H. VI. 201; cp. Hor. Odes II. 16. 35, 'bis Afro murice tinctae lanae.' Sailing down West African coast, N.H. II. 168, and cp. voyages of men of Gades. Tales of Fortunate Isles: dogs brought from the Canaries, N.H. VI. 203, 205.

p. **141**. Foundation of Iol Caesarea, S. 831. 12. 'Oppidum celeberrimum' according to Pliny, N.H. V. 20; 'urbs illustris,' Mela I. 30.

Inscriptions of royal servants, C.I.L. VIII. 9426, 9427, 9343–51. Cocleae of Iol very good, N.H. XXX. 45. 'Fabri argentarii,' C.I.L. VIII. 21106; 'argentarius caelator,' ibid. Sculpture, cp. new Apollo of Cherchel in *Monuments et Mémoires* (Piot), 1916, p. 35. Mosaic of Judgment of Paris, *Bull. Archéol.*, March 1921. Trades: Lanii, C.I.L. VIII. 9332; vestiarius, 20967; a myrepsus, 21097. Lamps from 'officina Sempronia' at Iol, C.I.L. VIII. 22644, no. 304 (cp. also *Bull. Archéol.*, March 1921); also peculiar lamps of district found in Baetica, C.I.L. VIII. 22642. 1 *h*, 2 *b*, and African lamps in Sardinia, C.I.L. VIII. S. III. p. 2213.

pp. **141, 142.** Tingis, about 30 miles from Belo on Spanish coast: a ferry there, S. 140, and cp. Mela I. 5. 26. Lixus faced Gades, and had another ferry, S. 825. 2; cp. Columella's account of 'munerarii' and shipping, in Colum. VII. 2. Siga opposite Malaca, N.H. V. 19, and cp. C.I.L. VIII. 19146. Malaca was 'ἐμπόριον τοῖς ἐν τῇ περαίᾳ νόμασι,' S. 156. A citizen of Iol at Tarraco, *Boletin de la real...*, 1915 (Inscr.). Cp. epitaph at Iol, 'Baetica me genuit tellus,' C.I.L. VIII. 21031. Cp. too dedications to Juba in Spain, as in C.I.L. II. 3417; and Otho's gift of revenues of Moorish cities to Baetica, Hist. I. 78.

p. **142.** Numidia. More cultivated, Mela I. 30; nothing save Numidian marble and wild beasts, N.H. V. 22. Yet some large towns, as Cirta and Bulla Regia. For wild beasts cp. Juv. IV. 100, and the 'munerarii' mentioned by Columella (above). For Numidian marble (quarries of Simitthu and elsewhere) cp. Hor. Odes II. 18. 4; 'columnas ultima recisas Africa,' Mart. VI. 42. 13 and IX. 75. 8, and also Juv. VII. 182. Temple at Bulla Regia of local marble, *J. des S.* 1914, p. 215. Many buildings and dedications of first century attest prosperity, *J. des S.* l.c. p. 215. Sheep, Georgics III. 339 ff. 'Vestiarii' at Cuicul, C.I.L. VIII. 20156. A Spaniard at Cirta, *Rev. Ep.* 1911, I. p. 193. A citizen of Madaura living at Emerita, *Boletin*, 1913.

pp. **143, 144.** Africa proper. Its fertility, Hor. Odes III. 16. 31. Wholly given to Ceres, N.H. XV. 8. Abounds in corn, Colum. III. 8. 4. The exceptional productiveness of Byzacium, Polyb. III. 23. 2 and N.H. XVIII. 94. Trees called 'milliariae,' N.H. XVII. 93. For Mago and farming see notes on p. 132. Hiding of corn underground, Bell. Afr. 65. 20,000 Attic medimni of corn to Rome, Plut. Caes. 55. 40 million modii of wheat annually sent to Rome, Jos. B.J. II. 386. Corn supplied to Tacfarinas, Ann. IV. 13. 3. Huge yield, Varro, R.R. I. 44. 2.

Vines and olives, Diod. XX. 8. 4. Oil in Byzacium, B.A. XCVII. 3; 300,000 litria of oil, Plut. Caes. 55. Oil from cedrus very good against decay, N.H. XVI. 197. Figs very good, N.H. XV. 69; cucumbers, XIX. 65; tuberes first sown in camp and transplanted, XV. 47; cp. Juv. V. 118. Coccus, N.H. XVI. 32, and purple, IX. 127; cp. S. 835. 18.

p. **145.** Specularis lapis recently found, N.H. XXXVI. 160. Salt, N.H. XXXI. 81. Cocleae of Iol, N.H. XXX. 45. Fisheries of Leptis, N.H. XXXI. 94; cp. city of Taricheia, near Thapsus, S. 834. 16. In Syrtis many small cities engaged in fishing, S. 835; and pickleries at Zuchis, S. 835. 18.

Quarries of Tunis, S. 834. 16; from Simitthu, N.H. xxxvi. 49; but 'tofus' used in lack of better, N.H. xxxvi. 166.

pp. **145, 146.** Carthage: a colony by Caesar, S. 833 fin.; 'καὶ νῦν εἴ τις ἄλλη καλῶς οἰκεῖται τῶν ἐν Λιβύῃ πόλεων'; 'iterum opulenta,' Mela 1. 34, N.H. v. 24. The young Carthaginian glass-worker, C.I.L. xiii. 2000. Navicularii of Carthage, *Notizie*, 1912, p. 435; 'curator navium Carthaginiensium,' *Notiz.* 1913, p. 353. Emperors probably keen on farming their vast domains, cp. N.H. xviii. 35, 'sex domini semissem Africae possidebant,' and Nero's confiscation of lands of Caesellius Bassus, Ann. xvi. 3 (sub fin.). For the imperial domains see Rostowzew's exhaustive treatment in 'Geschichte des Röm. Kolonates.' The importance of Africa as corn-bearing province grew slowly: it was Commodus who established an African corn-fleet, Hist. Aug., Commodus 17.

Pliny's list of cities in N.H. v. 23, 24 ff., among them Diarrhytos, Misua, Curubis, Leptis, Hadrumetum, Thapsus, Tacape, Sabrata and Oea. Many free cities. Quarrels between Leptis and Oea, Hist. iv. 50. Grazing-lands of Cinyps region, cp. Georg. iii. 312.

pp. **147, 148.** The Zarai tariff-list is given in C.I.L. viii. 4508.

Oil from Leptis, C.I.L. xv. nos. 2633 ff. and 3375 ff.; cp. *Mon. Antich.* 1918, p. 340. Amphorae from Tubusuctu, C.I.L. xv. 2634. Vinarii at Carthage, C.I.L. viii. 12574, and cp. 'oenopolae' in *C.-R. de l'Acad. des Inscr. et B.-L.*, 1906. 'Eborarii et citriarii,' C.I.L. vi. 33885. Seneca owned 500 citrus tables!, Dio lxi. 10. 3. 'Sordidas merces' between Africa and Sicily, Ann. iv. 13. At Thubursicum, father of knight a 'bonus agricola,' Dessau 7740. Granaries at Rusicade for corn-trade, C.I.L. viii. 7959, 7975; at Puteoli, Cic. de Finibus ii. 84. Merchants from Oea at Puteoli, C.I.L. x. 1684; cp. Tyrian agents.... For the excavations at Ostia and results see *Notizie degli Scavi*, 1912 and succeeding years.

Four-province mosaic, *Notiz.*, 1912, p. 206 (many other ship mosaics). 'Navicularii' of Misua, ibid. p. 172. 'Mensores frumentarii,' ibid. p. 347. 'Navicularii of Diarrhytus,' ibid. p. 388. 'Statio Sabratensium,' ibid. p. 435 (cp. fact that Vespasian married the daughter of a wealthy knight of Sabrata, Suet. Vesp. 3). Navicularii of Gummi, ibid. p. 435. Navicularii of Carthage, ibid. p. 435. Shipowners of Syllecte, ibid. 1914, p. 285. Merchants from Curubis, ibid. 1916, p. 328.

For ancient Africa the splendid 'Atlas Archéologique de l'Algérie,' by Stéphane Gsell, will be found invaluable for marking of sites and monuments, etc.

Boissier's 'L'Afrique Romaine' is excellent, but by now a little out of date. Toutain has published a good volume 'Les Cités Romaines de la Tunisie,' and there is the series of 'Notes et documents' published by the authorities at Tunis, starting in 1908. Cagnat has given a résumé of work done in Africa in the *Comptes-Rendus de l'Académie des Inscr. et Belles-Lettres* for 1915.

CHAPTER NINE: SPAIN

p. **150**. Justinus XLIV. 1. 4–5, Spain 'in omnia genera frugum fe-
cunda est': produces corn, wine, honey and oil, 'abstrusorum metal-
lorum felices divitiae: lini spartique vis ingens; minii certe nulla
feracior terra.' Pliny's enthusiasm for the mines, N.H. III. 30, 'metallis
plumbi ferri aeris argenti tota ferme Hispania scatet.' Cp. the 'terrae fe-
cunditas' in Bell. Hisp. 8. Justin l.c. speaks of the 'lenes cursus amnium.'

pp. **151, 152**. Republican milestones, C.I.L. II. 4956; and see also
the often-quoted passage of Polybius III. 39.

Bridge at Corduba, Bell. Hisp. 33. Also c. 36 mentions ships on
the Baetis as far as Hispalis.

The coast-road, S. 160. 9.

Milestones of Augustus, C.I.L. II. 4686 (Baetica), 4701, 4703 (Corduba), 4868, 4936, 4937, 4952–3 (Carthago Nova).

Tiberius' road-making, C.I.L. II. 4904, 4905 (to Aquitania); in
A.D. 14 and fifteen years later, Eph. Epig. VIII. 295 (Turiasso–Clunia),
219 (Bracara) and 210a; C.I.L. II. 4772, 4773a, 4777, 4778 (Bracara–
Asturica), 4869 (alternative route), 4651 (Emerita–Salmantica), 4935
(Montes Mariani), 4712 (repair of Via Augusta in A.D. 35, cp. *Ann.
Epig.* 1913, no. 11), cp. 4749.

pp. **153, 154**. Tiberius made Spaniards 'οὐ μόνον εἰρηνικούς, ἀλλὰ
καὶ πολιτικούς,' S. 156.

Claudius, C.I.L. II. 4954 (Carthago–Summum Pyrenaeum), and
4932 (near Castulo), 4644, 4645 (Emerita–Salmantica), and roads
between Bracara and Asturica, 4771.

Nero, C.I.L. II. 4884 (near Clunia), 4734 (repair of Via Augusta),
and 4657, 4719 (Emerita–Salmantica).

Vespasian, C.I.L. II. 4814 (yet another Bracara–Asturica road!), 4697,
4698 (repairing of Via Augusta and rebuilding of the bridges).

Trajan repairs Anas road, C.I.L. II. 4629; sees to road between
Emerita and Salmantica, 4667, and at Castulo, 4933.

For the North-West cp. Vespasian's reorganisation of the port
Brigantium as a Latin town, and the exploitation of the mines there.

pp. **154, 155**. The Durius, its good navigability, S. 153. 4. The
Tagus, its ships and gold, S. 151 (sub. fin.), and N.H. XXXIII. 66.
Description of the Baetis, its navigability, the bordering gardens and
so on, S. 142. The Anas too has metalliferous ranges around it (ibid.).

Trade to Italy great: exports of Turdetania, S. 144 ff. (ὁλκάδες
μέγισται πλέουσιν). Ferry at Belo, S. 140. 8. Malaca, 'ἐμπόριον τοῖς
ἐν τῇ περαίᾳ νόμασι,' S. 156. Carthago Nova, S. 158. 6. Export of
grass, S. 160. 9 (sub fin.). Dianium, S. 159; and Scombraria, ibid.
Tarraco, S. 159. 7. Seat of governor. 'Opulentissima,' Mela II. 90.
The harbour of the Artabri: imported tin, S. 175. 11. Trade with
Cassiterides. With regard to trade there see N.H. II. 167, quoted below.

p. **155**. Ostia–Tarraco, four days' sail, N.H. XIX. 4. Tarraco–Bilbilis, five days, Mart. X. 104. Icelus at Clunia ἑβδομαῖος from Rome, Plut. Galba 7. Gades–Ostia, seven days, N.H. XIX. 4. Gades–Tarraco, 'paucis diebus,' Bell. Civ. II. 21. Caesar was said to have reached Munda in 27 days from Rome, S. 160 (fin.); but the news of battle of Munda took from 17th March to 20th April to reach Rome, Dio XLIII. 42. 3.

pp. **156, 157**. For trade by sea cp. N.H. II. 167, 'a Gadibus... Hispaniae et Galliarum circuitu totus hodie navigatur occidens.' Cp. also S. 144 and 145. For the Testaccio finds see C.I.L. XV. p. 562, and cp. inscriptions quoted later.

The Tagus and its oysters, S. 152. The Exitani, S. 156. 2. Carthago Nova, 'πολλὴ ἡ ταριχεία,' S. 158. 6. Guild of 'piscatores et propolae,' C.I.L. II. 5929. Scombraria, S. 159. Gades and Southern voyage, N.H. II. 168, and cp. S. 99 and the tale there related. For fisheries see S. 145. 7, and for the various towns, S. 140. Discovery of pits at Belo, *Acad. des I. et B.-L.*, January 1918. Pickles equal to Pontic, S. 144. 6. Salt, S. 144. 6. Eye-salve recipe from rock-salt in Colum. VI. 17. 7.

pp. **157, 158**. For mineral wealth cp. Justin XLIV. 1. 4–5 and Pliny, N.H. III. 30. Exhausted mines reviving, N.H. XXXIV. 164, 'mirum in his solis metallis quod derelicta fertilius revivescunt.' Tiberius and Sextus Marius, Ann. VI. 19. The Societas of Ilucro, *Ann. Epig.* 1907, no. 135. 'Socii Sisapones,' C.I.L. X. 3964. The 'lex metalli Vipascensis,' C.I.L. II. 5181: therein are references to the 'lex metallis dicta,' and to the 'lex ferrariarum.' 40,000 men employed in mines at Carthago Nova, S. 147. 10. On slave-workers see Diodorus V. 35–38. 'Mercennarii' are mentioned in the Lex Met. Vip., and the other details in the text will all be found there. The mines at Baebelo and Aquitanian workers, N.H. XXXIII. 97. Adulteration, 'unde praeda societati,' N.H. XXXIII. 118. Cp. transportation of minium to Rome in Vitr. VII. 9. 4. 'Πλῆθος 'Ιταλῶν' working the mines, Diod. l.c.

pp. **159, 160**. The sands of Tagus and their gold, 'fluminum ramentis,' N.H. XXXIII. 66 and S. 146; cp. Sil. Ital. I. 234. Gold to be found near Calpe, S. 156. 2; in the mines of Marius (Montes Mariani), Ann. VI. 19; at Corduba, Sil. It. III. 401; among the Oretani, and at Cotinae, S. 142; at Carteia, Livy XXVIII. 3; in Lusitania and Asturia, N.H. XXXIII. 78 (cp. Sil. It. I. 231); and in Gallaecia, Mart. X. 17; among Turdetani, S. 146. A general description of methods of mining and gold-washing, of great interest, S. 146–7. Only $\frac{1}{30}$ of silver in Gallaecian gold, N.H. XXXIII. 80.

p. **160**. Silver: large profits made, Diod. V. 35. Found at Castulo, S. 148 (not worth working); at Carthago Nova, ibid.; at Ilipa and Sisapo, S. 142; in the N.W. of Spain, N.H. XXXIII. 96, 97; among Artabri, S. 147. The 'ἄργυρον ὄρος,' S. 148. 11. Silver mines at Ilucro, *Ann. Épig.* 1907, p. 135. 'Socii Sisaponenses,' *Boletin de la real...*, 1913. Finest silver found in Spain, N.H. XXXIII. 96.

272 NOTES

p. **161.** Lead: N.H. III. 30 and cp. XXXIV. 156. Baebelo mines yielded 300 lbs. daily, N.H. XXXIII. 97; found in the Ebro valley, N.H. XXXIV. 164, 165, and in Baetica, l.c. 164. as also in Capraria, one of the Balearic isles. Also among Madulingenses, N.H. IV. 118. But cp. N.H. XXXIV. 164, 'laboriosius eruto.' Also island of Plumbaria, S. 159; and Stephanus of Byzantium speaks of Μολυβδάνα near Malaca. Plumbarius, C.I.L. II. 6108.

pp. **161, 162.** Copper: at Corduba and in Montes Mariani, N.H. XXXIV. 4. In Turdetania, S. 146.

Iron in Cantabria, N.H. XXXIV. 149; cp. Mart. I. 49. Tempered at Bilbilis and Turiassio, N.H. l.c. 144. Works at Dianium, S. 159. 'Loricae Hiberae,' Odes I. 29. Loricarius, C.I.L. II. 3359.

Tin from Gallaecia, N.H. XXXIV. 156. Among the Artabri, and in land above Lusitania, S. 147. Tin from Cassiterides viâ the Artabri, S. 175. 11.

Minium, N.H. XXXIII. 118 (at Sisapo). Spanish minium brought to Rome, Vitr. VII. 9. 4. 'Minii certe nulla feracior terra,' Justin l.c.

Specularis lapis, N.H. III. 30. Quarries for marble, ibid. Spanish mica better than Cappadocian, N.H. XXXVI. 160. 'Lapicidinae' near Italica, C.I.L. II. 1131 (cp. 'marmorarius,' 1724). Pitch and red earth also exported, S. 144. Best red ochre in the Baleares, Vitr. VII. 7. 2.

p. **163.** For the fertility of Spain cp. passages cited earlier. Justinus, l.c., mentions 'frumentum, vinum, oleum, mel' as exports; cp. S. 144. 6. Host of exporters in many vessels, S. 142.

Good oil in small quantity from Turdetania, S. 144. Cp. N.H. XV. 1 and 17, on Spanish olives; also XVII. 31 for rich Baetic olive. Cicero's joke on oil in poetry in Pro Arch. X. 26. 'Olearii' ex Baetica, C.I.L. VI. 1625b. Cp. ibid. 1935 for Baetic oil-merchant. Cp. ibid. 29722 and II. 1481. Also Colum. V. 5. 15.

Wine: Laletane for 'copia,' Tarracon for 'elegantia,' also the vines of Lauro and Balearic isles, N.H. XIV. 71; cp. Sil. It. III. 369. Vines of Eastern coast, S. 164; cp. Mart. XIII. 118. Spanish wine in Petronius, Satyricon 66. 'Vinum Gaditanum' in *Bullet. Comunale*, 1879, p. 48. Despatched from Baetica in 'orcae,' Varro, R.R. I. 13. 6.

p. **164.** Flax. 'Splendorem lini' of crops near Tarraco and Saetabis in N.H. XIX. 10. Towels of Saetabis, Catull. XII. 14. Zoelic of Gallaecia, N.H. XIX. 10. Worked by Emporitae, S. 160. Prizes for weaving, Nic. Damasc. fr. 103. Lintearia (Tarraco), C.I.L. II. 4318a.

Esparto grass, S. 160. Cp. N.H. XIX. 30 and Mela II. 86.

Wheat: exported from Turdetania, S. 144. Baetica famous for its 'triticum,' N.H. XVII. 94, XVIII. 95.

Coccus exported in quantity from Turdetania, S. 144. Vegetable dyes, S. 163. 16. Coccus for half-payment of tribute near Emerita, N.H. XVI. 32. Figs, S. 163. Pistachio brought to Spain, N.H. XV. 91.

Galen VI. p. 613 places Spanish 'pruna' first.

p. **165.** Horses, N.H. VIII. 166 (from Olisipo), Mart. XIV. 199.

NOTES

Asturian 'esseda' horses, Sil. Ital. III. 335. Sheep and oxen in Turdetania, 'βοσκημάτων εὐπορία παντοίων,' 'ταλανταίους ὠνοῦνται τοὺς
κριούς,' S. 144. 6. Hunting in the woods, Senec. Controv. XVI. 22.
No wild beasts, S. 144. 6. Rabbits in Balearides, S. 168. 2.

pp. **165, 166.** Black sheep of Corduba, and fine wool, S. 144; cp.
also Colum. VII. 2. Milk of Gaditane cows, S. 169. Toga of Baetic
wool, Mart. X. 28. 5. Vegetable dyes, S. 163. 16. Dyeing, at Obulco,
C.I.L. II. 5519; cp. Eph. Epig. IX. 248, 'offector, infector.' Spanish
'sagum,' Livy XXIX. 3. At Saltigis, S. 144, and cp. N.H. VIII. 191.
Cerretani and Cantabri compete in export of hams, S. 162. 11. Sows
of Lusitania, Varro, R.R. II. 4. 11. Butter used by hill tribes instead
of oil, S. 155.

p. **166.** For pottery cp. C.I.L. II. 6254. 17a. 'Figlinae Medianenses'
in Baetica. Possibly Q. Fabius Rusticus was one of them (cp. Dessau,
6919). The pottery of Saguntum is praised by Pliny, N.H. XXXV. 160,
and its bottles by Juvenal V. 29, as also by Martial XIV. 107 and IV. 46.
Brickworks too at Maxilua, Vitr. II. 3. 4. Vases from the Ruteni
were imported to Saguntum, and have been found at Emporiae (*Rev.
Arch.* 1917, p. 114), also lamps from the factories at Iol Caesarea;
cp. some African colonies being under Baetic jurisdiction, as showing
close intercourse. Mommo's vases found in Spain, see Kisa, 'Das
Glas.'

Revival of mines in Baetica noticed, N.H. XXXIV. 165.

Margaritarius (Oriental), C.I.L. II. 496. Syrians at Malaca, Cag.-Laf.
I. 26. A citizen of Iol at Tarraco, *Boletin de la real...*, 1915. 'Negotians
salsarius' from Malaca, VI. 9677. Oil-merchants from Baetica, VI.
1625b. A Spaniard at Ostia, XIV. 397. A young merchant of Astigi
at Verona, V. 3365. Men of Calagurris at Nîmes, XII. 3167. Spaniards
from Bilbilis at Bordeaux, XIII. 612, 621.

CHAPTER TEN: ITALY AND THE
NORTHERN FRONTIERS

All routes, save the very old amber-route to the Padus valley from
the Danube, were practically of no importance till the exigencies of
frontier-defence turned them into military roads: trade followed of
course, and there were always the 'canabae' outside camps, but generally speaking Rhaetia, Noricum, Pannonia, Moesia, and even Dacia
contribute little of interest to the student of Roman trade and trade-
routes.

p. **171.** For the difficulty of the passes into Gaul cp. S. 204 and
such remarks as 'ὥστ' ἴλιγγον φέρειν τοῖς πεζῇ βαδίζουσι' and 'ἔθνη
λῃστρικὰ καὶ ἄπορα.' Cp. Caes. B.G. III. 1, 'iter per Alpes...magno
cum periculo.'

Augustus' pacification and road-making, cp. S. 204. 6, 'τὰς...
ὑπερβολὰς τοῦ ὄρους πρότερον οὔσας ὀλίγας καὶ δυσπεράτους νυνὶ
πολλαχόθεν εἶναι καὶ ἀσφαλεῖς ἀπὸ τῶν ἀνθρώπων καὶ εὐβάτους.' The
tribes 'τὰ μὲν ἐξέφθαρται, τὰ δ᾽ ἡμέρωται τελέως.' Cottius' roads,
Ammian. xv. 10. 2. Drusus' and Tiberius' campaigns, S. 206. 9, Vell.
II. 95, Hor. Odes IV. 4. 18 and 14. 7. Pass from Aquileia over Ocra,
'τὸ ταπεινότατον μέρος τῶν Ἀλπέων,' S. 207. 10. Native traders from
Danube, S. 214. 8. Road at Nauportus, S. 207. 10, and cp. Ann. I.
20 (soldiers employed on road-making).

pp. **172, 173**. The Ligurians, S. 202. 2. Wood-cutters, and putting
to sea, Diod. v. 39. As hired labourers, S. 165 (a very interesting
passage). Cularo, a customs-station, C.I.L. XII. 2225–7. Guild of
Transalpine merchants, C.I.L. XIII. 2029. Soldiers on guard, used
to quell disturbance at Pollentia 'e Cottii regno,' Suet. Tib. 37. 3.
Two routes from Augusta Praetoria, S. 205. 7 and 208. 11. From
Lemanus over Jura to Sequani: then on Agrippa's roads, S. 208. 11.
Sallustius' copper mine, N.H. XXXIV. 3. The Salassi and the river-
washings, S. 205. 7. Cp. N.H. XVIII. 182, 'Salassi cum subiectos
Alpibus depopularentur agros....'

pp. **173, 174**. Road through Tridentum started by Drusus and
completed by Claudius, 'quam Drusus pater Alpibus bello patefactis
derexerat,' C.I.L. v. 8002, 8003.

Maple in Rhaetia, N.H. XVI. 66. Larch brought to Rome for
building, ibid. 190, thus fulfilling Vitruvius' wish, who recounts many
fables about it, Vitr. II. 9. 14 ff. Rhaetian vines and wine, N.H. XIV.
16. 67. Imported for Augustus, Aug. 77.

Mustelae of Lake Brigantium, N.H. IX. 63.

Prosperity of Augsburg, Tac. Germ. 41 'in splendidissima provinciae colonia.' At Augsburg, C.I.L. III. 5816 (vestiarius), 5824 (ars
purpuraria), 5833 (ars cretaria), 14370 (porcarius) and also 12010. 48
(amphora 'liquamen scombri excellens M. Val. Maximi').

'Cives Romani negotiatores' at Brigantium, C.I.L. III. 13542,
5934 (Hispanus), 5824 (Greek), 5901 (Trevir), and 5797 (Trevir).

pp. **174, 175, 176**. Maroboduus flees to Tiberius, Ann. II. 63.
Lowest part of mountain-chain at Ocra, S. 314. Segestica at junction
of navigable rivers, 'ἁπάντων πλωτῶν,' S. 313. 2. Traffic from Italy
by river, S. 314, 'ποταμοί...καταφέροντες...τὸν ἐκ τῆς Ἰταλίας φόρτον.'
(Cp. jars of Aquileian merchant at Noricum, C.I.L. III. 6007. 5.)
Legionary headquarters at Poetovio, Hist. III. 1. Carnuntum as point
for invasion of Germany, Vell. II. 109. 5. A garrison there, N.H. IV.
80. At Brigetio, a dedication 'genio commerci et negotiantum,' C.I.L.
III. 4288. Maroboduus, S. 290, and cp. Vell. II. 108, 109. Roman
merchants attracted by 'ius commercii' offered, Ann. II. 62. The
amber-route explored, N.H. XXXVII. 45. Finds of coins farther North,
see Fredrich, *Zeitschrift d. Hist. Ges. für d. Prov. Posen.* XXIV. 1909.

The iron of Noricum: excellent working, N.H. XXXIV. 145, and cp.

Hor. Epodes XVII. 71. Iron-working and gold-washing at Noreia, S. 214. 8 (sub fin.).

pp. **177, 178.** Eastern branch to Segestica, Siscia, and Sirmium, and so to Danube, S. 314. Rise of Dacian power under Burebistas, S. 303. 11 ff. Trajan's conquest of Dacia, Dio LXVIII. 10 ff. Segestica as natural base for a Dacian war, S. 313. 2, and the river Marisus used for bringing supplies, S. 304. 13, even in Augustus' time. Gold-mines of Dacia, at Ampelum, C.I.L. III. 1297, 1312, and cp. 1997.

Trajan made 'iter per feras gentes a Pontico mari in Galliam,' Aur. Vict. 13. But cp. Ovid's remark on rarity of Western traders at Tomi in the first century, Tristia III. 12. 35–38.

Syrian merchants. In Pannonia, one died at Sirmium, C.I.L. III. 2006; another found at Celeia, III. 11701; and a trader from Antioch at Carnuntum, III. 14359². Two Syrians in Dacia, C.I.L. III. 1431, 7761. A Syrian, from Cyrrhus, at Aquileia, C.I.L. v. 785.

A Treviran merchant near Apulum, C.I.L. III. 1214. A Dacian merchant ('negotiator Daciscus') had a monument erected to his memory near Aquileia, probably where his agent dwelt, C.I.L. v. 1047.

CHAPTER ELEVEN: GAUL

pp. **180, 181.** Rome's connection with Massilia: she protected her from raids, Polyb. XXXIII. 8. 12; again, in 125 B.C. she went 'in auxilium Massiliensibus,' Liv. Ep. LX; a strip of land reserved, S. 180. Narbo, Cic. pro Fonteio v. 13, 'specula populi Romani.' Prohibition of vine and olive, Cic. de Rep. III. 9. 16. Romans in Gaul, Cic. pro Font. l.c. 11; over the passes into Switzerland, Caes. B.G. III. 1; on Western coast, IV. 20, 21. Penetration of Gaul with cheap wine and wares, Diod. v. 26. 3. Cp. Umbrenus who had many business interests in Gaul, Sall. Catil. 40. Roman citizenship a prize, Tac. Ann. III. 40. Hill towns replaced by lower settlements, *Ac. des Ins.* 1917, p. 53. Peace imposed on Gaul, S. 195. 2. Stop to barbarous practices, S. 198 and N.H. xxx. 13. Allobroges induced to adopt agriculture, S. 186. Altar of Rome and Augustus, S. 192. 2; cp. Dio LIV. 32.

p. **182.** Great rivers, fertile plains, crops of Gaul, S. 177. 2 ff.; cp. Mela III. 17, 'frumenti praecipue ferax.' Narbonensis 'magis culta et magis consita,' Mela II. 74. 'Italia verius quam provincia' according to N.H. III. 31. 'Pinguia Gallicis crescunt vellera pascuis,' Hor. Odes III. 16. Wealth of the Gauls, Dio LIX. 21. 2, 3.

Sea-route to Gaul, stormy and unpleasant, Suet. Claud. XVII. 2; bad shore, Massaliot watch-towers, S. 184. Usually by land, see previous chapter on Frontier Routes.

p. **183.** The Via Domitia and its milestones, Polyb. III. 39. Restored under Tiberius, C.I.L. XII. 5445, 5557, 5628 etc. Convenience and closeness of rivers, S. 177. 2.

Lugdunum: its position and wealth: it lies 'ἐν μέσῳ τῆς χώρας ὥσπερ ἀκρόπολις,' S. 208. 11. Agrippa's roads: (S. 208. 11) (1) to Southern coast, (2) to Aquitania and West, (3) N.W. to Bellovaci and Ambiani, (4) to the Rhine, (5) Vesontio–Jura–Nantuates–Italy.

p. 184. Drusus' campaigns: Vindonissa–Brigantia–Italy, cp. C.I.L. v. 8002–3. 'In tutelam provinciae praesidia ubique disposuit'; 50 forts along the Rhine; 'Bonnam Gesoriaco pontibus iunxit'; fleet at Bonna, Florus II. 30. 26.

The 'pontes longi' of Domitius in Germany, Ann. I. 63. Inscription to Tiberius at Bagacum, C.I.L. XIII. 3570 (road from Gesoriacum to Rhine). Fleet at Fectio under Germanicus, Ac. des Ins., 1916, June.

p. 185. Claudius journeys through Gaul by land and river, Claud. 17; Dio LX. 21. 3.

Roads in Brittany near Carhaix, C.I.L. XIII. 9016. Lugdunum to Mediolanum Santonum and Bordeaux, 8908, 8900, 8919. Also from Autricum to Alauna, 8976; Augustonemetum to Avaricum, 8920; Moguntiacum to Colonia (and presumably to Gesoriacum), 9145.

p. 186. Vespasian built from Argentorate into Rhaetia, C.I.L. XIII. 9082; Durocortorum–Divodurum (Nerva), 9053; he also built from Moguntiacum to Colonia Agrippinensis, 9146.

Trajan: Argentorate–Ariolica, C.I.L. XIII. 9078; Moguntiacum down Rhine to South, 9120; Colonia Agrippinensis to Noviomagus Batavorum, 9162. Other roads of his and Hadrian's are 8990, 9047, 9065, 9133, etc. Trajan's work: 'iter per feras gentes a Pontico mari in Galliam,' Aur. Vict. 13.

p. 187. Tin from Britain in 30 days down Rhone, Diod. v. 22. 4 ff.

Four routes to Britain, from river-mouths mostly: (1) Atax and Garonne, (2) through land of Arverni to avoid Rhone currents—Liger, (3) Rhone–Arar–Doubis–Sequana, (4) Rhone–Sequana–Itius, S. 189.

Merchants on this last route in Caesar's time, B.G. IV. 20, 21. Veneti once controlled trade, S. 194 (sub fin.). British embassies to Augustus, Mon. Anc. 32. Return of wrecked Romans, Ann. II. 24.

pp. 188, 189. Menapian vessels on Rhine, Caes. B.G. IV. 4. Commerce down Rhine to Itius and Britain, S. 199. 2, and see later chapters. Exploration voyage by Roman fleet, Mon. Ancyr. v. 26. The 'fossa Drusiana,' Ann. II. 8, completed under Nero, XIII. 53, with an agger. Corbulo's canal between Mosa and Rhenus, XI. 20; soldiers employed. Project of Arar–Mosella canal and completion of Gallic waterway, XIII. 53. Caligula's lighthouse opposite Britain, Calig. 46. Fleet at Gesoriacum for protection of commerce, C.I.L. XIII. 1. p. 561. Cp. inscriptions of 'nautae' of different rivers, given later.

pp. 189, 190. Gallia Narbonensis. 'Magis culta et magis consita ideoque etiam laetior,' Mela II. 74. 'Agrorum cultu...amplitudine opum, nulli provinciarum postferenda,' N.H. III. 31. Massilia, S. 179. 4 ff. Entitled to exact dues from those using Rhone canal: much wealth therefrom: their lighthouse towers, S. 184. Coral-beds, N.H. XXXII. 21, oyster-beds, 62, and tunny-fisheries, Aelian, Nat. Animal. XIII. 16. Fish-pickling of Antipolis, N.H. XXXI. 94. Olive and vine, but little corn because of rough soil, S. 179. 5. Their wine was παχὺς καὶ σαρκώδης (Athen. 27c and 152c), smoky (Mart. III. 8. 23), and often adulterated! (N.H. XIV. 68). School of medicine, N.H. XXIX. 9. Massiliots in Egypt, *Rev. Ét. Anc.* 1920, p. 50. Many Romans travel there for philosophy, S. 181. Exiles there, Ann. IV. 43, 44, XIII. 47; cp. Tac. Agric. 4.

p. **191**. Few harbours on coast, Mela l.c. Fisheries along Southern bend, S. 182; cp. Athen. VIII. 4. Naval harbour of Forum Julii, Ann. IV. 7. Minerals in West: iron-mines on bank of Atax, C.I.L. XII. 4398. Gold among the Tectosages, S. 187. 13; the treasure of Tolosa, S. 188.

An agricultural country, see Mela and Pliny l.c. Wool, N.H. XIX. 8. Export of hams, Varro, R.R. II. 4. 10. Cheese of Nemausus, N.H. XI. 240, and of Tolosa, Mart. XII. 32. 18. Allobrogic sweet wine, Colum. III. 2. 16. New wine of Vienna, N.H. XIV. 18; cp. Mart. XIII. 107. A 'diffusor' of Gallic wine, C.I.L. VI. 29722. Coloured pottery of the 'officina Aricii' at Vasio, *Rev. Ét. Anc.* 1911, p. 201. Figlinae among the Allobroges, C.I.L. XII. 2461.

p. **192**. Traffic: Fabri navales, C.I.L. XII. 700, 722 (at Arelate), 3165*b*, 'fabri tignarii,' *Ann. Ép.* 1910, no. 124. (Nemausus), guilds of sailors on various rivers, C.I.L. XII. 730, 731, 1797, 3316, and 'mercator Dubensis' in *Rev. Arch.* 1916, p. 210. Lead-stamps at Fréjus shew trade, C.I.L. XII. 5700. 2 *a*, *b*.

Riches of Vienna, Hist. I. 65, 66; silver statue to benefactor, C.I.L. XII. 5864. Harbour of Arelate; shipwright's epitaph, 5811. Nemausus, on main road to Spain, repaired by Tiberius: professions there, 3165 *b*, 3351, 3316, 2754. Men from Calagurris, 3167; lintearius, 3340.

p. **193**. Narbo, chief town of province, Mela l.c., 'μέγιστον ἐμπόριον τῶν ταύτῃ,' S. 181. 6. Its εὐκαιρία for trade, Diod. V. 38. 5.

Mosaic and inscriptions of Narbonese merchants at Ostia, *Notiz.* 1916, p. 326 (cp. 1913, p. 139). Among various trades we note: navicularius, C.I.L. XII. 4398; ampullarius, 4455; capistrarius, 4466; viminarius, 4522; gypsarius, 4479; faber limarius, 4475; solearius, 4510; pistor, 4503; fabarius, 4472; lardarius, 4483; lintearius, 4484; materiarius, 4467, and others.

Merchants at Narbo and at Rome, cp. C.I.L. XII. 4406, with the amphorae at Rome, XV. 3974–5.

pp. **193, 194**. Tres Galliae. 'Terra est frumenti praecipue et pabuli ferax, et amoena lucis immanibus,' Mela III. 17. 'ἡ δ' ἄλλη πᾶσα σῖτον φέρει πολὺν καὶ κέγχρον καὶ βάλανον,' S. 178. Export of corn to Rome in N.H. XVIII. 66. The 'naviculari marini' at Arelate chose as patron a 'procurator annonae prov. Narbon.,' C.I.L. XII. 672.

Lack of wine and oil in North, Diod. V. 26, cp. Varro, R.R. I. 7. 8.

Gauls brew ζῦθος, cp. Diod. v. 26. 2. To North 'ἡ μὲν ἐλαιόφυτος καὶ συκοφόρος ἐκλείπει,' and vine grows with difficulty, S. 178. The Viennese vines (see p. 191), and vines planted among the Bituriges, N.H. XIV. 27. For export of wine cp. 'Sum vetus v ann. Baeterrense,' C.I.L. XV. 4542, and N.H. XIV. 68, 71. Cp. vinarius who was head of Arar sailors, C.I.L. XIII. 1954, and a Trevir at Lugdunum who held same position, 1911. Oil appears to have come from Southern district too, cp. XII. 4499, 'olearius' and an 'olearius Aquensis' in VI. 9417. But one at Lyons, XIII. 1996, and cp. merchant who dealt in Baetic oil and wine from Lyons, and was president of Arar sailors, VI. 29722. Cp. XIII. 1999, 'neg. Italicus.'

pp. **194, 195.** Other vegetables and fruits; vaguely τἆλλα δὲ φύεται (same crops as in Italy (S. 178), also millet and acorns). Cherries in N.H. XV. 103–4, but no figs North of Cevennes, S. 178. Peaches, N.H. XV. 39.

No land save marsh-land uncultivated: inhabitants compelled to give up fighting and become γεωργοί, S. 178.

pp. **195, 196.** 'Pinguia Gallicis crescunt vellera pascuis,' Hor. Odes III. 16. 35. Thick-fleeced sheep of Belgae: herds owned by Romans, S. 196. 3. Export of hams and sausages, Varro, R.R. II. 4. 10, 'pernae, tomacinae, petasones.' Pickled pork from region of Sequana, S. 192. 2. Belgae supply cloaks and pork to Rome and Italy in abundance, S. 197. Ham 'de Menapis,' Mart. XIII. 54, cp. Edict. Diocl. IV. 8. 'Galliae universae tela texant' (Cadurci, Caleti, Ruteni, Bituriges, Morini), N.H. XIX. 8 ff. Bolsters and quilts made by the Cadurci, N.H. XIX. 13; cp. Juv. VI. 537. Burrarii of Med. Santonum, C.I.L. XIII. 1056. Flax woven among Cadurci too, S. 191. A sagarius at Lyons, C.I.L. XIII. 2008. A lintearius from the Veliocassae, 1998. Trevir vestiarius, 542; sagarii at Vienna, XII. 1928, and at Paris, XIII. 3037. A clothes-cleaner at Lyons, XIII. 2023. At Milan, 'sagarius et pellarius,' v. 5928; a sagarius of the Mediomatrices, 5929. A 'negotians vestiarius' from Gaul in Pola (Pais, 1096). Varieties of Trèves and Arras, Edict. Diocl. XIX. 54 and 61; cp. XIX. 32, 'βίρρος Νερβικός' (Cumont). Gallic cloaks, Mart. XIV. 128.

pp. **196, 197.** Working of metals among the Gauls, Caes. B.G. III. 21 (among Aquitani) and VII. 22 (iron-working at Avaricum).

Gold-mines among Tectosages, S. 187. 13; treasure of Tolosa, S. 188; cp. riches of Luerius, king of Arverni, S. 191. Easily found among the Tarbelloi, S. 190.

Silver-mines among Gabales and Ruteni: in latter country one worked by bailiff of Tiberius and imperial slaves, C.I.L. XIII. 1550; cp. Suet. Tib. 49. 2. 'Argentarii,' C.I.L. XIII. 1963, 2024. Yet change of ownership may have been slow, see S. 148. 10 (Spain). A poor mine across Rhine, worked by legate and soldiers, Ann. XI. 20. Bituriges, 'argentum incoquere,' N.H. XXIV. 162.

Copper-mines owned in Gaul by Livia, N.H. XXXIV. 3. Mines of

NOTES 279

copper at Vaudrevange, C.I.L. XIII. 4238. Worked at Lyons, 2901.
Mines of iron and working among the Petrucorii, S. 191. Iron-mines
on the Atax let out, C.I.L. XII. 4398. 'Ferrariae' at Anicium, XIII.
1576–7. 'Magnae ferrariae' at Avaricum, Caes. B.G. VII. 22. 'Fabri
ferrarii' at Lyons, C.I.L. XIII. 2036. Iron-works at Dijon, 5474.
'Loricarii' of Aedui, 2828. Later still a 'procurator ferrariarum' at
Lyons, 1797. Vast remains near Sambre valley, Cumont, pp. 38–9,
and in Brittany, Jullian v. p. 209.

p. **198**. Marble quarries in Aquitania: first exporters, C.I.L. XIII.
38. A 'marmorarius' at Agennum, 915, and cp. 122.

Yet Pliny has no praise for Gallic silver or gold, N.H. XXXIII. 96,
and cp. XXXVII. 203. Britain and Spain surpassed her production in
tin and lead and silver.

pp. **198, 199**. See especially Déchelette, 'Vases Céramiques ornés
de la Gaule Romaine.'

Arretine pottery imported, Déchelette, 'Vases,' pp. 9, 15; cp.
Samian ware in camps, C.I.L. XIII. 10009 passim. Figlinae among
the Allobroges, XII. 2461. Augustan pottery at Vetera, *Bonn. Jahr.*
fasc. 122, 1913, p. 210. Samian ware at Fectio, *Ac. d. I. et B.-L.* 1916,
June. Lamps from Lugdunum at Vindonissa, *Rev. Arch.* 1919, p. 398,
and also decorated ware, *Rev. Ét. Anc.* 1920, p. 146. Mommo's ware
at La Graufesenque among Ruteni, C.I.L. XIII. 10010, no. 1374,
XII. 5686, no. 602. Arvernian and Rutenian pottery at Ruscino, *Rev.
Ét. Anc.* 1920, p. 128. In Rhine valley at Tabernae, C.I.L. XIII. ii.
p. 164, especially too at Trèves, XIII. 10013. 1–3; cp. Fölzer, 'Die
Bilderschüsseln.' The Atisii exported ware (Allobrogic), C.I.L. X.
8048. 2. Lugdunum ware found in England, VII. 1334. 1 and 14.
Rhine pottery in Britain, Cumont, op. cit. p. 69. Gallic ware exported
into Italy by end of first century, *J.R.S.* IV. p. 27. Ars cretaria,
at Lyons, in C.I.L. XIII. 1906 and 2033 (a Trevir), and at Cologne,
8224 and 8350. Cp. large number of Treviri found as traders over
Gaul.

p. **200**. Glass. See especially A. Kisa, 'Das Glas im Altertum,'
and Morin-Jean, 'La Verrerie en Gaule....'

Egyptian glass found north of the Alps, Déchelette, 'Manuel,'
II. p. 789. Sand-tempering of glass spreads to Gaul, N.H. XXXVI. 194.
Ware of Artas in France, Kisa, p. 10. Sidonian glass on Rhine banks,
Bonn. Jahr. 1888, p. 86. Syrian ware not imported after first century,
Kisa, p. 736. Works at Lyons, cp. C.I.L. XIII. 2000 (young worker from
Carthage); high prices, N.H. XXXVI. 195. Chief centre in region of
Normandy and the Channel: note ὑαλᾶ σκεύη as imported to Britain
early, S. 200. 3 (from Caleti?, S. 189). Frontinus and his workshops,
C.I.L. XIII. 10025, no. 38 (cp. Morin-Jean, op. cit., pp. 170 ff.). In
Cologne and Rhine valley, Cumont, p. 72 (probably later); at Tabernae,
C.I.L. XIII. 2. 164.

p. **201**. Terra-cotta images: workshops at Bordeaux, C.I.L. XIII.

10015. 77; in Brittany, 10015. 85; among Arverni, 10015. 38. Cp. glassworks of Norman region, the masses of scoria in Brittany, and Claudius' roads in that region, and trade with Britain.

pp. 201, 202. Merchants from foreign parts. At Burdigala; two Spaniards from Bilbilis, C.I.L. XIII. 612; a Spaniard, 621; a Trevir merchant, 634; a German, 618; two Greeks, 619, 620; one from Nicomedia, 625; Syrians, 632.

At Lyons: a place of exile, cp. Herod Antipas (Jos. XVIII. 252). The African young glass-worker, C.I.L. XIII. 2000; a man from Puteoli, 2022; merchant from Rome who was a navicularius of Puteoli, 1942; a Greek, 2005 (and cp. 2007); a Syrian, 2448; an embroidery merchant from Syria, 1945.

A Lydian aurifex among Helvetii, C.I.L. XIII. 5154; a mosaic-maker from Puteoli, 3225; a man from Beyrouth, XII. 3072; merchant from Nicomedia, XIII. 4337; Bithynians, 6851.

Spaniards at Burdigala (see above), and in Narbonensis, C.I.L. XII. 412, 3332, 4377.

p. 203. Traffic in Gaul itself. Lamps of Lugdunum at Haltern and Vindonissa on Rhine, *Rev. Arch.* 1919, p. 398. Decorated ware, cp. *R.É.A.* 1920, p. 146. Merchandise of North Gaul into Germany by sea way, Willers, 'Neue Untersuchungen.' Terra sigillata at Fectio, *Ac. des I. et B.-L.* 1916. Treveran merchants at Lugdunum, also a Tribocus, C.I.L. XIII. 2018, 2029, 2033. The sailors of Paris and their monument, 3026. Merchants at Burdigala from various parts: a Trevir, 634; Bellovaci, 611; Ruteni, 629; Parisii, 626; Sequani, 631. 'Sagarius Carnutensis' at Lyons, 2010. Trevir at Agedincum, 2956; a Nervian at Cologne (Brambach, 418). Geese driven on foot from Morini to Rome, N.H. x. 53. 'Strepentibus ab utroque mari itineribus,' Hist. II. 62.

p. 204. Traffic out of Gaul. Sailors at Fectio, C.I.L. XIII. 8815. Pottery merchant to Britain, XIII. 8793. Vases of Trèves found at London, Fölzer, op. cit. p. 701, and compare other merchants to Britain at Cologne and Castel, C.I.L. XIII. 8164a, 7300. But vases from Ledosus more plentiful in Britain, Oswald and Pryce, T.S., pp. 12 ff. Trevir merchant to Britain at Burdigala, C.I.L. XIII. 634. Vases from Ruteni at Saguntum and Emporiae, *Rev. Arch.* 1917, p. 114. At Mevania and Milan, trading with Gaul, C.I.L. XI. 5068, v. 5911. A Mediomatrix at Milan, v. 5929. Treviri in Rhaetia, III. 5901, 5797, and at Apulum, III. 1214. A Gaul at Cliternia, IX. 4172. Direct voyage to Egypt, Sulp. Sev. Dial. I. 1–3. Narbonese pottery in Egypt, C.I.L. III. 14148. 8. Cp. Massiliots there, see p. 190. Exceptional instance: hired Aquitani in mines at Baebelo, in N.H. XXXIII. 97. An 'unguentarius' from Lyons at Rome, C.I.L. VI. 9998.

pp. 204, 205. The wealth of the Gauls, Jos. B.J. II. 364 (Agrippa's speech). 'Are the Jews "πλουσιώτεροι Γαλάτων," who have "πηγὰς τῆς εὐδαιμονίας ἐπιχωρίους" in their land?' 'τοῖς ἀγαθοῖς σχεδὸν ὅλην ἐπικλύζοντες τὴν οἰκούμενην.' The Arverni retained Zenodorus for an enormous fee to make an image of their god, N.H. xxxiv. 45–7.

Gallic pottery had beaten Italian export by about A.D. 50, and appears at Hofheim about A.D. 100, T.S., p. 4. La Graufesenque and Lezoux earliest: Lezoux imported to Britain in second century, T.S., p. 12. The East Gallic pottery begins towards end of first century, T.S., p. 11.

CHAPTER TWELVE: BRITAIN

pp. **208–210.** Early notices. Much lead in the island, little iron: copper imported: plenty of timber, Caes. B.G. v. 12. Many cross over to island for Druid learning, B.G. vi. 13. 11. Merchants from Gaul, iv. 20. 3. Control of trade by Veneti, S. 194 (sub fin.). Tin dug in Britain, Diod. v. 22. Taken to Ictis and across sea to Gaul, v. 22. Taken to Massilia and to Narbo, Diod. v. 38. Gallic coins have been found in Falmouth and South.

Many chieftains send embassies to Augustus: no heavy tolls, S. 200. 3; cp. mention in Mon. Ancyr. 32. Yet land still to conquer, Panegyr. Messal. 149; cp. Hor. Odes iii. 5. 3. Augustus' 'policy,' Tac. Agric. 13; he very nearly did go, Dio liii. 25. 2. Claudius' conquest of Britain, Dio lx. 19. Agricola's pacific measures, Tac. Agric. 19, 20, 21.

pp. **211–213.** A country of woods, plains, and great rivers, Mela iii. 6. 50, 51. No milestones before Hadrian: hints from camps and colonies. Londinium the great centre, Ann. xiv. 33. Area between Trent and Severn secured (reading 'cunctaque cis Trisantonam et Sabrinam'), Ann. xii. 31. Army in land of Decangi, xii. 32; cp. too pigs of iron from Flintshire before A.D. 70, C.I.L. vii. 1204, 1205. Conquest of South, Suet. Vesp. 4; and pigs from Mendips of A.D. 49, C.I.L. vii. 1201; probable date for Isca and Glevum. Lindum (cp. 'Vict. Hist. Northants,' i. 214). Expedition to Mona, Ann. xiv. 29. Frontinus among Silures overcomes difficulties of country, Agric. 17. Policy of advanced forts, c. 14; cp. Agricola's placing of garrisons on new districts, c. 20. Natives compelled to work on roads, c. 31; and cp. reference to 'devortia itinerum,' c. 19. Hadrianic milestones at three points: one near Leicester, C.I.L. vii. 1169, another near Lancaster, 1175, and a third near Conway, E.E. vii. 1099. The Hadrianic wall, Spartianus, Hadr. 11, and see the full account by Collingwood in *J.R.S.* xi. p. 37. Four routes to the island, S. 199. 2. ''Ιδιῶται μύριοι διαβαίνουσι,' Aristides, Orat. Aeg. 355 (Dindorf).

p. **213.** For sea-communication only with Cornwall we have a parallel in Mauretania.

pp. **214, 215.** Corn exported from Britain, S. 199. 2; at first only grown in the South, Caes. B.G. v. 14. Soil very fertile, though crops are late, owing to moisture of climate, Agric. 12. Corn exacted as tribute: in granaries, Agric. 19 (cp. c. 31). Cp. in fourth century

Julian's export of corn from Britain to Rhine, Zosimus III. 5 (cp. Epist. ad S.P.Q. Ath. p. 279 D).

Herds, hides, and hunting-dogs exported, S. 199. 2. The geese of Britain, N.H. x. 56. Olive and vine not grown, Agric. 12. The cherry acclimated, N.H. xv. 102; also the apple, cp. *Archaeol.* LXI. p. 213.

pp. **215, 216.** Gold, silver, and iron, S. 199. 2 (exported). Same list in Agric. 12, 'pretium victoriae.' Tin from Britain, Diod. v. 22 and 38. Lead ('nigrum plumbum'): law of limit; used for pipes, N.H. xxxiv. 164. Lead-mines in Mendips, C.I.L. VII. 1201; near Wroxeter, VII. 1209; among the Decangi, VII. 1204, 1205 (cp. E.E. VII. 1121 at Chester, date A.D. 76); near Tamworth (A.D. 76), E.E. IX. 1264; near Matlock at Lutudaron, E.E. IX. 1266. Copper in North Wales, E.E. IX. 1258–61. Tin very mysterious: one solitary 'massa' in Cornwall, E.E. IX. 1262; see Haverfield in 'Mélanges Boissier,' p. 251 and Rice Holmes' exhaustive discussion in 'Ancient Britain,' p. 499. Iron worked in Sussex and Forest of Dean: hoards of iron tools at Silchester, *Archaeol.* LII. p. 742, LVII. p. 246. Iron-workings at Ariconium, *The Times*, Oct. 6th, 1922. For minerals generally see Haverfield, *Rom. Occup. of Britain*, pp. 254 ff., and Wheeler, *Prehistoric and Roman Wales*, pp. 268 ff.

p. **217.** 'Britanniam aperiat,' Sen. ad Polyb. 13. British sheep, S. 199. 2. Woollens at Venta Belgarum, Notit. Occ. XI. 60. British cloth, Edict. Dioc. XIX. 36. Lichen dyes; dyeing works at Silchester, *Archaeol.* LIV. p. 460. Basket-making, Martial XIV. 99, 'barbara bascauda.' British oysters, N.H. IX. 169 and XXXII. 62, and cp. Juv. IV. 141 (from Richborough); but the pearls were poor and of a darkish colour, N.H. IX. 116; cp. Aelian, De Nat. Animal. xv. 8.

p. **218.** Clay in Britain ('creta argentaria'), N.H. XVII. 45. Samian ware imported from Gaul (see Gaul); at Din Lligwy, in Anglesea, *Arch. Cambrensis*, 1908, pp. 183 ff. The Castor ware, manufactured there, possibly originally from Germany, Walters, 'Catalogue of Roman pottery in British Museum,' p. 397. New Forest ware, ibid. p. 410. Ware named after Upchurch in Kent, ibid. p. 415. There was much importation of Samian ware, Oswald and Pryce, 'Terra Sigillata,' pp. 4–5, 12, and 33, 35 ff.

p. **219.** Seneca as usurer, Ann. XIII. 42, 'Italiam et provincias immenso faenore hauriri,' cp. Dio Cass. LXII. 2. Merchants from Rhine valley to Britain, C.I.L. XIII. 8164a (Cologne), 7300 (Castel), and 'negotiator cretarius' at Walcheren, 8793. Pottery from East Gaul mostly in North, T.S., p. 33, though ware from Trèves and Rheinzabern found at London, T.S., p. 35. Italian pottery before conquest, p. 5, ceased after Flavian era. Ware from Ledosus most common, acme in Antonine age, p. 12; bulk of pottery at Balmuildy from there, cp. Miller, 'The Roman Fort at Balmuildy,' p. 68.

pp. **219, 220.** Crowd of merchants, Aristides, Orat. Aeg. 355. At London, Tac. Ann. XIV. 33, and note the high total of those massacred, 70,000. A Trevir and a Mediomatrix at London, C.I.L. VII. 36. 55.

A Biturix at York, 248. A Sequanus, 69. A Greek at Lindum, 190.
Barates from Palmyra in second century, E.E. IV. 718a. Prune-kernels
from Damascus found, Sagot, 'La Bretagne R.' p. 284. For the trade
from N.E. Gaul cp. the interesting inscription in Eph. Epig. IX. 1182,
in which Nonius Romanus from the Moselle district makes a dedication
to his local god (Mars Lenus) at Caerwent. Later notices of trade and
artisans in Eumen. Paneg. Const. Caesari 21; cp. also Amm. Marcell.
XVIII. 2, 3, 'annona a Britanniis sueta transferri.' A *Sevir* of York at
Bordeaux: *Ann. Épig.* 1922, no. 16

pp. 220, 221. Agricola thought of subjugating Ireland: one legion
necessary! Tac. Agric. 24; more known 'per commercia et negotia-
tores,' Juv. II. 160, 'ultra | litora Juvernae.' See Haverfield's article
in Pauly-Wissowa: coins mostly in North, one of Nero, some of
Trajan and Hadrian, usually later. Cp. article in *Class. Quarterly*
for 1922, by Knox McElderry.

CONCLUSION

p. 224. Amount of voyaging, Philo, 'Quod omnis probus liber sit,'
65, who speaks of '$\pi\epsilon\lambda\acute{a}\gamma\eta$ $\emph{ἄπλωτα}$ $\tau\grave{a}$ $\kappa\alpha\theta$' $\emph{ἑκάστην}$ $\emph{ὥραν}$ $\tauο\hat{υ}$ $\emph{ἔτους}$
$ναυκλήροις$ $\emph{ἐμπλεόμενα}.$' Seneca, ad Paul. 2, 'alium mercandi prae-
ceps cupiditas circa omnes terras, omnia maria, spe lucri ducit';
cp. Ovid, Tristia I. 2. 75, 'Non ego divitias avidus sine fine parandi, |
Latum mutandis mercibus aequor aro.'

p. 226. Kidnapping to 'ergastula,' Scribonius Largus 231.
Augustus' measures against the practice, Suet. Aug. 32. Cp. Tiberius'
examinations, Suet. Tib. 8, and cp. 37. Hadrian abolishes them,
Spartianus, Hadr. 18. Soldiers of civil war in brigandage, App. Bell.
Civ. V. 132. Footpads in Pomptine marshes, Juv. III. 307. Reluctance
to sail in winter: many passages citable, but cp. following for Empire
period, J. XVI. 15, approach of winter makes voyaging risky; Jos.
B.J. IV. 632, fear of winter-voyaging makes Mucian lead army through
Cappadocia and Phrygia. Cp. the 'violentia' of Agrippina, which
made her sail even in winter! Ann. III. 1. 1.

pp. 226, 227. Wind holding ships up. Voyage from Alexandria
hindered by Etesians from July 20th onward, cp. Caes. B.C. III. 107,
Tac. Hist. II. 98 and IV. 81. Again the region of Hellespont very bad
for winds (Anytus and Greek instances), and cp. Herod being held
up off Cos by strong N. wind for several days, J. XVI. 16. Sudden
storms in Gulf of Lyons, wrecking on Stoechades, cp. Claud. 17. 2
and Tac. Hist. III. 43.

pp. 227, 228. Question of corn-supply made emperors careful;
cp. Augustus' cleaning of Egyptian canals, by soldiers, Aug. 18. Law
against hindering of corn-supply, Digest XLVII. 11. 6. Bounties for
corn-merchants, Ann. II. 87. Dependence of Italy, Ann. III. 54.
Harbours of refuge for corn-ships, J. XIX. 205-7. Only fifteen days'

supply left in city, Ann. XII. 43. Exemptions for merchants and foreigners, Ann. XIII. 51. Rewards for winter-supplies, Claud. 18, 19. Harbour at Ostia, Claud. 19, 20. Arrival of fleet at Puteoli, Senec. ad Lucil. 77. 1. Yet Ostia still unsafe, Ann. XV. 18. Trajan's measures: storing in granaries: careful conservation, in Pliny, Paneg. 29–31.

pp. **228, 229.** General harbour and sea-works. Work on port of Ostia, Claud. 20, 1, 3, a lighthouse added. A lighthouse near Boulogne, Calig. 46. Fleet stationed at Boulogne, C.I.L. XIII. p. 561. A harbour at Antium, Nero. 9. Projected canal from Ostia, Nero. 16. Trajan's improvements at Ostia, Juv. XII. 75; cp. Cohen 365, 366. A new port at Centumcellae, Pliny, Ep. VI. 31. 15 ff. A harbour at Ancona, 'accessum Italiae tutiorem navigantibus reddiderit,' C.I.L. IX. 5894. Project of digging Corinthian isthmus, Calig. 21, Nero. 19. Cp. Hadrian's new harbour at Lupiae, Paus. VI. 19. 9.

pp. **229–232.** Roads. Augustus repairs Via Flaminia, other roads allotted to nobles, Aug. 30, cp. Dio LIII. 22. The imperial post, Aug. 49; attempted change by Claudius, C.I.L. III, Suppl. 7251. Nerva remitted tax from Italy, Eckhel VI. 408, 'vehiculatione It. remissa.' Bad state of Italian roads, Ann. III. 31. Tiberius and roads, Tib. 31. Claudius uses gladiators for their repair, Claud. 24. 2. (All references to new roads under respective provinces.) Once again Trajan is prominent: road through Pomptine marshes, Dio LXVIII. 15. Galen describes his roadmaking in Meth. Med. IX. 8. Cp. Dio LXVIII. 7. 7.

pp. **232–234.** Roman arms and commerce, N.H. XXVI. 19. Nero sets up shops and shelters on Thracian roads, C.I.L. III. 6123. Juba's work on Arabia, N.H. XII. 56 ff. Nero's expedition to Aethiopia; map of Aethiopia, and centurions, N.H. XII. 19, VI. 181, 184. Corn brought from Moesia and beyond by Plautius Silvanus, C.I.L. XIV. 3608. Warships on Black Sea, B.J. II. 16. 4, 'εἰρηνεύουσι θάλασσαν.' Proposed expedition to Caspian Gates, N.H. VI. 40, and Nero. 19. Protection of trade by Black Sea and Phasis, Arrian, Perip. 9. 5. Indian trade viâ Caspian, N.H. VI. 52.

Arrian's report to Hadrian mentioned in Arrian, Perip. 1. Information from Suetonius Paulinus in N.H. V. 11 ff. Maps: 'orbis terrarum chorographiae,' Vitr. VIII. 2. 6. Inscription of legionary, χωρογραφήσας, in July 33 A.D., given in Ditt., O.G.I.S. 205. Expeditions into Africa, Ptol. 1. 8. 4. Fragment of itinerary; Cumont in *Syria*, VI. p. 1.

pp. **234, 235.** Soldiers engaged in trade, Ann. XIII. 51 (cp. c. 35, 'nitidi et quaestuosi'). Knights busy in the provinces, Ann. XVI. 27. Veterans return to provinces in which they had served, Ann. XIV. 27. Merchants in India, Perip. *passim* and Ptol. Proleg. 1. 17, and N.H. VI. 101; in Ireland, Tac. Agric. 24; in Atlantic, Hor. Odes I. 31. 14; cp. Aristides, Orat. Aeg. 355; in Black Sea, Arrian, Perip. 9. 5; in Suabia, Ann. II. 62; in Red Sea, Diod. III. 18. 3, and at Charax, N.H. VI. 139.

p. **236.** Brickworks of Domitius Afer, Frank, 'Econ. Hist.,' p. 175.

Calvia Crispinilla's pottery, C.I.L. III. 12010. 2; and cp. Tac. Hist. I. 73. For Traulus cp. Ann. XI. 36 and C.I.L. III. 12010. 7. Baltic expedition, N.H. XXXVII. 45. Maes Titianus and China, Ptol. I. 12.

p. **237**. Besides Egypt we must remember too the Emperor's ownership of mines.

Juba's purple-works, N.H. VI. 201. Annius Plocamus' freedman, VI. 84.

Red lead of Ephesus best, N.H. XXXIII. 114; yet most brought from Spain, ibid. 118. Spanish plums in Galen, VI. p. 613.

p. **238**. For details of traders see chapters on provinces, but cp. the migration of Ephesians to Rome in Vitr. VII. 9. 4.

Alexandrian gladiators, C.I.L. VI. 10194 and v. 3465. Alexandrian musicians at Cologne, C.I.L. XIII. 8343.

p. **239**. Honesty of Roman trading noticed by Chinese: 'they have no double prices,' see chap. VI. Good coinage, see N.H. VI. 85. Cp. Epict. IV. 5. 2, and later story of Cosmas, XI. 448 D. Cp. testimonies to Empire in Epict. IV. 3. 13. 'We may travel at all hours,' and in Irenaeus, Contra Haereses IV. 46. 3 (quoted as chapter heading). N.H. XIV. 2, 'Quis enim non communicato orbe terrarum maiestate Romani imperii profecisse vitam putet commercio rerum et societate festae pacis?'

INDEX

Date Due